Ten Biblical Concepts

Ten Biblical Concepts

You Think You Know but Probably Don't

Yung Y. Yang

WIPF & STOCK · Eugene, Oregon

TEN BIBLICAL CONCEPTS
You Think You Know but Probably Don't

Copyright © 2025 Yung Y. Yang. All rights reserved. Except for brief quotations in critical publications or reviews, no part of this book may be reproduced in any manner without prior written permission from the publisher. Write: Permissions, Wipf and Stock Publishers, 199 W. 8th Ave., Suite 3, Eugene, OR 97401.

Wipf & Stock
An Imprint of Wipf and Stock Publishers
199 W. 8th Ave., Suite 3
Eugene, OR 97401

www.wipfandstock.com

PAPERBACK ISBN: 979-8-3852-4497-3
HARDCOVER ISBN: 979-8-3852-4498-0
EBOOK ISBN: 979-8-3852-4499-7

VERSION NUMBER 04/30/25

All Scripture quotations, unless otherwise indicated, are taken from the ESV® Study Bible (The Holy Bible, English Standard Version®), Copyright © 2008 by Crossway, a publishing ministry of Good News Publishers. Used by permission. All rights reserved.

Scriptures marked (NKJV) taken from the New King James Version®. Copyright © 1982 by Thomas Nelson. Used by permission. All rights reserved.

To my wife, Jane, for being my conversation partner and editing the entire manuscript; to our children, Eugene, Benjamin, and Laura, for their ongoing support; and finally, to Dr. Song Nai Rhee, a lifelong friend and mentor.

Contents

Preface | ix
Introduction | xiii
Abbreviations | xxii

1. Faith | 1
2. Doubt | 20
3. Sin | 33
4. Salvation | 50
5. The Kingdom of God | 74
6. Election and Predestination | 97
7. Repentance | 118
8. Death and Afterlife | 133
9. Heaven and Hell | 152
10. Eternal Life | 176

Bibliography | 195

Preface

BIBLICAL ILLITERACY IS A critical issue facing American Christians today.[1] It is most apparent as a lack of understanding of fundamental biblical words and concepts, such as *faith*, *sin*, and *salvation*. This illiteracy too often leads to miscommunication, misinterpretation, and misapplication, hindering the development of a robust Christian faith and worldview. As a result, Christians may struggle to engage in meaningful prayer, worship, and spiritual practice, ultimately impacting the vitality of Christianity in America.

I wrote this book as a resource for busy and practically minded laypeople. I focus on ten commonly used but often misunderstood essential biblical concepts: *faith*, *doubt*, *sin*, *salvation*, *the kingdom of God*, *election* and *predestination*, *repentance*, *death* and *afterlife*, *heaven* and *hell*, and *eternal life*. Each entry includes a concise but thorough study of the topic, including common misunderstandings, word study, biblical teaching, relevant doctrine, and practical implications.

This book fills a gap in the current literature on the topic. J. I. Packer's *Concise Theology* and R. C. Sproul's *Essential Truths of the Christian Faith* are helpful quick references for biblical words. Still, they are concise by design and do not provide significant detail. At the same time, there are also multivolume handbooks that may be overwhelming for laypeople. This book offers a middle ground and is a valuable guide for a deep but digestible understanding of foundational biblical words in a single volume.

My niche as a Christian writer stems from my perspective as an analytically minded layman. I spent my entire thirty-five-year career as

1. Mohler, "Scandal of Biblical Illiteracy"; Parsons, "Infallible Words."

ix

an economist and developed an inquiring and inquisitive mindset. As a Christian layperson, I apply my analytical skills to comprehend and communicate the fundamental truths of Christian beliefs. Furthermore, my background as a macroeconomist enables me to grasp the overarching narrative of the entire Bible and utilize this macro perspective to elucidate how each biblical word and concept fits into God's overall plan of salvation. My goal is to distill the insights of theologians, both past and present, and present clear and logical explanations tailored for busy laypersons and church leaders.

I approach the subject in each essay by considering what the Bible teaches. My theological education is influenced by the Reformed tradition, which is associated with theologians such as John Calvin (1509–1564), Francis Turretin (1623–1687), Herman Bavinck (1854–1921), Geerhardus Vos (1862–1949), and Herman Ridderbos (1909–2007), as well as modern-day theologians like J. I. Packer (1926–2020), R. C. Sproul (1939–2017), John Stott (1921–2011), Timothy Keller (1950–2023), Michael Horton, John Piper, Sinclair Ferguson, and Kevin DeYoung, among other prominent theologians.

I have been looking for a book that connects the Bible's story with the Christian view of the world and life that uncovers life's more profound meaning and purpose. I am in my early eighties and the search is more urgent. The meaning of death, the afterlife, and eternal life has become a practical interest. As my pursuit of biblical truth and life's meaning has become more pressing, I have observed that any serious engagement with church friends about these two topics was always hindered by a lack of common ground in understanding key biblical words like faith, sin, and salvation.

I have attempted to distill a lifetime of Christian learning into an accessible resource that supports other believers in understanding foundational biblical truths. I hope readers will be transformed through a deeper understanding of the saving work of Christ and its significance for life's meaning and purpose.

About the Author

I was born into a Christian family in South Korea in the early 1940s and attended missionary middle and high schools. When I enrolled at Seoul National University (SNU) to study economics in 1960, I was a struggling college student, barely able to pay tuition from the money I earned from tutoring. Like any SNU student in the 1960s, I was full of hope and pride. However, somewhat different from my peers, I earnestly sought to connect life's more profound meaning and purpose with traditional Christian teachings. Studying and earning money from tutoring kept me occupied during the weekdays. Attending worship services and Campus Crusade for Christ meetings kept me busy on Saturdays and Sundays.

After college, I pursued busy corporate and government research careers in Seoul, Korea, for several years during the mid-1960s. I now had a family and decided to move to the United States to pursue graduate studies in economics at the University of Oregon. I finished a PhD in 1974 and started my professional career at California State University, Sacramento, teaching and conducting economic research. During my thirty-five-year academic career, I published numerous refereed journal articles in prestigious journals like the *Review of Economics and Statistics*, published by Harvard University. I also served as the journal's editorial collaborator (referee) and the president of the Korea-America Economics Association. In retrospect, I had a reasonably successful professional career.

I have consistently studied the Bible and theology throughout my career while serving in the church. As I prepared for retirement, I realized I had a strong desire to reconnect with the serious exploration of life's meaning and purpose through Christian truths that I pursued during my college years in the 1960s. In 2008, I enrolled in Bible and theology classes at Fuller Seminary. I was fortunate to regularly engage with Dr. Song Nai Rhee, a lifelong friend and retired professor of biblical studies. Through his encouragement, I pursued a two-year guided self-study program in theology and biblical studies at Northwest Christian University (now Bushnell University) in Eugene, Oregon, earning a master of philosophy in theology in 2014. Since then, I have continued to study theology and biblical studies, enjoying them thoroughly.

Introduction

We had just completed our Sunday morning Bible study at a church in San Diego in May 2022. Our discussion focused on salvation from sin.

As I was about to gather my Bible and lecture materials, my close friend raised a final question with all sincerity, gesturing with both hands raised: "By the way, what is salvation anyway? You keep referring to sin and salvation as if we all understand it." To appreciate the seriousness of his inquiry in discussing the meaning of sin and salvation, it's essential to know that he has been a Christian his whole life. He is a brilliant retired professor from a well-established state university in the Midwest. Having known him well, I sensed that he was asking this question out of genuine interest in the truth claims of Christianity. Unfortunately, words like sin, death, faith, and salvation are often used so frequently, both inside and outside the church, that their biblical meanings have lost their freshness and vitality. In other words, these terms have become overused, clichéd, and unoriginal.

In his famous 1946 essay "Politics and the English Language," George Orwell (1903–1950) argued that the deteriorated state of the English language correlated with the degraded political situation. In a summary and analysis of the essay, Oliver Tearle argues that Orwell believed political writers tend to use stock phrases instead of words with precise meanings.[1] Although some critics may consider Orwell's writing too idealistic, the crucial issues raised in his essay about the degraded use of the English language in politics remain relevant and valid in Christianity today.

Words are important. They play a critical role in effective communication, expressing our thoughts and emotions, building relationships,

---

1. Tearle, "Summary and Analysis."

influencing and persuading others, and more, depending on the context. By using words, we communicate the importance, relevance, or significance of something. When we say something matters, we mean it has an impact, influence, or consequence. Therefore, choosing our words carefully and using them appropriately is crucial to ensure clear understanding and effective communication in various aspects of life. Miscommunication often arises when words are misunderstood or used ambiguously.

The foundational truths of Christianity are expressed through theological propositions using biblical words, phrases, and concepts. We believe that all biblical words are God-inspired, infallible, and thus essential for us to understand. However, some words stand out as especially important, as they are the main building blocks for communicating these truths, particularly in the doctrine of salvation. These words include *belief/faith, doubt, repentance, election, eternal life, death* and *afterlife, heaven* and *hell, the kingdom of God, salvation, sin,* and so forth.

One may observe that these biblical words share several common characteristics. The first distinctive feature is that they are familiar and frequently used. Secondly, these biblical words are closely related to each other. Let's use the first four biblical words, faith, doubt, repentance, and election, to illustrate their close relationships. The Bible teaches us that faith is not the absence of doubts; faith keeps us believing even amid our doubts. Faith requires repentance; faith gratefully accepts and receives election. The doctrine of election helps Christians see that it is God's grace that saves them, which in turn moves them to humility, confidence, joy, praise, faithfulness, and holiness in their lives.

Thirdly, they are often misunderstood or used ambiguously. As a result, communicating the intended message for learning and sharing knowledge can be difficult. A shallow and vague understanding of these words and concepts is common among laypersons and Christian leaders. Ironically, the familiarity with these words both within and outside the church leads people to assume they understand the meaning when, in fact, they do not. Many adults have only a superficial, shallow, or vague understanding of these words, no better than a child's. They did not take the time to learn them when they were younger, and now they remain apathetic about learning these essential biblical words. Unfortunately, this situation has never been worse than it is in our current generation.[2] There

---

2. This is the same conclusion that was reached in an editorial remark by Burk Parsons. Parsons, "Infallible Words."

is a crying need for a robust understanding of these key biblical words and concepts, which recognize the multifaceted meaning of orthodoxy.

Additionally, some biblical words and concepts seemingly oppose each other, and a balanced understanding is essential. For instance, let's take faith and doubt as an example. Christianity emphasizes faith in God and Jesus Christ. However, the Bible also acknowledges moments of doubt, even from prominent figures like Abraham (Gen 17:17). A balanced approach recognizes the importance of faith while acknowledging that doubt is a natural part of the human experience. Other examples may include heaven and hell, love and the judgment of God, and grace and the wrath of God. This balanced approach doesn't mean these concepts lose their meaning. Instead, it allows for a more nuanced understanding of these vital biblical words for practical Christian living. Finding balance in some biblical words can be an ongoing process as individuals grapple with their faith journey.

To emphasize the importance of correct understanding of these biblical words, I would like to quote what Rick Warren, in his most recent book, writes,

> Pursuing God's dream for your life is a walk of faith, and the very first step is placing your faith in Jesus Christ to forgive your sins. That's the starting point. Jesus has already offered you his forgiveness. There is nothing left for you to do but to believe and receive.[3]

In this short paragraph, he uses terms like "God's dream for your life," "a walk of faith," "placing your faith in Jesus Christ," "forgive your sins," and "believe and receive." You may notice several biblical words chosen here for examination. This amply shows the importance and the necessity of understanding the true meaning of these biblical words in communicating the vital truth. Granting that pursuing God's dream is the goal, what does "a walk of faith" mean? What is faith? Is faith a belief in Christian doctrines and teachings? Hebrews 11:1 says "faith is the assurance of the things hoped for, the conviction of things not seen." The biblical concept of faith includes beliefs in Christian doctrines and much more. The idea of faith is simple, complex, and comprehensive. Understanding the true meaning of faith is hard enough, but what does "a walk of faith" mean? The plain meaning of walking is to move on foot at a regular pace. But the *Baker Expository Dictionary of Biblical Words*

---

3. Warren, *Created to Dream*, 27.

explains that in the New Testament, the verb "walk" (*peripateo* in Greek) can be used in two primary senses: literally, to refer to physically walking, and metaphorically, to refer to a way or manner of life.[4] What is intended here is the latter sense of living by faith, not by sight.

In 2 Cor 5, Paul describes the Christian walk as one based on faith rather than sight (v. 7). Here, faith encompasses more than merely believing in Christian doctrines. It signifies embracing a true story of the universe—one marked by love, loss, promise, and costly rescue, in which we all have a part to play. This raises important questions: How can one accept this understanding of faith? Without fully grasping the completeness of Christ's work, how can we claim that all we need to do is to believe and receive? While faith and sin are familiar terms, they are also complex, carrying deep meaning and significance that requires thorough understanding.

One of the main challenges for Christians, especially for laypersons, is that practically all of the ten biblical concepts chosen here have some problematic elements, which often lead to misunderstandings. Therefore, it is necessary to state, clarify, dispel, and rebuff them. Only after that can we present the patterns of usage of the biblical concept in Scripture before we present historic Christian beliefs.

As mentioned earlier, survey data shows an alarmingly low level of biblical knowledge among modern Christians. And the situation has never been worse than it is in our generation. Even when people recognize the importance of understanding the meaning of biblical words in Christian life, they often seek quick explanations in just a few words or sentences. However, to fully comprehend the significance of these words, it's essential to delve into word study, the pattern of usage in the Scriptures, and the entire biblical story rather than settling for a brief, on-the-fly answer.

What might have contributed to the development of this deplorable situation? One powerful cause is the subtle influence of the secularity of the modern age, even in the church. People in this new age are not interested in religion, including Christianity. People are too busy in their ordinary lives, pursuing pleasures and happiness. They do not take Christianity seriously enough to be interested in learning its foundational truth, and many view it as irrelevant. A well-known theologian, J. I. Packer, captured such laid-back features of modern-day Christian life

---

4. Longman and Strauss, "Walk," *BED* 881–82.

beautifully and humorously in his book *Hot Tub Religion*. The following is a direct quote:

> It struck me that the hot tub is the perfect symbol of the modern route in religion. The hot tub experience is sensuous, relaxing, floppy, and laid-back: not in any way demanding, whether intellectually or otherwise, but very, very nice, even to the point of being great fun. Many today want Christianity to be like that and labor to make it so.... Meantime, many churches, evangelists, and electronic religionists are offering occasions which we are meant to feel are the next best thing to a hot tub—namely, happy gatherings free from care, real fun times for all.... No wonder, then, that when a Western man turns to religion, what he wants is total tickling relaxation, the sense of at once smooth, supported and effortlessly invigorated: in short, hot tub religion. He asks for it, and up folk jump to provide it. What hot tub religion illustrates most clearly is the law of demand and supply.[5]

The law of demand and supply refers to their interactions in determining market outcomes. He meant to convey that what people want/demand in Christianity is a hot tub–like laid-back experience, and many church leaders labor to provide (supply) just that. In other words, what the congregation wants/demands from Christianity is a relaxing, easy, and not demanding or intellectually challenging study experience, which determines what is provided/supplied. This is the case of demand determining supply.

Of course, this is not authentic Christianity. Christians need to endeavor to know God's truth and God himself. The Christian's goal in life is to know, love, and worship God as the true God of the Bible. In pursuing these goals, learning and understanding foundational biblical words is crucial.

Another powerful influence of the modern age is the influence of the belief system, of both young and old, dubbed "moralistic therapeutic deism" (MTD in short). This also reflects the modern culture as a whole. First, it is a deism, a particular understanding of God. According to this view, God exists, created the world, and defines our general moral order but is not personally involved in man's affairs. But this particular deism is "about inculcating a moralistic approach to life. It teaches that central to living a good and happy life is being a good, moral person. That means being nice, kind, pleasant, respectful, responsible, at work

---

5. Packer, *Hot Tub Religion*, 68–69.

on self-improvement, taking care of one's health, and doing one's best to be successful."[6] Adherents to this view care about receiving therapeutic benefits from religion."

To them, religion is not about repentance from sin, keeping a Sabbath, living as a servant of sovereign divinity, building character through suffering in God's love and grace, etc. "Rather, what appears to be the actual dominant religion among U.S. teenagers is centrally about feeling good, happy, secure, at peace. It is about attaining subjective well-being, being able to resolve problems, and getting along amiably with other people."[7]

Behind the somewhat related powerful influences of modern secular culture, the church's third and closest problem is its failure to provide an organized setting for adult Christian education. Until the late 1960s in the United States, the church offered educational opportunities for adult education, such as the serious learning of biblical words and concepts in the context of broad Christian education. But since then, these opportunities have slowly dried up for various reasons. Now, not many churches provide such learning opportunities. But, as J. I. Packer points out, "Christianity is not instinctive, nor is it picked up casually without effort. Faith must be learned and taught, so some of the catechumenate (the organized setup for giving instruction) is essential to a church's life."[8]

In writing this book, I aim to offer opportunities for individuals both within and outside of churches to explore and understand essential Christian beliefs. The book focuses on ten pivotal biblical words and concepts: *faith, doubt, sin, salvation, the kingdom of God, election, repentance, death* and *afterlife, heaven* and *hell,* and *eternal life*. Each concept is covered in a concise and rigorous essay, briefly introducing the subject's importance, central issues, and common misunderstandings. I provide a word study, primarily based on *the Baker Expository Dictionary of Biblical Words*, before briefly presenting the pattern of usage of the biblical words chosen in the Scriptures, which is followed by historic Christian beliefs. On the topic of faith, for instance, I examine first *what* faith is and what it involves. Those who are analytically minded are bound to ask the *why* of faith and the basis of Christian beliefs and continue on to ask *how* to experience it (the method of obtaining it) and further ask *so what* about faith. In other words, what difference does it make to have faith? The critical question is,

6. Mohler, "Moralistic Therapeutic Deism."
7. Mohler, "Moralistic Therapeutic Deism."
8. Packer, *I Want*, 14.

Is belief in God epistemologically justified? Much progress has been made recently in the knowledge of God, and I attempt to bring some insights into the essays. To conclude each essay, I typically select a relevant sermon by Charles Spurgeon and provide a concise summary. This helps to reemphasize the key features of the biblical word studied alongside Spurgeon's unique sermonic appeal to the subject.

To those who regularly attend weekly worship service, sermons in those services can provide opportunities to learn about Christian truth. However, preaching does not offer much help because it consists primarily of the proclamation of gospel truth and ordinarily assumes both the preacher and congregation to be sure of the meaning of biblical words and concepts. Usually, the assumption is unrealistic, and the reality is a vague and shallow understanding or outright misunderstanding of these biblical words. This results in poor communication between the speaker and hearers. Some serious seekers and doubters may even be bothered by what appear to be unexamined assumptions. Ordinarily, preaching in worship is not the proper place for seriously examining, challenging, and testing the intellectual basis of the fundamentals of Christian faith. Our great need is to somehow learn the way of basic training of Christian truth. I want to provide such opportunities to learn them by writing a solid book for adults in the modern secular culture.

In carrying out our task, we rely first on the Christian Bible and three well-established resources, known for their reliability and wide acceptance among biblical scholars, in examining ten key biblical concepts in Christianity. First, we turn to relevant portions of classic teachings from John Calvin's *Institutes of the Christian Religion*, David Hall and Peter Lillback's *Theological Guide to Calvin's Institutes*, and Herman Bavinck's four-volume set of *Reformed Dogmatics* and his book *The Wonderful Works of God*. Secondly, we consult two well-known encyclopedias: *The Baker Expository Dictionary of Biblical Words* and the four-volume set of *The International Standard Bible Encyclopedia*. Additionally, InterVarsity Press's two volumes on the *Dictionary of Jesus and the Gospels* and the *Dictionary of Paul and His Letters* are helpful for the brevity of their discussions on the subject. Third, as we take up each key biblical word and concept, at least two well-known and respected biblical scholars' works are chosen as additional references. For examining sin, for instance, Cornelius Plantinga's *Not the Way It's Supposed to Be: A Breviary of Sin* was used as the go-to source. For salvation, we turn to John Murray's *Redemption Accomplished and Applied*, Bruce Demarest's *The Cross and*

Salvation: The Doctrine of Salvation, and Herman Ridderbos's *Paul: An Outline of His Theology*, a classic on Pauline theology.

Who Needs to Read This Book, and Why

This book is written by a layperson for those who take the Christian faith seriously. Who in their right mind, without serious interest in Christianity in this modern age of speed and busyness, would spend their precious time learning the basics of the historic Christian faith? Only those who take the Christian faith and life seriously enough will be interested in carrying on the demanding task of learning biblical words and concepts. Yet the rewards from learning are bountiful and well worth the effort. Learning them is a matter of life and death, both now and eternally. This is not the book for those who only want a laid-back, easy, and comforting experience in Christianity. I have the following circumstances of life in mind as I write.

First, I consider those people who were born and grew up with a Christian upbringing. They were raised and taught about Christianity early on from a young age. In the process, they accepted Christianity as their faith through their upbringing. As they grow up through adulthood, they keep their faith, remain Christians, and become active in the church. As they mature, they must explore their faith more seriously and sincerely. This is usually the prompting of the Holy Spirit, and I strongly suggest you follow your instinct to learn and relearn the basics of Christian truth.

Second, I have in mind those who became Christians through personal conversion or evangelism and yet did not have opportunities to learn the basics of Christianity. In the case of individual conversion, one may have decided to become a Christian after searching or reflecting. It may have come through a gradual learning process about Christianity through reading good books like *Mere Christianity* by C. S. Lewis or *I Want to Be a Christian* and *Knowing God* by J. I. Packer. For others, a sudden change in circumstance or an unusual spiritual experience may explain why they became Christians. In the case of conversion through evangelism, it was through the efforts of another person, usually a family member, friend, or missionary. Regardless of the particular circumstance in which they became Christians, they need to learn the basics of Christianity. This book can serve as a guide.

As is well known, we must continue to grow and mature once we become Christians through upbringing, personal conversion, or evangelism. Growing up and living the Christian life necessitates constant learning and spiritual discipline. When one stops learning, Christian life becomes stagnant, but it slowly starts to die sooner or later. This book may be used as a good resource and for group discussion.

Third, I consider those who experienced a period of questioning and doubt, with skepticism in their journey of Christian life. Others might have been turned off either by the perception of hypocrisy among church leaders or by negative experiences (such as judgment, exclusion, or abuse) with church members. Maybe they all led to disillusionment about Christianity. As a result, they have struggled with doubts and skepticism about Christianity itself. Some others may find reconciling Christian teachings with scientific or historical knowledge challenging. The perceived conflict between some aspects of Christian teachings and scientific and historical knowledge may have led to doubts and skepticism about Christianity. This is essentially an intellectual challenge from modernity.

Fourth and finally, some people have found traditional Christianity irrelevant to them in the busy and practical life of modern times, especially amid social and cultural views shifting to more liberal and progressive attitudes. Christians live in the contemporary and secular world, and any serious Christians would consider some doubts and questions on the truth claims of Christianity as part of living Christian life in the midst of it. A firm and good grip on the simple and deeper meaning of essential biblical words and concepts is a necessary tool to cope with the impact of modern society. This book clarifies some misunderstandings and confusions about them and hopefully helps contribute to viewing Christianity with new eyes.

Abbreviations

BED	Baker Expository Dictionary of Biblical Words
DJG	Dictionary of Jesus and the Gospels
DPL	Dictionary of Paul and His Letters
ESV	English Standard Version
ISBE	International Standard Bible Encyclopedia
LXX	Septuagint
NKJV	New King James Version
NLT	New Living Translation
NT	New Testament
OT	Old Testament
TDNTA	Theological Dictionary of the New Testament: Abridged in One Volume
v.	verse
vv.	verses
WSC	Westminster Shorter Catechism

CHAPTER 1

Faith

WHAT DOES IT MEAN for the Christian to say, "I believe"? What is faith? We know that faith is the instrumental means of justification for our salvation. Why faith and faith alone? Because it is through faith alone that we lay hold of or appropriate the sole basis of our justification—namely, the righteousness of Christ in his obedience. So, faith itself is not the righteousness upon which God declares us righteous but the sole means of salvation. We often use phrases like "true faith" and "saving faith" to distinguish genuine and authentic faith in the Scripture to keep us from misunderstanding, misappropriating, and misstating it.

In Heb 11, we find examples of genuine and saving faith. By faith, we understand that the universe is created by the word of God (v. 3). From Abel to Abraham (vv. 4–19), all men of the OT heroes (vv. 20–40) lived exemplary lives by faith.

Herman Bavinck defines biblical faith as a "trust-filled surrender to God and his word of promises," focusing on trust, surrender, and obedience to God as the required elements of faith.[1] For Calvin, faith was personal confidence in God's kindness towards us, revealed to our minds and sealed in our hearts by the Holy Spirit. Thus, in grasping the concept of faith, the believer's heartful knowledge of God and his love for us was emphasized.

The language of faith (belief, confidence, conviction, faithfulness, reliability, trust, etc.) is essential to human relationships, and the word

---

1. Bavinck, *Holy Spirit*, 96.

faith is versatile and can be used in different contexts and situations. Here are some examples to illustrate this point:

1. Religious Faith: She has unwavering faith in God. Her faith guides her through difficult times.

2. Trust or Confidence: They trust the team to deliver results. I have faith (confidence) in your success.

3. Belief or Conviction: She believes in people's goodness despite the challenges. His political faith shapes his views on social issues.

4. Loyalty or Allegiance: The soldier had faith in his comrades on the battlefield. I have faith that my friends will support me.

5. Complete Trust: Faith in a relationship is crucial for success. The business partners have faith in each other's decisions.

6. Optimism for the Future: Things are rough right now, but he has faith that they will work out for the best and that things will improve despite the current challenges.

7. Worldview: Faith in science and reason is central to his worldview.

The above examples shows that *faith* is used in various situations. Faith is also a complex and multifaceted concept that can be used and interpreted in numerous ways, depending on cultural, religious, philosophical, and individual perspectives. Therefore, to understand the actual and intended meaning of the word faith, it is necessary to pay close attention to the pattern of usage and context in which the word is used.

As briefly mentioned, many biblical terms, including faith, are often widely misunderstood. Given that, it may be helpful to show some examples of misunderstanding; discussing some familiar misunderstandings at the outset raises interest in the topic and provides valuable benefits. First, it may help identify gaps in knowledge and areas needing further explanation or counter a misunderstanding. Second, it can also help promote a deeper understanding of faith. Stimulating curiosity, identifying gaps in knowledge, and highlighting different perspectives on faith from the outside would help us improve our understanding of faith. Misunderstandings about the word faith in Christianity, often called Christian faith, abound. Below are a few well-known examples of misconceptions about the Christian faith.

Misunderstandings of Faith

1. The Christian faith is a blind belief.

This is not true. Christian faith is based on knowledge, reflection, history, and personal experience. Apologetics, a branch of theology, offers reasoned arguments and evidence supporting Christian beliefs. Christian faith is a deep trust in God and his promises based on evidence from the Bible and creation. Christians believe in God's existence and character as revealed in the Bible, and they trust him even when they don't have all the answers. Christian faith involves an informed and credible approach based on Scripture, history, and personal experiences, which encourages intellectual engagement, critical thinking, open-mindedness, and a willingness to question assumptions and learn. This approach fosters intellectual integrity and strengthens one's faith.

2. Faith is the opposite of reason.

This oversimplification does not adequately capture the complexity of the relationship between faith and reason, which has been debated for centuries. Some people believe that faith and reason are incompatible, while others believe they complement each other. There is no easy answer to this question, which essentially depends on how one defines faith and reason.

Human reasoning is a powerful tool to acquire knowledge, but faith and reason are not necessarily in conflict. Christians believe that faith and reason are essential in comprehending the world and their place in it. Faith provides a framework for understanding the world and human life, while reason enables us to examine, test, refine, and improve our understanding of the world. We will delve further into the relationship between faith and reason, particularly in light of what we learn from modern epistemology on the nature of knowledge.

3. Faith is only for the weak-minded.

It is often claimed that faith is only for the weak-minded, but this notion is not entirely accurate and is frequently used to attack Christianity. This idea is attributed to Friedrich Nietzsche, a German philosopher. However, there are several issues with this notion.

First, it is a sweeping generalization that does not apply to all people with faith. Many intelligent and thoughtful people believe in God, and their faith does not make them weak-minded. Second, this notion is based on the assumption that there is only one way to think about the world, which is through reason. This assumption dismisses the idea that faith can be a rational way of thinking. Third, this notion dismisses people who have faith by suggesting they are weak or inferior. This is not true since people with faith come from all walks of life and are just as intelligent and capable as anyone else. Faith is not a sign of weakness; instead, it is a sign of strength.

It takes strength to believe in something we cannot see or prove. Choosing to have faith requires a humble mind, courage, and conviction. The notion that faith is only for weak minds is a harmful generalization that should not be taken seriously.

What Is Faith?

We will discuss the notion of faith in the context of Christianity, and when we say faith, we mean faith in God of the Scripture and Jesus Christ. While we focus on the nature and concept of faith in God in what follows, it is desirable to include a brief discussion on the reason for such faith (*why* faith?) and the method of obtaining it (*how* to have faith?). In addition, I would like to add some discussions on the difference it makes to have faith in God (*so what* about faith?) in our lives.

To understand the true and deep meaning of the biblical word "faith," we must first conduct a brief word study, relying on reliable expository dictionaries, such as the *Baker Expository Dictionary of Biblical Words*, published in 2023. Another reliable source is the *Theological Dictionary of the New Testament*,[2] which has been used as the main staple of any serious New Testament (NT) word study.

Baker Dictionary lists two entries for the English word "faith": one for the Old Testament (OT) usage and another for the NT usage.[3] The Hebrew basic stem for "faith" from which other stems (faith, faithful, faithfulness) derive is 'āman'. The basic idea of 'āman' is constancy. When it is used for things, it means "continual," and when it refers to people, it has the

---

2. Kittel and Friedrich, *Theological Dictionary*.

3. The discussion of these terms draws from Longman and Strauss, "Faith, Faithful, Faithfulness," *BED* 281–83.

connotation of "reliability." The Greek word for the English word "faith" is *pistis*. The semantic range for *pistis* covers faith, faithfulness, belief, firm conviction, guarantee, assurance, honesty, and integrity. *Baker Dictionary* notes that *pistis* has three primary connotations. First, faith can convey the active sense of believing in, trusting, or committing to someone based on the reliability of the one trusted. Second, *pistis* can signify faithfulness, the state of being someone in whom trust, commitment, or belief can be placed. Finally, in a few instances, *pistis* signifies that which is believed, a body of teaching or belief—namely, doctrine.

From the dictionary definition, we learn that one word, "faith," means so many things, depending on the contents of faith and its context. For a clear understanding, paying close attention to the context where the word "faith" takes place and the usage pattern is necessary. In a word, "faith" does not exist in a vacuum, without contents and context.

Before we delve into the details of the question of what faith is, it is helpful to discuss a few words close to the word "faith." First, "believe" is a verb that generally means to accept that something is true or exists without necessarily requiring evidence or proof. It is commonly used when expressing acceptance of a statement, fact, or proposition. For example, "I believe the earth revolves around the sun" or " I believe it will rain tomorrow." A closely related phrasal verb is "believe in"; it has a broader and often deeper meaning in that it implies trust, faith, or confidence in a person, idea, or concept. For example, "I believe in you" suggests acknowledging someone's capabilities and expressing confidence and support in their abilities or potential. One can argue that "believe" conveys a sense of accepting a proposition based on evidence or reason. In contrast, "believe in" can involve a more decisive element of faith or trust, extending beyond just acknowledging facts.

Before we take up the biblical concept of faith, it would also be helpful to discuss the role of faith and two other sources of gaining human knowledge: reasoning and experience. As is well known, reasoning, faith, and experience are three fundamental sources of human knowledge that have played a crucial role in shaping our understanding of the world and us in it. Each source contributes to our knowledge in unique ways and complements each other.

First, reasoning is the process of logical thinking, analysis, and deduction. It allows us to make inferences from known facts and principles to arrive at conclusions. Reasoning is necessary for scientific inquiry, analysis, and critical thinking. It also enables us to evaluate empirical evidence, identify patterns, and form logical arguments. Secondly, faith refers to accepting or believing in something without concrete evidence or proof. It is often associated with religious beliefs but also encompasses a broader sense of accepting something as true without necessarily verifying its truthfulness. Good examples are when we say, "I believe that the earth revolves around the sun," or "I believe that the solar system is just one of many planetary systems in the universe." We gain knowledge by trusting and accepting what others pass on to us without fully understanding it and verifying its veracity. In a sense, faith in other people's faith is often the source of gaining knowledge. For our purpose, we need to point out that faith provides a framework for understanding the world and guides our decisions more confidently, not necessarily with absolute certainty. But since absolute certainty is hard to come by in real life, faith is desirable and a necessary element in our lives. Third, we also gain knowledge through experience, relying on observations, sensations, and environmental interactions. The interplay of these three sources of knowledge is essential for a comprehensive and fuller understanding of the world and our place in it.

Let's focus now on the basis and reason for faith in God (*why* faith). It is based on the revelation of God himself and his faithfulness. This declaration is an integral part of the traditional and classic Christian belief that God has revealed himself to humanity through creation (Rom 1:19–20), his written word in the Scriptures (2 Tim 3:16, Heb 1:1–2), and his Son, Jesus Christ (John 14:6, Acts 10:38). The declaration of this truth, often called *kerygma* (proclamation), is encapsulated in the apostolic proclamation. Then, the *kerygma* serves as the basis for comprehending faith as a response to God's revelation. Next, on *how* to have faith in God, we show that faith is not a work we can earn or achieve; it is a gift from God. Finally, as to the difference faith in God makes in our lives and the question of *so what*, we can provide answers by listing several benefits faith provides in Christian life. First, faith provides a personal relationship with God, a source of love, comfort, and guidance. Second, faith in God through Jesus Christ provides eternal life, a relationship with God that will never end. Third, it provides hope for the future and a sense of purpose in life. Fourth and finally, faith in God transforms our lives, enabling us to live with love, joy, and peace.

Faith in Christianity does not exist by itself; it coexists with hope and love. The importance and necessity of faith, along with hope and love, is best captured by the "ode of love" by Saint Paul in the last summary verse of 1 Cor 13: "So now faith, hope, and love abide, these three; but the greatest of these is love" (v. 13). Though this is called the "ode of love," one should note that faith comes first among the three, indicating its primary importance. Being instructed to always abide by those three things should also tell us that they are the core theological truths. Paul's exhortation, "Be watchful, stand firm in the faith," in 1 Cor 16:13 teaches us that constant trust (faith) undergirds our relationship (love) and supports our outlook of both the present and future (hope). From this, one can see that faith, hope, and love constitute not only core theological truths but also core theological virtues and essential elements of Christian life. The more relevant but sobering fact for our purpose is that faith is the most neglected element among the three.[4]

C. S. Lewis's Understanding of Faith

In what way do some prominent Christian authors understand the word "faith"? One can learn substantially from C. S. Lewis in his well-known book *Mere Christianity* and G. K. Chesterton in his equally well-known book *Orthodoxy*.[5] The explanation of faith C. S. Lewis offers in chapters 11 and 12 of his book is somewhat lengthy and involving. Thus, we will present the main line of his thoughts here.

He first notes that Christians use the word "faith" in two senses: one is a plain and ordinary sense and another in a high sense. First, "faith" means simply accepting Christian doctrines and teachings as true. What puzzled people and Lewis himself was why embracing Christian doctrine itself viewed as a virtue. Lewis raises a pertinent question about why faith as accepting Christian doctrines is good and moral. Lewis used to think that reasonable man makes his decision based on evidence. Earlier in his life, he presupposed that the human mind is entirely ruled by reason. But that is not the case in real life. He then explains the relationship between reason and faith, on the one hand, and senses and emotions, on the other, by using anesthetics as an example. He knows by sound evidence and prior experience that anesthetics are perfectly safe, and a properly-trained surgeon does not start the operation until he is knocked out. The following is what he writes about his experiences:

---

4. Brown, *Is Faith Obsolete?*, 20.
5. Lewis, *Mere Christianity*; Chesterton, *Orthodoxy*.

But that does not alter the fact when they have me down on the table and clap their horrible mask over my face, a mere childish panic begins inside me. I start thinking I am going to choke, and I am afraid they will start cutting me up before I am properly under. In other words, I lose my faith in anesthetics. It is not the reason that is taking away my faith; on the contrary, my faith is based on reason. It is my imagination and emotions. The battle is between faith and reason on one side and emotion and imagination on the other.[6]

To further illustrate the relationship between reason and faith on the one hand and emotions and moods on the other hand, he offers his second example of a man and a pretty girl of his acquaintance. He knows she is a liar, cannot keep a secret, and ought not to be trusted, but his senses and emotions win over his reason every time he is with her. Then he defines faith as "the art of holding on to things your reason has once accepted, despite your changing moods."[7]

In two examples, C. S. Lewis showed that reason and faith can work together against emotions and moods. Some believe faith and reason are opposing forces, but that's untrue. In his latest book, Kevin DeYoung points out that the church's top theologians have emphasized that faith and reason are not in conflict. DeYoung concludes that, according to the historic Christian tradition, reason is a support and not a threat to genuine faith when appropriately used.[8]

We all know that emotions and moods will change, and our outlook on the whole thing changes as they change. The uprising of emotions and moods against your reason and the sense of your authentic self continues anyway. He realizes faith is necessary because it teaches one to control emotions and moods. This realization helps explain Lewis's puzzle on why Christians view faith as a virtue, which finally makes sense. Lewis suggests that one must train in the habit of faith.

Lewis then turns his attention to the Christian's second or higher sense of faith by utilizing the notion of humility in several areas. First, when we seriously attempt to practice some Christian virtues, like resisting temptations or evil impulses inside us, we learn sooner or later that we are bound to fail. Then we discover some truth about ourselves, teaching us humility for our inability. Second, we also discover that everything we have

---

6. Lewis, *Mere Christianity*, 186.
7. Lewis, *Mere Christianity*, 188.
8. DeYoung, *Daily Doctrine*, 17–18.

(reasoning ability and the ability to move part of our body) is first given to us by God. This is another reason why we must keep humility as our basic attitude. Those who learn and experience humility at heart will discover their "bankruptcy," completely lacking in their ability to live as God originally intended. Lewis then notes that until one has discovered the fact of bankruptcy, he cannot get into the right relationship with God. Discovering bankruptcy involves a change in attitude from being confident about our ability and efforts "to the state in which we despair of doing anything for ourselves and leave it to God."[9] Leaving it to God and embracing what God has already provided is to put all our trust in Christ so that Christ somehow will share the perfect human obedience with us.

Finally, Lewis concludes his discussion of the second sense of faith as follows:

> But the difficulty is to reach the point of recognizing that all we have done and can do is nothing. What we should have liked would be for God to count our good points and ignore our bad ones. . . . Thus, if you have really handed yourself over to Him, it must follow that you are trying to obey Him. But trying in a new way, a less worried way. Not doing these things in order to be saved, but because He has begun to save you already. Not hoping to get heaven as a reward for your actions, but inevitably wanting to act in a certain way because a first faint gleam of Heaven is already inside you.[10]

Biblical Concept of Faith

Now, let us take up the biblical concept of faith. We may start from the first verse of chapter 11 of the letter to the Hebrews. Hebrews 11 is usually known as the "Hall of Faith"; its first verse is generally understood to be a good definition of faith. The verse states, "Now faith is the assurance [confidence] of things hoped for, the conviction of things not seen" (Heb 11:1).

Different translations may vary slightly, but the essence remains the same. This definition emphasizes two critical components of faith:

1. Confidence in what we hope for. Faith involves a deep trust and assurance in the promises and truths of God. It is not based solely

---

9. Lewis, *Mere Christianity*, 197.
10. Lewis, *Mere Christianity*, 197–98.

on what we can see or experience in the physical realm but extends to the realm of hope and belief in the spiritual reality. Additionally, faith is associated with hope—a firm assurance of things hoped for. Christians are called to place their hope in the promises of God, including salvation through Jesus Christ.

2. Conviction about what we do not see. Faith is not dependent merely on tangible evidence. It involves a conviction and certainty about things beyond our cerebral comprehension and immediate perception. It goes beyond empirical evidence and relies on trust in the character of God and his revealed will in the Bible.

So, we learn from the first verse of Heb 11 that the two critical components of faith are confidence in what we hope for and conviction in what we do not see. Though this first verse of chapter 11 is often understood as the definition of faith, it teaches us two critical elements of faith but is not a complete definition of faith. It is also true that Scripture does not contain a full definition of faith. Yet, one can view the first verse as more or less an operational definition. Consider verse 2 and the remainder of chapter 11 to understand why.

Verse 2 states, "For by it the people of old received their commendation." This verse provides the reason ("for," or *gar* in Greek) to undergird the assertion in verse 1 and sets the stage for the subsequent examples of faith by various biblical heroes of faith in Heb 11 by repeating "by faith." The central point is that whatever the faith is, all heroes of faith in the Bible attained their goal by faith. In other words, whatever else may determine faith to be, they all appropriate and utilize it to accomplish the task at hand. Many succeeded in attaining the goal, but many failed and suffered. And yet they are all commended for keeping their faith in God despite facing challenges and uncertainties. Whatever faith we determine it to be, it was utilized and was in operation. Because of this operational aspect of faith, we can view the first verse of Heb 11 as the definition of faith in an operational sense. Chapter 11 encourages believers to persevere in faith and trust in God and his promises.

Earlier, we mentioned faith, hope, and love as three essential elements of Christian life that should be abided by. Now, I want to turn our attention to how they relate. Robert McAfee Brown, in his *Is Faith Obsolete?* discusses this question. Here is what he said, and it was well stated:

> It was surely a sound instinct that led the apostle Paul, even in a "hymn to love," to begin his concluding summary sequence

with a reference to faith, for whatever else we determine faith to be, we must surely understand it as a way of appropriating something that is already available to us, provided for us out of the past, and about which we make some kind of decision, for or against. It is out of whatever *faith* we affirm that we can look ahead to what is still to come and (depending on the content of the faith) be enabled to adopt a stance of *hope* for the future. And it is out of a creative tension between past and future (i.e., between faith and hope) that we can form the ingredients for dealing with the present, a stance that (once again depending on the content of the faith and hope) can be an embodiment of *love*. . . . All that really needs to be insisted upon, for the discussion to proceed, is that faith has a capacity to undergird hope and love and to provide both the content and the context in which they flourish most creatively, for fruits of hope and love can nourish and deepen the faith from which they spring, and there is considerable evidence in human lives that such an interplay is always in process.[11]

So far, we have started with the dictionary definition of faith, described C. S. Lewis's notion of faith, and briefly discussed chapter 11 of the letter to Hebrews and Robert McAfee Brown's discussion of the interrelationship between faith, hope, and love.

John Calvin's Definition of Faith

Let us now finally take up a classic and formal definition of faith from John Calvin's *Institutes of the Christian Religion*, published in 1559. Following is a direct quote from the *Institutes*:

> We shall now have a full definition of faith if we say it is a firm and sure knowledge of the divine favor toward us, founded on the truth of a free promise in Christ, revealed to our minds, and sealed on our hearts, by the Holy Spirit.[12]

Calvin's definition of faith may be restated to say faith is a strong and unwavering belief in God's love for us based on the promise that God will save us through Jesus Christ. This belief is not just in our minds; it is also deeply rooted in our hearts and given to us by the Holy Spirit.

---

11. Brown, *Is Faith Obsolete?*, 17–18.
12. Calvin, *Institutes*, §3.2.7.

Calvin's definition of faith encapsulates the core concepts of his Reformed theology. This highly condensed definition can help us substantially understand faith better. Let us first summarize four critical components with a brief explanation.

1. Faith is a firm and sure knowledge. This highlights the intellectual aspect of faith. It is a deep understanding of God's character and promises, not a vague or uncertain belief about God and his character. And this knowledge is not acquired through human reasoning or effort but is revealed by God's grace. To know God in this way involves a personal and intimate knowledge of God himself.

2. Faith (as a "firm and sure knowledge") demonstrates the divine favor toward us. This underscores the relational aspect of faith (toward us). Faith is not mere intellectual assent but a heartfelt trust in God's goodness and love for us. It is the recognition of God's willingness to forgive and accept us despite our shortcomings.

3. Faith is a gift founded on the truth of free promise in Christ. This affirms the sure and objective foundation of faith. Faith is not based on our own merits or achievements but on the promises of God made through Jesus Christ, thus highlighting the centrality of Christ in the Christian faith.

4. Faith is a relationship involving the whole person ("revealed to our minds, and sealed on our hearts"). God's favor toward us highlights the relational aspect of faith-knowledge, and it is revealed to *our* minds and sealed in *our* hearts. We can, therefore, see that the nature of promise comes to us in personal terms so we can respond in our personal lives. We should also note that Calvin mentions both mind and heart. That it is revealed to our mind shows us that faith is not a blind leap but a rational acceptance of the revealed truths about God, his promises, and salvation. Stress on the heart alone would reduce faith into emotional sentimentalism. Finally, the Holy Spirit enlightens our minds to understand God's truth in the Scripture and stirs our hearts to embrace them. This inward work of the Spirit confirms and seals our faith, providing assurance and peace.

John Calvin's definition of faith is concise, condensed, complete, and thorough. Therefore, it is widely accepted as the simple and best definition of faith. Nevertheless, Søren Kierkegaard criticized Calvin's definition of faith for its overemphasis on objective knowledge and neglecting the subjective experience of faith. In his *Fear and Trembling*, Kierkegaard argued that true faith is not about having all the answers but having the courage to embrace uncertainty and trust in God even in the face of doubt.[13] Friedrich Nietzsche criticizes Calvin's definition of faith in his *Genealogy of Morals* as a "slave morality" that stifles human creativity and freedom.[14] Nietzsche argued that doubt is essential for intellectual growth and personal responsibility and should not be suppressed in the name of faith. To him, Calvin's definition of faith does not account for the reality of doubt and uncertainty in Christian life. Kierkegaard and Nietzsche correctly pointed out a symbiotic relationship between faith and doubt. Still, it is reasonable to agree that Calvin's definition of faith is the most broadly accepted. It has been most influential in developing Reformed theology and theology in general. Given that, we must dig deeper for a thorough and deep understanding of what is involved and contained in each of the four critical components of Calvin's definition of faith.

For this purpose, let us first summarize the four key components of Calvin's definition of faith as follows:

1. A firm and sure knowledge of God
2. A knowledge of divine favor (God's love) to us
3. Salvation as a gift founded on God's promises through Jesus Christ, not based on our own merits or achievements, thus highlighting the centrality of Christ in the Christian faith
4. A relationship involving the whole person (not just in our minds but also deeply rooted in our hearts)

Reviewing the four key components of the definition of Calvin's faith above, we readily find that no serious Christians will question the validity of the second component (God's love) and the third component (the gift through Jesus Christ) in grasping the concept of faith. The first and last components of Calvin's definition of faith entail the idea of knowledge in general and the concept of knowledge of God in particular, and they are the subject matter in the study of knowledge (epistemology). Epistemology deals with what knowing something, someone, or even God means and involves.

---

13. Kierkegaard, *Fear and Trembling*.
14. Nietzsche, *Genealogy of Morals*.

Epistemology is a branch of philosophy concerned with the nature, sources, and limits of knowledge. It investigates the relationship between knowledge, truth, belief, justification, and evidence. Those specializing in it seek to understand what constitutes knowledge, how we acquire it, and what justifies our beliefs. Gaining some basic knowledge in epistemology would help us better understand the nature of knowledge and its relationship to our beliefs, experiences, and the world around us because it provides the necessary framework and knowledge to navigate a world filled with information, opinions, and conflicting claims. However, epistemology is a complex and ever-evolving field, and it is a difficult and demanding task for the average informed person to acquire even a working knowledge in it.

For those serious about studying epistemology from the perspective of Christianity, I found works by Alvin Plantinga, Michael Polanyi, and Esther Lightcap Meek helpful. Alvin Plantinga (born 1932) is an American philosopher who has significantly contributed to various fields, including epistemology, philosophy of religion, and logic. His best-known and influential work concerns a "warrant" theory of knowledge and his evolutionary argument against naturalism.[15] Michael Polanyi (1891–1976) was a Hungarian-British chemist and philosopher best known for his work on personal and tacit knowledge.[16] Esther Lightcap Meek (born 1953) is an American philosopher. Her works, based largely on Polanyi's earlier works, are the best introduction and guide for informed readers, both accessible and critical.[17]

Let us now return to our primary subject: the knowledge of God as a firm and sure knowledge of God. We have already learned that this is not just our intellectual knowledge of God but is deeply rooted in our hearts. Several good books are available on this topic. What comes to mind first is *Knowing God*, a well-known Christian classic by J. I. Packer.[18] The lesser-known but most thorough treatment of this topic is John Frame's *Doctrine of the Knowledge of God*, which is part of a broad series called A Theology of Lordship.[19]

A concise summary of J. I. Packer's teachings, more accessible for our purpose, follows. It consists of two small segments: (1) five basic

15. Plantinga, *Warranted Christian Belief*; Plantinga and Tooley, *Knowledge of God*.
16. Polanyi, *Personal Knowledge*.
17. Meek, *Loving to Know*; Meek, *Longing to Know*.
18. Packer, *Knowing God*.
19. Frame, *Doctrine*.

truths or five foundational principles of the knowledge about God (found in chapter 2 of *Knowing God*), and (2) what knowing God involves (found in chapter 3).

Here are the five basic principles of Christian knowledge of God. They also serve as a guide for the contents and shape of his book and the first step to gaining such knowledge.[20]

Five Basic Truths of Knowing God

1. "God has spoken to man, and the Bible is His Word, given to us to make us wise unto salvation."
2. "God is Lord and King over His world; He rules all things for His own glory, displaying His perfections in all that He does, in order that men and angels may worship and adore Him."
3. "God is the Savior, active in sovereign love through the Lord Jesus Christ to rescue believers from the guilt and power of sin, to adopt them as His [children], and to bless them accordingly."
4. God is triune; within the Godhead are three persons: the Father, the Son, and the Holy Spirit. "The work of salvation is one in which all three act together, the Father purposing redemption, the Son securing it, and the Spirit applying it."
5. "Godliness means responding to God's revelation in trust and obedience, faith and worship, prayer and praise, submission and service. Life must be seen and lived in the light of God's Word. This, and nothing else, is true religion."[21]

What Knowing God Involves

The second important segment of J. I. Packer's book *Knowing God* deals with what knowing God involves. The concept of "knowing" is a complex one that philosophers have debated for centuries. When we say we know the city, it means that we deeply understand its culture, history, people, and places. It means knowing more than the tourist attractions; it involves knowing the city's history, neighborhood landmarks, and

---

20. Packer, *Knowing God*, 20.
21. Quotes of these five points taken from Packer, *Knowing God*, 39–41.

unique character. When we say we know a person, it's more complex because it involves deeply understanding their thoughts, feelings, and motivations. It takes understanding who that person is, not just who they appear to be. To know a person requires far more time to be with that person, listen attentively, and ask questions. J. I. Packer further notes that knowing someone is more complex because people keep secrets. Because of this, the quality and extent of our knowledge of other people depends more on how much the other person is willing to let us know his or her personal and confidential matters. When a person we get to know is superior to us in rank and position, intellectual distinction, or professional skill, knowing that person depends entirely on his or her willingness to open up to us.

God is the almighty Creator and the Sustainer of the world, and the Lord of hosts, and he revealed his secrets and plans in the Scripture. He invites us here to be his children and begins to talk to us through his words and truths. How would you then respond to his initiatives? God the Son, the second person in the triune Godhead, comes to you and invites you as a friend, asking you to be his partner for his work; such a generous offer is a staggering thing to think about.

J. I. Packer summarizes what the activity of knowing God involves as follows:

> What, then, does the activity of knowing God involve? Holding together the various elements involved in this relationship, as we have sketched it out, we must say that knowing God involves, first, listening to God's Word and receiving it as the Holy Spirit interprets it, in application to oneself; second, noting God's nature and character, as his Word and works reveal it; third, accepting his invitations and doing what he commands; fourth, recognizing and rejoicing in the love that he has shown in thus approaching you and drawing you into his divine fellowship.[22]

Then, J. I. Packer turns his attention to the manner, or the way, of knowing God. The Bible uses analogies of a son knowing his father, a wife knowing her husband, a subject knowing his master, and a sheep knowing its shepherd. These analogies emphasize a relation in which the knower "looks up" to the one known, and the latter takes responsibility for the former. The Bible teaches us that we know God in the way

---

22. Packer, *Knowing God*, 37.

described above through knowing Jesus Christ (a proof verse for this point is found in John 14:9).

J. I. Packer summarizes what knowing God is by making three points below:

1. Knowing God is a personal and relational journey as he opens up to us. It involves direct and personal encounters. What matters most is the depth of our intimate knowledge of God. As in loving relationships, knowing God also involves a mutual knowing by being more keenly aware of each other as the object of love and enjoying the other.

2. Knowing God calls for involvement of our entire being—our thoughts, our choices, and our emotions.

3. It is by God's grace that we are able to know him. Knowing God is not something earned or achieved, but is a gift freely given. Those who embrace his provision by grace know him by faith because he first singled them out by grace.

Combining the three points above, J. I. Packer describes what is involved in God's knowing of us as follows:

> Here, God's knowledge of those who are his is associated with the whole purpose of saving mercy. It is a knowledge that implies personal affection, redeeming action, covenant faithfulness, and providential watchfulness toward those whom God knows. It implies, in other words, salvation, now and forever, as we hinted before.[23]

This is, indeed, a "momentous knowledge" that is the source of "unspeakable comfort."[24] Why? Because God knows the real me, with warts and all, yet accepts me as who I am.

Another valuable source of information on the knowledge of God as a firm and sure knowledge of God, deeply rooted in our hearts, is available from a series of sermons delivered by Charles Haddon Spurgeon under the same topic, the knowledge of God. He was born in 1834 and called to be a pastor in 1854 at nineteen at London's famed New Park Street Chapel in Southwark.[25] This was the largest Baptist congregation

---

23. Packer, *Knowing God*, 41.
24. Packer, *Knowing God*, 42.
25. Ort, "Who Is Charles Haddon Spurgeon?"

in London at that time. He is known to have delivered nearly thirty-six hundred sermons by his death in 1892.[26] There are at least three sermons on this very topic.[27] Out of these three sermons—the most closely related and informative sermon is titled "Heart-Knowledge of God" and delivered in 1874—Spurgeon elaborates on the heart-knowledge of God as follows:

> It is not enough to know that our creator is the Jehovah of the Bible, and that he is perfect in character, and glorious beyond thought; but to know God, we must have perceived him, we must have spoken to him, we must have been made at peace with him, we must have lifted up our heart to him, and received communications from him. If you know the Lord your secret is with him, and his secret is with you; he has manifested himself unto you as he does not unto the world. He must have made himself known unto you by the mysterious influences of his Spirit, and because of this, you know him. I cannot explain this knowledge, but it is delightful to remember that many of you understand what it means by experience.[28]

By replacing Calvin's phrase for faith as "a firm and sure knowledge" of God with Spurgeon's "heart-knowledge" of God, as described above, Calvin's formal definition of faith may be reimagined as *a heart-knowledge of God and his love for us founded on the gift of Jesus Christ in pursuit of godliness and purpose of life.* This condensed definition of faith teaches us that knowledge of God is not merely intellectual assent to certain doctrines or dogmas; it is a deep-seated conviction that God is real and has a personal and intimate relationship with each individual believer. This belief is rooted in the heart, not just in the mind. Oh, how badly do we Christians need to have "deep-rooted faith" in our hearts? Those who trust in God and his love through Jesus Christ are like a tree planted by the water. They will always have a source of nourishment and refreshment; they will not be afraid of heat or drought; they will bear fruit in season (Jer 17:7–8). The heart-knowledge of God and his love for us in Jesus Christ, the human expression of the invisible God, undergirds a personal and intimate relationship with a living God, which

---

26. For access to a complete collection of Spurgeon's sermons, see https://www.spurgeongems.org/spurgeon-sermons/.

27. Among them are sermons titled "Immutability of God," "Do You Know Him?," and "Heart-Knowledge of God."

28. Spurgeon, "Heart-Knowledge," 2.

is often understood as faith. In defining faith, some, like John Calvin and J. I. Packer, emphasize the heart-knowledge of God and his love for us in Jesus Christ. In contrast, many others emphasize an intimate and personal relationship with a living God. But they are like one and the other side of the same coin.

A common theme in Christianity is that faith needs to be applied in life. Faith is not just something to be believed in but something to be lived out in everyday life. This means that Christians should strive to put their faith into action by loving God and others, serving others, and living a life consistent with their beliefs.

This practice of faith takes many forms, including prayer, study, worship, and service to others. Through these activities, Christians cultivate their relationship with God and grow in their understanding of his will for their lives. As they do so, faith becomes increasingly integrated into their daily lives, shaping their thoughts, words, and actions.

Living by faith may be compared to playing golf well. The analogy between faith and golf is apt because it highlights the importance of knowledge and practice. Just as a golfer needs to know the rules of the game and the proper techniques for swinging a club, so does a Christian need to have a basic understanding of Christian doctrine and the principles of living a Christian life. However, knowledge alone is not enough. To play golf well, a golfer must practice regularly and develop the necessary muscles. And by repeated practice, a golfer develops muscle memory. Similarly, Christians must practice putting their beliefs into action to live out their faith. This "muscled faith" is needed, a solid and rugged faith, especially when one faces challenges and difficulties.

This practice of faith is not always easy. It requires effort, perseverance, and a willingness and desire to grow amid challenging life situations. The practice of faith requires trust or commitment to Christ and the ability to sustain the contradiction between this challenging present reality and the future hope, and to live out of that tension with a clear vision. However, the rewards of a life lived in faith are immeasurable. As Christians grow in their faith, they find that they can increasingly love God and their neighbors, find joy even while suffering, and live with hope for the future. In conclusion, faith in God is a gift that offers us a transformative relationship with God, eternal life, hope, purpose, and personal transformation. It is a journey worth taking by all means.

CHAPTER 2

Doubt

IN EXAMINING THE WORD "faith," we proceeded as if God's revelation in the Bible is self-evident and authoritative enough for us to continue with full conviction and faith in God and the Scripture. Doubt did not enter into our discussion. However, doubt is complexly intertwined with faith, and it is important and necessary to examine doubt in the context of faith in Christianity. It is so because many Christians wrestle with doubt from time to time—even some well-known Christian leaders have been plagued by times of doubt. Abraham and Moses in the Old Testament and John the Baptist, Saint Peter, and doubting Thomas in the New Testament struggled with doubt at one time or another. Socrates is believed to have famously said, "The unexamined life is not worth living." In our own lives, there are times when doubt arises, especially in our pains and sufferings. We may question, Where is God? Does he hear my payers? Is he the heavenly Father who loves and cares for his children? And am I his child even if he seems distant, far from my struggles and sufferings?

Given doubt's importance and potential ever-presence, examining doubt and its relationship to faith is only proper. Furthermore, it is desirable to discuss doubt immediately after we examine faith for another reason. It is because doubt is the most closely related word to faith, forming part of a two-part concept—dichotomy—in Scripture. A dichotomy means a division between two things that are or are represented as being opposed or entirely different. For instance, when considering the word blessing, we must know the distinction between blessing and its opposite, cursing. We find a similar parallel between wisdom and foolishness. So is the parallel between faith and doubt. Examining both words together or one after another is desirable to appreciate the link and bring distinction and contrast between them. If we study only one word without the other, we will do a great disservice to a rich and full understanding of the word under consideration.

Two Views on the Normalcy of Doubt

In examining doubt in the context of Christianity, a vitally important question is the appropriate attitude toward it. Specifically, is doubt a normal and healthy human experience, both within the faith and outside, or is it something abnormal and undesirable, something to avoid if possible? While most Christian writers readily agree that doubt is found both in faith and without it, there are two perspectives. To answer this question, we need to know whether or not doubt is built into the inherent nature of human beings. If so, it is reasonable to argue that doubt is an inherent and unavoidable state. If not, it is something unnatural and to get out of, if possible. We will explore this question more fully when we examine the nature and character of doubt later. For now, we will start by reviewing what is written on the question by two prominent and respected theologians. J. I. Packer, a renowned theologian, has written briefly on doubt and presents one view on this question of the nature of doubt as follows:

> Well, what is doubt? It is a state of divided mind—"double-mindedness" is James's concept (James 1:6–8)—and is found both *within* faith and *without* it. In the former case, it is faith infected, sick, and out of sorts; in the latter, it belongs to a struggle either toward faith or away from a God felt to be invading and making claims one does not want to meet. In C. S. Lewis's spiritual autobiography, *Surprised by Joy*, you can observe both these motivations successively.
>
> In our doubt, we think we are honest, and certainly try to be; but perfect honesty is beyond us in this world, and an unacknowledged unwillingness to take God's word about things . . . often underlies a person's doubt about this or that item of faith. Repeatedly this becomes clear in retrospect, though we could not see it at the time.[1]

---

1. Packer, *I Want*, 25.

Let us examine Packer's view. First, his view on doubt is a nuanced perspective on faith and doubt. While he recognizes that doubt is not necessarily incompatible with faith, he argues that doubt is a condition characterized by a divided mind, echoing the "double-mindedness" from the letter of James. As he says, double-mindedness is "found both *within* faith and *without* it. In the former case, it is faith infected, sick, and out of sorts; in the latter, it belongs to a struggle either toward faith or away from a God felt to be invading and making claims one does not want to meet."[2] Whatever he had intended to communicate with this description of doubt, it is clear from the immediate context that doubt is both negative and undesirable. In other words, it is not normal or healthy. This view overly emphasizes the unsettling and possibly negative aspects of doubt. Yes, there is such a thing as destructive doubt. However, many people will readily agree that doubt is natural and normal within faith and can strengthen faith with many potential benefits. Whether doubt is healthy or destructive depends largely on how you deal with it. A more detailed discussion on this point will follow when we discuss ways to deal with doubt later.

Alister McGrath, another renowned theologian, presents another view on doubt. His is also nuanced but more positive view of doubt. He first notes that doubt is not unbelief. Some ideas closely related to doubt, like belief, faith, doubt, skepticism, and unbelief, will be discussed later. He then notes that doubt is natural even within faith. Many authors have famously grappled with the idea of doubt. In his work *Anna Karenina*, Leo Tolstoy's character Levin, while in confession, tells a priest that it is a near-constant state of existence for him.[3] Why do we humans doubt? It comes from our human weakness and frailty. We humans, including believers, lack the confidence to trust fully in God and long for certainty in what we believe. In this imperfect world, achieving the absolute certainty is practically is impossible. Given that, it seems wise to heed McGrath's advice to learn to be relaxed about doubt.

He further notes that

> doubt is like an attention-seeking child. The more attention you pay to it, the more attention it demands. By worrying about your doubts, you get locked into a vicious cycle of uncertainty. So how does doubt become unbelief? Unbelief is the decision

---

2. Packer, *I Want*, 25.
3. Tolstoy, *Anna Karenina*, part 5, ch. 1.

to live as if there is no God. It is a deliberate decision to reject Jesus Christ and all He stands for. But doubt is something quite different. Doubt arises within the context of faith. It is a wistful longing to be sure of the things in which we trust. But it is not, and need not, be a problem. Just because I can't prove my faith in God doesn't mean it is wrong.[4]

This somewhat lengthy quotation helps delineate several important factors in examining doubt. First, he recognizes the basic principle that while doubt is not unbelief, it may become unbelief. Second, it highlights doubt as a natural and normal activity in Christian life. He argues then that "it is not, and need not, be a problem." While doubt may be unsettling, it is a crucial aspect of human cognition. It allows us to refine our beliefs, make informed decisions, and engage in meaningful intellectual pursuits. Embracing doubt rather than suppressing it can lead to a greater understanding of our faith, personal growth, and a more nuanced appreciation of the world around us. Third, McGrath explains three sources of doubt. Doubt comes about first because of our human weakness and frailty, lack of confidence to trust God fully, and our longing for certainty in all life matters. As long as there are so many unknowns and uncertainties in our lives and the world, doubt is normal, natural, and inevitable. In the same article, McGrath notes that doubts also arise through our lack of humility. It is true that we are often led to believe that there are no answers to tough questions on Christian truths, when we simply have not yet found answers to difficult questions.

Considering the two views on the appropriate attitude to doubt, I find that my personal view is much closer to that of McGrath because the innateness and inevitability of doubt make much more sense. When we think through it, we realize that belief, faith, doubt, skepticism, and unbelief are natural and normal parts of the human experience in our search for truth and meaning. Alister McGrath has published a book-length treatment of the nature of doubt and how to grow and thrive amid uncertainties and doubt.[5] Philip Yancey's two well-known books, *Disappointment with God* and *A Skeptic's Guide to Faith*, would also be helpful to those who struggle with doubt.[6] Both authors examine doubt in a

---

4. McGrath, "When Doubt Becomes Unbelief."
5. McGrath, *Doubting*.
6. For Yancey's further views on doubt in the Christian context, see also Yancey, "Faith and Doubt."

Christian context and strongly espouse a positive approach to dealing with doubt in the Christian community.

Misunderstandings of Doubt

As with the misunderstood word "faith," there are many misconceptions about doubt. To illustrate the importance of the issue of doubt and the reality check for debunking the misconceptions, let us begin with a few examples of misconceptions of doubt in Christianity.

1. Doubt is the opposite of faith.

Doubt and faith are not opposites; faith is not about blind certainty but about trusting God in good and bad times, even when we do not have all the answers. Doubt is a natural and normal human experience, just like faith; it can be a helpful avenue for strengthening our faith. Doubt can also become unbelief. A possible harmful effect of this misconception is that it makes those holding the misconceived view feel shameful or guilty about their doubt.

2. Doubt is a sign of weak faith.

Doubt is not a sign of weak faith. Instead, doubt is a sign of strength. It takes courage to question our beliefs and to wrestle with difficult issues. When we face our doubts, we demonstrate our commitment to truth and our willingness to grow in our faith. Those who hold this misconception may feel discouraged and give up on their faith.

3. Doubt is a sin.

Doubt is not a sin. It is an ordinary human mental state and emotion, and God understands our doubts. The Bible is full of examples of people who doubted God, and God never condemned them for it. God often used their doubts to draw them closer to him. The book of Job provides a good example of this. The Psalms and Lamentations in the OT are full of complaints, questions, and doubts about God's love and goodness. Those who hold this erroneous view may feel a lot of fear and anxiety.

4. We should never talk about our doubts.

It is important to be honest about our doubts with God and with trusted friends and mentors. Talking about our doubts can help us process them and find answers to our questions. It can also help us connect with other people struggling with similar doubts.

Definition of Belief, Faith, Doubt, Skepticism, and Unbelief

Before examining the nature and sources of doubt, let us define the terms closely related to doubt. They are *belief, faith, doubt, skepticism,* and *unbelief*. We will use these terms repeatedly; thus, defining them closely at the outset is important. Precise definitions of these terms will help clear confusion about doubt and related terms. Below are concise descriptions of these terms with brief explanations.

Belief: Belief is a general term for accepting something as true or real. It can be based on personal experience, evidence, or authority. Belief can be strong or weak and can be accompanied by varying degrees of certainty.

Faith: Faith is a strong belief or trust in something or someone without concrete evidence or proof, going beyond what can be rationally established. Faith is often associated with religious belief but can be applied to other areas of life, such as personal relationships or societal norms. In Christianity, faith is trust in a God who has shown himself worthy of that trust. Faith can provide a sense of purpose, meaning, and comfort in the face of uncertainty.

Doubt: Doubt is a state of uncertainty or lack of conviction about something or someone. It can arise from a lack of evidence, conflicting information, or personal experiences that challenge existing beliefs. Doubt can be a healthy and productive part of the learning process, as it encourages critical thinking through questioning our assumptions and seeking further understanding. Doubt can also be destructive, shriveling faith until it dies.

Skepticism: Skepticism is a critical attitude towards claims or ideas, demanding evidence or proof before accepting them. Skepticism is not the same as unbelief; rather, it is a way of evaluating the strength of evidence and identifying potential flaws in reasoning. Skepticism is essential for scientific inquiry and critical thinking.

Unbelief: Unbelief is a mental state characterized by the absence of belief in something or someone. It is the opposite of belief and may stem from a lack of evidence, a personal experience, or an authority. The strength of unbelief can vary and may be accompanied by varying degrees of certainty.

Belief, faith, doubt, skepticism, and unbelief are all mental states that describe varying degrees of certainty or uncertainty in our search for truth and meaning. It is important to note that the opposite of either belief or faith is not doubt but unbelief. Doubt is placed between belief and faith on the one hand and skepticism and unbelief on the other. This highlights doubt's ambivalence as it sits between these two groups. James 1:8 compares the person who doubts to a wave of the sea, unstable in all they do, thus implying double-mindedness. To believe is to accept something as true, to disbelieve is to reject it, and to doubt is to be in a state of indecision between the two, thus being double-minded. Though doubt is unsettling, it can be a productive part of the learning process. Unbelief or unfaith, on the other hand, is a voluntary decision to reject faith.

Nature of Doubt and Its Sources

What is the doubt? It is not the absence of faith but the questioning of one's beliefs and faith. In other words, one can only doubt what one already believes. The Christian believes there is a God, and when doubting, he questions the existence of God. The atheist, by definition, believes that there is no God, and when doubting, he questions his belief that there is no God. So, by doubting his belief in the nonexistence of God, he fears that God may exist. When a communist doubts, for instance, he questions Karl Marx's vision of the utopian society. These observations lead us to conclude that doubt presupposes faith or belief. In Christianity, it is common for us to have faith with questions. We need to confront this sooner or later in our Christian lives.

Doubt, within the Christian context, refers to a state of uncertainty or questioning about one's belief, faith, or understanding of spiritual matters. It is a normal and often inevitable part of being human. To understand why and how doubt arises, we need to examine the nature and sources of doubt, such as the inquisitiveness of human nature, the mystery of God, the complexity of the Christian narrative, and personal disappointment in faith's journey. Below, we have presented each source of doubt with a brief explanation.

1. Nature of Faith: Faith is inherently trusting in something or someone beyond verifiable empirical evidence. Though we deeply long for absolute certainty in everything we believe, such certainty is impossible. Furthermore, the things in life that matter the most, such as respect for human life, democratic ideals, or religious beliefs (like Christianity), cannot be proven with certainty beyond any doubt. The same goes for the choice of worldviews. We commit ourselves to the great worldviews without waiting for perfect proof and assurance. Therefore, this element of trust in upholding any of these worldviews without empirically verifiable evidence implies a willingness to embrace uncertainty and accept the possibility of being wrong. Doubt is a natural consequence of accepting this inherent uncertainty. In a world of perfect certainty, there is no need or role of faith.

2. Human Nature: Humans are naturally inquisitive and curious beings, constantly seeking answers and explanations for the world around them. This innate inquisitiveness and curiosity can lead to questioning accepted beliefs, including those within Christianity. Doubt, in this context, serves as a mechanism for intellectual exploration and personal growth.

3. Mystery of God: Christianity centers on the transcendent nature of God, a personal being beyond human comprehension. This inherent mystery can lead to questions and uncertainties as individuals strive to reconcile their limited understanding with the vastness and complexity of the divine. In light of the mystery of God, doubt is a natural consequence.

4. Complexity of the Christian Narrative: The Christian faith encompasses vast and complex narratives spanning centuries of history, diverse interpretations, and hard-to-understand and challenging concepts. Gripping the entirety of this narrative demands difficult theological questions, and doubt is a natural outcome.

5. Personal Experience of Faith: Faith is not merely an intellectual exercise but a deeply personal and experiential journey. Individuals

encounter challenges, setbacks, disappointment, tragedy, and unanswered prayers, naturally leading to questions about God's presence and plan.

Doubt can arise for various reasons and can be unsettling. However, it can paradoxically serve as a catalyst for deeper understanding and stronger faith. By confronting doubt and engaging in honest inquiry, individuals can refine their beliefs, strengthen their convictions, and develop a more resilient and authentic faith. In summary, doubt is not an enemy of faith but an inherent and natural companion on the Christian faith journey. By embracing doubt as an opportunity for exploration, questioning, and personal growth, individuals can deepen their understanding of their faith and strengthen their relationship with God.

Types of doubt are closely related to the sources of doubt, and let's turn our attention to different types of doubt below:

1. Intellectual Doubt: This type of doubt arises from intellectual challenges, questions, complexity, and uncertainties about certain aspects of Christian doctrine and theology. More often than not, doubt arises from the incompatibility of Christian faith with the human pursuit of knowledge, like science and philosophy. This is a serious challenge for both young and old Christians in the modern secular world, where humanism, relativism, and scientism are prevalent.

2. Emotional Doubt: Doubt can be an emotional experience, often linked to personal struggles, suffering, traumatic experiences, or disappointment with God. Individuals may grapple with doubts about the goodness of God in the face of adversity or the meaning and purpose of their own lives. Two members of the cell group of our church lost their spouses in their fight with cancer, and their doubts about the power and goodness of God were serious and genuine. In the end, one gave up her faith in God; another kept her faith in God and continued.

3. Relational Doubt: Doubts can also arise in the relationships within the Christian community or with God. The real or perceived failure of church members and leaders often leads individuals to question the authenticity of their faith in God or the presence of God in their lives. This doubt often results in the baby being thrown out with the bath water. In this case, doubt becomes unbelief.

4. Moral Doubt: Moral dilemmas and ethical questions can bring doubt about the moral framework of Christianity. Believers may struggle with questions of right and wrong, seeking to align their actions and decisions with the evolving standard of values in secular society.

We have already learned that doubt is not the opposite of faith and is a natural and normal experience of human life. Doubt is a state of uncertainty or lack of conviction about something or someone you have faith in. It can arise from a lack of evidence, conflicting information, or personal experiences that force re-examining existing beliefs. We also learn that doubt can be a healthy and productive part of the learning process, as it encourages critical thinking through questioning our assumptions and seeking further understanding of our faith. At the same time, doubt can be destructive when doubt becomes unbelief.

Healthy Doubt, Honest Doubt, and Destructive Doubt

Depending on motivation and its impact, there are different types of doubt: healthy, honest, and destructive. Healthy and honest doubts can have a positive effect as they can enhance our understanding and appreciation of our faith. However, if doubts become destructive, they can lead to a loss of faith, disillusionment with Christianity, and a sense of disconnection from God. Therefore, it is crucial to comprehend their differences to navigate our faith journey and develop a positive relationship with God in our spiritual journey. What would be the distinguishing factors between different types of doubts? The motivation to raise the doubt comes first. Is the doubt arising from a genuine desire to attain truth and understanding, or does fear, anger, or resentment drive it? The honesty, sincerity, and integrity to confront doubt openly are closely related to motivation as a determining factor. Secondly, another important determining factor is the nature and content of the questions and the way and manner in which we ask questions.

Healthy and honest doubts are born from a sincere desire to seek truth and personal growth in faith. Such doubts are often sparked by curiosity, a willingness to learn, and an openness to critical thinking and exploration. Honest doubt requires an open and sincere attitude, integrity, readiness to confront difficult questions, and honest self-examination. On the other hand, destructive doubt is motivated by fear, cynicism, and negativity. When doubts arise about seemingly negative historical events in the OT, favoring Israel and punishing its neighboring nations, they can develop into a negative view of God's capriciousness, leading to a negative and cynical view of the OT, which ultimately leads to a rejection of the authenticity of the Bible. The rejection of the Bible is tantamount to the rejection of Christianity.

Illustrations and examples can help differentiate between healthy, honest, and destructive doubts. Let's consider doubting God's existence as an example. Honest and healthy doubt can arise when we reconcile an almighty God's existence with the world's suffering and evil. In contrast, destructive doubt may question the notion of God as a human invention. For instance, Ludwig Feuerbach argued that God was a projection of human desires and fears. An example of destructive doubt based on Feuerbach's argument could be, "Did man create God, instead of God creating man?"

Another example is doubting the authority of the Bible. Healthy and honest doubt can be raised when seeking clarification on unclear or contradictory passages. In such cases, one may explore different interpretations or engage in respectful dialogue with others. However, destructive doubt can question the Bible's authenticity as a divine revelation. Karl Marx expressed this doubt by criticizing inconsistencies, the Bible's support for existing social hierarchies, and its promotion of passivity and obedience.

When and How Does Doubt Become Unbelief?

Alister McGrath suggests that we should consider our faith a lifeline to God.[7] Then he compares a lifeline to an umbilical cord, linking us to God and providing a channel through which his life-giving sustenance of grace can reach us. Unbelief severs this link, and faith will wither away like a branch broken off a vine. Doubt can either strengthen or weaken our faith. If you keep focusing on your doubts, they may grow and become destructive, leading to the downfall of your faith. To illustrate this point, McGrath compares doubt to an attention-seeking child. The more you pay attention to it, the more demanding it becomes, creating a vicious circle that's hard to escape. By feeding our doubts in our

---

7. The ensuing discussion draws from McGrath, "When Doubt Becomes Unbelief." For the umbilical analogy, see also McGrath, *Doubting*, 121.

thoughts, we allow Satan to have his way, as portrayed in *The Screwtape Letters* by C. S. Lewis.

Alister McGrath identifies three possible ways in which doubt can lead to unbelief. The first way is when someone has unrealistic expectations of faith. Human beings crave security and certainty and often feel they should be sure about everything they believe. However, in reality, except for logical propositions (the whole is bigger than the part) and mathematical equations ($2 + 2 = 4$), many important things in life cannot be proven with complete certainty. For instance, questions about God's existence and his nature, human nature and destiny, and the universe are all significant and can impact how we think, live, hope, and act. But no one can claim to have the complete truth about these matters.

As McGrath points out, we cannot see or touch God nor demand that he publicly demonstrate his existence or character. Our knowledge of God comes only through faith. However, the human mind often desires more than faith, asking for a sign or proof to remove all doubt. In Matt 12:38–42, some scribes and Pharisees demanded such signs and proofs, but Jesus rebuked them for their unrealistic attitude towards faith. You will likely encounter difficulties and doubts if you require absolute certainty in your faith. This can lead to unbelief, and doubt becomes an obstacle to faith.

To fully appreciate how doubt turns into disbelief through the first route, we must understand the nature of faith in Christianity. Believing in God requires an act of faith, and so does the decision not to believe in God. Similarly, accepting Christianity or Jesus as the Son of God and the risen Savior demands a leap of faith, and so does the decision to reject both. Both accepting and rejecting faith in Jesus requires faith because nobody can prove anything with absolute certainty beyond any doubt. Whether accepting or rejecting, every attitude relies on faith, not certainty. That's why there always remains an element of doubt in both cases. To capture the essential nature of faith based on these observations, I will quote McGrath's description of faith below:

> Faith is not belief without proof but trust without reservations—trust in a God who has shown himself worthy of that trust. To use a Trinitarian framework: God the Father makes those promises; God, the Son confirms them in his words and deeds; and

the Holy Spirit reassures us of their reliability and seals those promises within our hearts.[8]

The second way Alister identifies that doubt becomes unbelief is by focusing on ourselves in an unhealthy and negative way. This can lead to feelings of hopelessness. Instead, we should look outward to the living God who gave us our faith and promised to be with us through good and bad times. Doubt can be compared to a spoiled child who seeks attention, as mentioned earlier. The more attention we give it, the more it demands. Therefore, instead of feeling overwhelmed by doubt, we should see it as an opportunity to strengthen our faith by reorienting our minds.

Thirdly and finally, doubt can turn into unbelief when one's faith is weak and underdeveloped. A faith that refuses to mature is susceptible to spiritual warfare, where internal struggles and external forces can challenge one's beliefs. A feeble foundation in faith may not withstand these challenges, leading doubt to eventual unbelief. Therefore, it is crucial to make a diligent effort to learn, renew, deepen, and consolidate one's faith in God and his character by getting to know him intimately, loving him deeply, and serving him. McGrath's analogy of reinforced concrete is an appropriate image for reinforced faith in God.

---

8. McGrath, *Doubting*, 25.

CHAPTER 3

Sin

IN EVERYDAY LANGUAGE, SIN is understood to mean doing something bad, mean, or immoral, such as lying, stealing, cheating, hurting, or killing. Committing such acts against fellow human beings is already a serious offense. The concept of sin in Christianity is primarily related to God. It refers to disobeying God's will or law, which results in a deplorable human condition. Kevin DeYoung puts his finger on the essence of sin by stating, "Sin is both a condition, inherited from Adam (Rom 5:12–21), and an action, manifesting itself in thought, word, and deed, which, when full-grown, gives birth to death (James 1:15)."[1] Sin is often defined as "missing the mark." The mark is the norm of God's law, and "missing the mark" means falling short of God's glory. "For all have sinned and fall short of the glory of God" (Rom 3:23). Two major characteristics of sin are that it is universal across time and human culture, and sin corrupts the whole human person. In this regard, the universality of sin and human depravity is a simple assumption of Scripture. The graveness of sin is even more significant in Christianity because it is seen as an active rebellion against God and his laws. God is the Creator and Sustainer of the world and mankind, and violating his will and law is a serious and heinous offense.

Charles H. Spurgeon captures the essence of sin in his sermon "The Deep-Seated Character of Sin," delivered in 1868, based on Jer 17:1, as follows:

---

1. DeYoung, *Daily Doctrine*, 116.

> Sin is a want of conformity to the will of God; sin is disobedience to God's command; sin is a forgetfulness of the obligations of the relation that exists between the creature and the creator. This is the very essence of sin. Injustice to my fellow creature is truly sin, but its essence lies in the fact that it is sin against God, who constituted the relation which I have violated.[2]

In his sermon, Spurgeon identifies three types of sin. The first is the *sin of omission*, which is a failure to conform to the will of God, not doing what you are commanded. The second type is the *sin of commission*, which is disobedience to God's commands and laws. It involves committing acts and deeds that God prohibits by crossing the boundaries set by God. Finally, there is the *sin of forgetfulness*, which refers to our failure to remember our obligation as creatures to our Creator. This sin covers the rest of all other sins we commit.

Sin is a complex concept with theological, philosophical, and psychological dimensions. Various Christian traditions may have different perspectives and approaches to understanding the nature and origin of sin and how to overcome it. Some traditions focus more on individual sin, while others focus on sin's systematic and societal aspects, such as injustice and oppression. Nevertheless, different traditions share some commonalities: sin is universally pervasive and deep-rooted, and there is a solution to the problem.

The verse from Rom 3:23 ("For all have sinned and fall short of the glory of God") quoted earlier, most forcefully expresses the universality of sin. We often say that "nobody is perfect" or "to err is human," and these casual comments also capture the universality of sin across cultures and periods.

In the same sermon referred to earlier, Spurgeon provides a vivid explanation of the intrinsic and deep-rooted nature of sin in the hearts of humans. He bases his explanation on Jer 17:1, which states, "The sin of Judah is written with a pen of iron; with a point of diamond it is engraved on the tablet of their heart, and on the horns of their altars." The prophet Jeremiah uses this powerful image to illustrate the permanence and deep-rootedness of sin Spurgeon continues to expound that humans love sin, and it is not an accidental occurrence but a deliberate choice. By his disposition, man selects evil, rejects good, and goes against God.

---

2. Spurgeon, "Deep-Seated Character," 2.

Understanding the severe consequences of sin can help us realize that all other problems we face in life are insignificant compared to the damage sin can cause. Sin can twist our character, a fundamental aspect of our humanity—including our thoughts, emotions, speech, will, and actions—and turn it into a weapon that can harm others. Kevin DeYoung again spotlights the root of our fundamental problem by saying that our fundamental problem is not bad parents, schools, or circumstances. "Our fundamental problem is a bad heart. And every single one of us is born into the world with it."[3] The idea of sin, whether as a deprivation or an active, corrupting, and destructive force, is depressing and disheartening. That's why we avoid discussing it and would rather mumble, fudge, or trivialize it. Nowadays, the word *sin* is mostly used to describe indulging in decadent candy and chocolate on dessert menus.

Why do we need to bring out the topic of sin and examine it? For what purpose do we restate the Christian doctrine of sin by tracing the origin and examining the nature of sin? The purpose of doing that is not to make us feel guilty or punish us but to provide a framework for comprehending our brokenness in humanity and allowing God to heal us. It reminds us that we are all flawed and need to seek redemption.

Common Misconceptions of Sin

As mentioned, sin usually means doing something bad or immoral, in everyday language. Below are a few common misconceptions about sin and a brief evaluation of each.

1. Sin is an act of wrongdoing. It is doing something bad, like indulging in drunkenness, smoking, talking behind a person's back, swearing, or doing something cruel, like beating and hurting.

This statement captures some common perceptions of sin as specific immoral actions. However, in Christianity, sin is not limited to external actions but refers to internal conditions in human nature, which determine attitudes and motivations. According to Christian teachings, sin involves falling short of God's standards and manifests itself in thoughts, words, and deeds. Paul also speaks of sin in a summary fashion as a mode of human existence outside of Christ. For Paul, therefore, sin is

---

3. DeYoung, *Daily Doctrine*, 118.

not, in the first place, an individual act or condition to be considered by itself. Instead, it is the supra-individual mode of existence, from which one can only be redeemed by being taken up in the new-life context revealed in Christ (Col 2:13).

2. Sin is committing immoral actions, like cheating, lying, stealing, and killing.

Similar to the first statement, this misconception focuses on specific immoral actions. While these actions are generally considered sinful in Christianity, it's important to note that sin is not solely defined by outward behavior but also by the condition of the heart and separation from God.

3. Sin is only breaking God's rules.

This statement captures an aspect of Christian theology in that it is understood as a violation of God's commandments or divine law. This emphasizes the legalistic aspect of sin, but it is limiting because sin is not just breaking God's rules; it is about the broken relationship between God and humans and how it affects our choices in our thoughts, emotions, will, and actions.

4. Man can overcome sinning through teaching and education.

While teaching and education can contribute to moral development and understanding, Christianity teaches that sin cannot be overcome through human ingenuity or effort. The solution to the problem lies in what God has done for us in Jesus Christ. Overcoming sin requires a more profound heart transformation through faith in Jesus Christ. According to Christian beliefs, salvation and the power to overcome sin come through a personal relationship with Jesus Christ.

5. Original sin is imagined and invented to control people.

This statement reflects a skeptical view of original sin, suggesting it may have been created to control individuals. It is important to note that beliefs about original sin vary among Christian denominations, but the concept is generally rooted in theological interpretations of biblical passages. From a Christian perspective, original sin is not invented but is seen as a theological explanation for humanity's universal fallen state.

Word Study of Sin

Our primary goal through word study is to determine what the word under consideration can mean (to determine the semantic range), what it means based on the context, and which sense is most in line with the immediate context in the flow of thought.[4]

The Hebrew Bible has many words for the concept of "sin," and each has its distinct meaning. This indicates that sin is a complex concept that can be described from different perspectives. In the Hebrew language, the verb "sin" (*chata*) means "to miss" or "to fail," with an additional connotation of "making an error." This can also be extended to mean sinning against God. The most significant aspect of these extended meanings of "sin" is that they show that sin is primarily seen as an act against God. This is evident in David's prayer of repentance for his sins against Bathsheba, where he says, "Against you [God], you only, I have sinned [*chata*]" (Ps 51:4a). This is the primary usage of the verbal root in the OT.

In the New Testament, the words *hamartano* (which means "to sin," as a verb) and *hamartia* (which means "sin," as a noun) are closely related to the idea of sin. The verb *hamartano* refers to committing impious, immoral, or unjust actions. In Rom 3:23, Saint Paul states that "all have sinned [*hamartano*] and fall short of the glory of God," clearly demonstrating the universality of sin. The noun *hamartia* is a term more commonly used among Christians to refer to sin, and it can mean anything from failure or error to transgression against a deity. In the Bible, *hamartia* refers to acts of impiety or unrighteousness—violations of God's standards of holiness. To Paul, sin is not just a violation of God's will and law, but instead, it is a destructive force that corrupts all of humanity.

Biblical Understanding of Sin

The concept of sin has played a central role in Western cultures for centuries, shaping its religious, legal, and governmental legislation and

---

4. The discussion that follows draws from Longman and Strauss, "Sin," *BED* 744–46.

philosophical landscapes. Sin is probably most foundational to Western religions, especially Christianity. It defines the relationship between humans and God, shapes concepts of morality, salvation, and the afterlife, and determines religious institutions and moral compasses. With modernization and secularization during past centuries, the influence of sin in these areas is somewhat weakened. However, the biblical concept of sin as any act and disposition against God and his law, as well as the power to corrupt human thought, word, and deed, is upheld in the Christian tradition.

What I aim to accomplish here is to provide a brief and in-depth understanding of the historical and traditional Christian views of sin with its whole reality and grave consequences. Those who are interested in the modern treatment of the concept of sin are encouraged to consult two excellent sources. The first is a book-length treatment of sin, *Not the Way It's Supposed to Be: A Breviary of Sin*, by Cornelius Plantinga Jr., and *Biblical Critical Theory: How the Bible's Unfolding Story Makes Sense of Modern Life and Culture* by Christopher Watkin.[5] Substantive issues to be focused on are the origin of sin, the nature of sin, total depravity, and the dynamics of sin, as well as the gospel and sin. These are primarily based on the well-known *Reformed Dogmatics* volumes and the lesser-known but equally informative book *The Wonderful Works of God*, both by Herman Bavinck; *Institutes of the Christian Religion* by John Calvin; and *The International Standard Bible Encyclopedia* (*ISBE*), as well as those works by Plantinga and Watkin referred to above.[6]

The Origin of Sin

Our fallen world is not how it was originally meant to be. This is the idea behind the title of Cornelius Plantinga's well-known book on sin. When God created the world, he looked down with delight on the works of his hands, for it was all very good (Gen 1:31). However, sin crept in stealthily, and its devastation was catastrophic. But the origin of sin remains a mystery. We may speculate that when God created humanity, he chose to

---

5. Plantinga, *Not the Way*, chs. 4–6.

6. While works on sin by Calvin and Bavinck are substantial and mature, the most comprehensive and thorough treatment of sin is found in chs. 1–4 of Bavinck, *Sin and Salvation*; Bromiley, "Sin," 518–25; and a chapter titled "Sin and Death" in Bavinck, *Wonderful Works*, 203–41.

take Adam and Eve on the perilous path of covenantal freedom, which left open the possibility of their rebellion, resulting in sin and death.

Let's follow the Genesis story of the fall. According to Gen 2:9, there were two trees in the garden for which God had a particular purpose: the tree of the knowledge of good and evil and the tree of life. Since the tree of life does not surface again in the story of sin, we may proceed to God's permission to eat every other tree of the garden, but the prohibition is not to eat from the tree of the knowledge of good and evil. By violating the command of God and eating, they would make themselves like God in the sense that they would position themselves outside and above God's law and determine and judge, like God, for themselves what good and evil was.

Genesis 3:1a introduces a serpent, the most cunning of all the wild animals the Lord God had made. This animal is a beast like any other. Still, the Bible strongly implies that the serpent of Gen 3 is to be identified with the devil (Rev 12:9). This recognizes the entrance of superterrestrial power in explaining the origin of sin. Genesis 3:1b describes an encounter of the serpent with the woman with a low-key and innocent-sounding question: "Did God actually say, 'You shall not eat of any tree in the garden'?" This question stealthily elevates her to a position to judge herself on what God has said. This is a powerful and effective way to invite her to doubt God's word.

In Gen 3:2–3, it is recorded that the woman spoke to the serpent, saying, "We can eat from all the trees in the garden, but God has said, 'You must not eat from the tree that is in the middle of the garden, and you must not touch it, or you will die.'" Two important points can be taken from this passage. Firstly, Eve exaggerated God's commandment by including the instruction not to touch the fruit, which suggests that she may have been secretly dissatisfied with God's decree. Secondly, Satan subtly implied that God was an uninterested deity who did not have Eve's best interests at heart, making her more susceptible to his temptation and leading her to participate in the serpent's wicked plan.

In Gen 3:4–5, "the serpent said to the woman, 'You will not surely die. For God knows that when you eat of it, your eyes will be opened, and you will be like God, knowing good and evil.'" The statement made by the serpent is only partially true and is mostly a lie. The half-truth is that eating the fruit will make Adam and Eve like God, as confirmed by God in Gen 3:22. However, the Hebrew word for "to know" can also mean "to choose." As explained by Watkin, God knows good and evil by recognizing them and having the authority to decide what is good and evil.[7] If Eve were to know good and evil, it would mean she is trying to take God's place and make decisions based on her judgment of good and evil.

While the four verses in Gen 3:2–5 describe the nature and the process of temptation, verses 6–13 describe the anatomy of sin. For our purpose, let's focus on verse 6: "So when the woman saw that the tree was good for food, and that it was a delight to the eyes, and that the tree was to be desired to make one wise, she took of its fruit and ate, and she also gave some to her husband who was with her, and he ate."

In explaining the role of verse 6 with earlier verses on the nature of temptation, David Atkinson, in his commentary on Genesis, points out that verse 6 describes the process of moving from casting doubt on God's trustworthiness ("Did God say . . .") to casting doubt on the truth of his word ("You will not die").[8] This decrying of the character of God is the primary root of all the disorders that follow in the story. From then on, temptation yields to disobedient action.

So far, we have used the earlier portion of Gen 3 to explain the origin of sin, focusing on how Adam and Even sinned by rebelling against God. This initial sin is often known as the "original sin." However, the original sin in Christian theology is a technical term (Latin: *peccatum originale*). It refers to mankind's hereditary sinful dispositions as part of human nature, originating from Adam's fall. According to this doctrine, Adam's sin caused all human beings to be born with a fallen nature. The idea is not that we are sinners because we sin, but we sin because we are sinners.

The debate about human nature is ongoing. Some argue that humans have the potential for good and evil, altruism, and selfishness. They suggest that we should recognize this duality instead of relying solely on the idea of original sin. Others argue that upbringing, cultural norms, and individual experiences shape human behavior. They believe that we must consider these external factors when examining human nature. While these factors can influence behavior, they don't fully explain why evil has been prevalent in all cultures throughout history. All serious Christians agree on the universality, solidarity, stubbornness, and historical momentum of sin. For many, the biblical story of the origin of sin offers a compelling explanation for the state of the world. Without this doctrine, the world as we know it would be incomprehensible.

---

7. Watkin, *Biblical Critical Theory*, 112.
8. Atkinson, *Message of Genesis*, 85.

More recently, historical criticism and modern evolutionary theory have questioned the historicity of the fall and have challenged the fall's authenticity. According to geology and other fields of natural sciences and prehistoric studies, the concept of an original moral perfection and the subsequent fall of human beings, as described in the Genesis account, is susceptible to questions. These fields suggest that early human ancestors emerged from darkness and have progressively improved their lives. On this challenge from some natural sciences, Herman Bavinck suggests that defense of the truth of the fall would be on firmer ground if one takes a position not in the paradisal story but based on data of experience amid sinful reality as a fact of life. Those interested in his arguments may consult the relevant discussions in his *Reformed Dogmatics*.[9]

Total Depravity

In the Reformed tradition of Christianity, total depravity is closely connected to the idea of original sin. Virtually every traditional and historical church has a creed or confession that acknowledges something very serious happened to the human race due to the first sin committed by Adam and Eve. However, "original sin" is often misunderstood as the first sin, in the popular arena. We need clarification in two areas. Firstly, many usually think the original sin refers to the first sin. But historically, that's not what original sin has referred to in the church. As R. C. Sproul aptly points out, the doctrine of original sin defines the consequences of the first sin on the human race. Secondly, the word "total" in total depravity doesn't mean the maximum (utter or complete degree) of depravity. In other words, total depravity doesn't mean every human being is as sinful as possible. It means that the fall was so significant and serious that it affected every part of the whole person. As a result, the whole person (body, mind, will, and spirit) has been infected by the power of sin. R. C. Sproul suggests that a good term to replace total depravity is "radical depravity" because the meaning of the term "radical" (with its roots in Latin *radix*) is to permeate to the core of a thing.[10] The Reformed view is that the effects of the fall extend or penetrate to the core of our being. Since the core or the very center of our existence is often identified in English with the heart, total

---

9. Bavinck, *Sin and Salvation*, 36–39.
10. Sproul, *Essential Truths*, 147–48.

depravity reminds us of a sermon title of Spurgeon's sermon on the deep-rootedness of our sin in our heart, mentioned earlier.

According to Bavinck, the concept of total moral human depravity might seem hard to accept and even incomprehensible to some.[11] However, this is a clear teaching of Scripture and is confirmed by the experiences of our daily lives. The doctrine of incapacity for good is a religious confession, which means that we cannot do any good in the eyes of God. But the doctrine of total depravity is not meant to make us feel guilty or punish us. Instead, it provides a framework to understand our inherent brokenness as human beings. It reminds us that we all have flaws and need to seek redemption. To conform ourselves to the image of Christ, we must be regenerated and renewed and have our hearts transformed by the Holy Spirit. Nonetheless, even this change does not completely eliminate sin, and we must wait for our glorification in heaven.

Christians can comfortably believe in the biblical origin of sin based on Scripture, church history, and the truthfulness of the narrative to understand the world as we know it. In his article by the same name, Trevin Wax presents three answers to the question, "Why Should I Believe in Original Sin?"[12] The first and primary reason we believe in original sin is that it is taught in the Scripture. Romans 5:12–21 is a well-known passage that explains how death came into the world through Adam's sin and how life is now made possible through Christ. Paul does not explicitly state how Adam's sin and the sins of humanity are connected, but there is a clear implication that there is a link between them. The doctrine of original sin is a church doctrine constructed by combining various biblical texts to explain the deep-rooted corruption of the human heart. This is similar to how the doctrine of the Trinity was constructed. There are many Bible verses to support the notion of original sin. Still, the prominent ones are found in Rom 3:23 and 6:23; 1 Cor 15:22; and many of Jesus' teachings in Matt 23 and Mark 7:20–23.

Second, there are two views in the debate on the will to sin, between Augustine and Pelagius in church history. The traditional view, which Augustine supported, is that sin begets sin. In the case of Adam and all his descendants, a sinful state follows a sinful deed. Pelagians, on the other hand, deny this consequence of sin. They believe that the will that sins is entirely free to sin or not to sin, ignoring the habit-forming dynamic aspect

---

11. Bavinck, *Sin and Salvation*, 78.
12. This discussion draws from Wax, "Why Should I Believe."

of sin. However, Scripture and our experience testify that every act of the will arising from antecedent impulses and desires has a retroactive impact and reinforces it. This is how sin becomes a habit, and those who commit sins become servants of sin. Herman Bavinck argues, "Sin gives birth to sin. In the case of Adam and all his descendants, a sinful state follows a sinful deed. . . . Guilt and pollution go hand in hand. Due to God's judgment, Adam's disobedience plunged all his posterity into guilt, pollution, and death. This is the condition into which we are born."[13]

Third and finally, biblical texts regarding the origin of sin can be pretty bleak and uncompromising. They draw attention to the fact that we are inherently flawed sinners and that our hearts are corrupted to the very core. We can't perform any good deeds for God on our own. In his earlier blog, Trevin Wax highlights three reasons why he finds this grim state, instead, encouraging. Firstly, the concept of original sin gives hope to those who may see themselves as failures. Secondly, it helps us to understand that we are all equal in the eyes of God. This is because it puts us all on the same level, regardless of our social status, wealth, education, or any other factors that may differentiate us. Lastly, and most importantly, original sin directs us towards the necessity of the gospel and the salvation that can only be found through Jesus Christ. This is God's only provision and answer to original sin.

The Nature of Sin

In the Hebrew Bible, there are many words for "sin," but the basic meaning of the Hebrew verb for "sin" (*chata*) is "miss." The Greek equivalent of this verb is *hamartano*, which means "fall short" or "a lack of."[14] For instance, Rom 3:23 reads, "All have sinned and fall short of the glory of God." This information shows that the primary meaning of the word "sin" points to a lack of conformity to God's will, often called the sin of omission. However, the idea of sin as privation (the absence of a quality ordinarily present) is incomplete. Instead, the essence of sin lies in knowingly breaking God's commandments, which originate from a heart that rebels against God. In this sense, sin is an active rebellion against God and his commandments.

---

13. Bavinck, *Sin and Salvation*, 77.
14. Longman and Strauss, "Sin," *BED* 744–46.

Sin is hereditary in that Adam and Eve's original sin is passed down to all subsequent generations, resulting in everyone being born with a natural inclination toward sin. Some interpretations emphasize that this inclination doesn't equate to automatic guilt for Adam's sin but rather a vulnerability and tendency toward making sinful choices.

Sin is a universal reality in all people everywhere. It acknowledges the imperfection inherent in the human condition. It doesn't necessarily imply that all sins are equivalent in severity or that everyone is inherently evil. Instead, it highlights the human capacity for both good and bad choices.[15]

Man's sinfulness is deep-rooted and fixed, as expounded in Spurgeon's "Deep-Seated Character of Sin" sermon (referred to earlier), based on Jer 17:1. Sin is not a mere accident but rather something that man takes pleasure in because it is deeply ingrained in his heart. Removing sin from the human heart is impossible for humans to achieve themselves. However, as mentioned in Ezek 36:26–27; 37:14; 39:29; and Joel 2:28–29, God promises to give believers a new heart.

Sin is not a standalone entity but a parasite that lives off its host. On the parasitic existence of sin, G. W. Bromiley's entry on sin in *ISBE* points out the negative or parasitic quality of clinging to what is good and destroying the good host, which is further elaborated in Plantinga's book.[16] Plantinga first points out that while Saint Paul understands the works of sin (luring, enslaving, and destroying), he does not explain where sin comes from nor defines the nature of sin or how it is transmitted. In answering this omission, Plantinga's graphical explanation of the parasitic aspect of sin is similar to Bromiley's entry in *ISBE* and is worth a direct quotation:

> So the biggest biblical idea about sin, expressed in a riot of images and terms, is that sin is an anomaly, an intruder, a notorious gate-crasher. Sin does not belong in God's world, but somehow, it has gotten in. In fact, "sin has dug in, and, like a tick, burrows deeper when we try to remove it." This stubborn and persistent feature of human sin can make it look like as if it has a life of its own, as if it were an independent power or even a kind of person. . . . Victory passages typically follow the big Pauline sin passages, and these (especially Rom. 8:31–39, in which all the trumpets are sounding) present the main biblical

---

15. See Gen 3–11 and Rom 5:12–21 (especially 5:19).
16. Bromiley, "Sin," 518–25; Plantinga, *Not the Way*, 88–89.

teaching: sin is a fearfully powerful spoiler of the good, but it cannot finally overpower either the original or the renewed project of God in the world.[17]

The biblical view of sin's nature presented thus far can be summarized as deeply rooted and fixed; sin is deeply ingrained in human hearts. Sin is not a standalone entity but a parasite living off its host. Herman Bavinck adds another nature of sin as an active and destructive power, depriving humans of moral perfection. Bavinck bluntly states, "Sin is a privation of the moral perfection human persons ought to possess and includes active transgression. Having no existence on its own, sin is ethical-spiritual in nature, though it always comes to expression in concrete terms. It is a deformity, a departure from God's perfect law by rational creatures who can know God's will. Because in its existence it has no real right to exist, sin a riddle, a mystery."[18]

In his writing, Plantinga raises the question of how sin can be both dominant and doomed, powerful and insignificant. He explains that this apparent contradiction arises because sin is like a parasite. Sin has no power of its own; rather, it steals power, persistence, and plausibility from other sources. It is not an entity in and of itself but rather a spoiler of entities—a leech that feeds on the host organism.

The impact of sin is vast and long-lasting, affecting human history. It is practically impossible to list all its effects, but we can summarize them by stating that they are overwhelmingly negative. Sin corrupts (as highlighted in Rom 5:12–21), pollutes, and disintegrates. One of its most damaging effects is how it shatters relationships on every level. It disrupts people's relationships with God and their relationships with other people and the world around them.

Human Depravity: Dynamics of Sin

The story of the fall teaches us that sin is a corrupting force that can progressively spoil the goodness of creation. It is not just a particular sin but a multiplying power that makes all sins more destructive. Because of this dynamic power, sin as a corrupting force can be best likened to spiritual AIDS, as it is a mysterious, systematic, and progressive attack on our spiritual immune system. Eventually, it breaks down and makes us vulnerable

---

17. Plantinga, *Not the Way*, 88.
18. Bavinck, *Sin and Salvation*, 126.

to multiple self-seeking sins, progressively making life more miserable. Therefore, sin is a dynamic and progressive phenomenon.

On this dynamic aspect of sin, Cornelius Plantinga compares the dynamics of sin to that of addiction.[19] Both sin and addiction share common features of dynamics. By repeating pleasurable acts of sinning, habit-forming behavior escalates tolerance and desire. Sin begets sin; repetition of sinning helps form a habit of heart; habitual sinning increases tolerance for the remorse of sinning and even creates a desire for more sin. Ultimately, this downward spiral makes the sinner a slave to sin. The same dynamic process is equally applicable to addiction. As in addiction, this is why sin persists and moves the general tragedy of sin forward with the progressive and lethal character of moral evil.

Sin and Gospel: Gospel as Solution to Sin?

Having learned of the grim nature of sin and its consequence on the miserable state of mankind and the downward spiral through dynamics of sin in the preceding sections, it is natural to ask whether there is any hope for the solution to sin's penalty and its power.

Yes, there are solutions. However, the solutions proposed vary, depending on different views of the nature of sin.[20] The biblical view focuses on the sin's deep-rootedness and fixedness ingrained in human hearts. The non-biblical and standard view is that sin does not live in man or come out of him but attaches itself to him from without. By nature, according to the non-biblical view, man is good; his heart is uncorrupted. Evil lies in the circumstances, environment, and society in which man is born and reared. Take these circumstances away through reforming society—for instance, by equal distribution of goods to all men—and man will naturally be good. There will be no more reason for him to do evil. This view has been held by many since the eighteenth century, but disillusionment with the goodness of humans is also widely shared.

Others sought the origin of sin in man's sensual nature. Man has a soul but also a body, which has sinful tendencies and inclinations, impure desires, and base passions. This view received some support from the theory that man descended from an animal and is still an animal in his

---

19. For the dynamic aspect of sin, see the chapter titled "The Progress of Corruption" in Plantinga, *Not the Way*, 52–77.

20. This section relies mainly on Bromiley, "Sin," 523–24.

heart. Going back to much earlier thought, sin takes its point of departure in matter. In the ancient past, this was a favorite view. One can push a similar line of logic further to arrive at a view taught by some philosophers that God himself is nothing but a dark nature and a blind force.

The non-biblical and standard views on the origin of sin differ. Still, they share a common belief: they do not attribute the origin of sin to the will of the individual but instead to circumstances, society, sensuality, the body, and matter. According to these views, man is entirely free from blame. If this is true, then sin did not begin at the time of the fall but was inherent in creation. Consequently, redemption from sin would be impossible because sin is an intrinsic part of existence, which is miserable and heartbreaking.

The Bible presents good news! The gospel is God's answer to the penalty and the power of sin. Old Testament patriarchs and prophets have already walked in the light and hope of the coming messianic deliverance. The gospel is the good news that God has fulfilled his promises in Jesus Christ, the Savior for sinful people. It is interesting to note that the first message he preaches is, "Repent, for the kingdom of heaven is at hand" (Matt 4:17). One of the critical questions in the substantive issues of the gospel is how to deal with the penalty and power of sin. The doctrine of imputation teaches us that our sins are transferred to Christ on the cross, and his righteousness is transferred to us by faith. This is excellent news for all of us.

The gospel first exposes the reality of sin's grim nature and grave consequences, as presented in the preceding sections. Some respond by repenting and embracing their sins when the gospel is preached. Others may reject it and continue to live a sinful life. Regardless of the responses of those who hear it, the gospel offers a solution to the problem of sin in several ways. First, it teaches us that sinless Christ takes the curse of sin to himself and thereby redeems us—for it is written, "Christ redeemed us from the curse of the law by becoming a curse for us" (Gal 3:13). Second, by taking to himself our sin and the resulting death, Christ destroys sin in his own body. Romans 8:3b says, "By sending his own Son in the likeness of sinful flesh and for sin, he condemned sin in the flesh." Christ's death in his body, which is the penalty of our sin, is thus the death of sin so that there is liberation/salvation from both the penalty of sin and the power of sin. Third, Christ, through his death and resurrection, enables and warrants all who believe in him to die with him and rise in and with him. There are many Pauline verses on believers dying and rising in and with him. What do they mean? Considering several well-known verses, such as Rom 6:2–14 (especially 6:7, 14); Gal 2:20 and 5:24; and Col 3:5, we learn that we died to sin and the old way of life. Therefore, sin will have no dominion over us, and we are no longer a slave to sin under the law but under grace (Rom 6:14). As a result, we rise and live in newness of life with a new identity and new purpose of life, which is life in and through the Spirit.

What Difference Does the Doctrine of Sin Make?

So far, we have discussed a wide range of topics related to sin. We have examined common misconceptions about sin, its origin, the concept of total depravity, its nature, and its dynamics, along with the gospel as a solution to sin. Now, we come to the final question of what difference the doctrine of sin makes. The doctrine of sin plays a significant role in Christian life and theology in several key ways.

First, the doctrine of sin provides a framework for understanding the fundamental problem with human nature. As mentioned earlier, our fundamental problem is not bad parents, bad schools, or dire circumstances. Our fundamental problem is an evil heart. All humans are born with a sinful nature, inherited from Adam and Eve's original rebellion against God. This sinful nature corrupts every aspect of our being, including our minds, will, emotions, and physical bodies. Because of sin, we are separated from God and unable to save ourselves through our own efforts. This understanding of human sinfulness highlights our need for divine salvation and redemption. This also explains why simply trying to be a "good person" is neither good enough nor possible until and unless our hearts are changed and our minds are renewed (Rom 12:2).

Second, the doctrine of sin provides a lens for interpreting the world. It explains the presence of evil, suffering, and death as consequences of humanity's fall from grace. This doctrine, drawn from Gen 3, as examined in detail under the "Biblical Understanding of Sin" section, presents a Christian worldview on evil, suffering, and death.

As to evil, there are three things to be said: (1) sin explains the origin of moral evil in the world; (2) the doctrine of sin posits that evil is not created by God but is a result of human choice; and (3) the doctrine suggests that humans have an inherent tendency towards sin (the original sin).

There are also three points to suffering: (1) the fall of humanity is seen as the root cause of various forms of suffering; (2) physical pains, emotional stress, and relational conflicts are viewed as consequences of living in a fallen world; and (3) suffering is often interpreted as a result of either personal or the general sinful state of the world.

On death, there are again three points: (1) in Christian theology, death is not seen as part of God's original design for creation; (2) the doctrine of sin presents death as a consequence of the fall, introduced as a punishment for disobedience; and (3) both physical and spiritual death are attributed to the effects of sin.

Third, sin doctrine helps us recognize personal sin in our lives. While Christians are forgiven and given a new nature, the sinful nature still remains and must be actively fought against. Christians are called to "put to death" (Col 3:5) sinful desires and behaviors and strive for holiness by relying on the Holy Spirit's power. Recognizing personal sin creates an attitude of humility, recognizing our ongoing need for God's grace and forgiveness. This also promotes, among believers, mutual support, accountability, and encouragement in living out our faith.

Fourth, understanding sin and its consequences, along with the gospel as its solution, leads to a profound appreciation of God's grace. Believers find hope in the assurance that forgiveness is always available through Christ, regardless of their past.

Finally, understanding the severe consequences of sin encourages Christians to share the gospel with others. This awareness helps Christians see nonbelievers as equally needing God's grace.

CHAPTER 4

Salvation

SALVATION OR *SAVE* IS a versatile word with different meanings in various aspects of our lives. It can refer to actions related to preserving, protecting, being efficient, or rescuing. We refer to saving money, saving lives, saving energy, saving documents, saving time, saving passwords, saving on discounts, and saving witnesses. Likewise, the Bible uses the term *salvation* or *save* in various ways. In its simplest form, the verb *to save* means to be rescued from a dangerous or threatening situation. The exodus from Egypt was the greatest event of salvation in the OT; Old Testament history is full of stories of deliverances (salvation) from Israel's neighboring nations. In this regard, the idea of salvation in the OT emphasizes a nation's political and military dimension during the exilic and pre-exilic periods in Jewish history. In the NT, the idea of salvation differs from that of the OT in that the emphasis is on spiritual redemption from sin and reconciliation with God. In this sense, salvation is deliverance from the wrath and judgment of God.

The Bible uses the term *salvation* in many ways and several tenses. The verb "to save" is used in every possible tense of the Greek language: we were saved, we are being saved, we are saved, we will be saved. The Bible speaks of salvation in terms of the past, present, and future.[1] The central idea of the Bible is that salvation is a result of God's saving actions, and the main message of the whole Bible is salvation.

---

1. For past, present, and future salvation, see Marshall, "Salvation."

What is salvation in Christianity, and what does it signify when someone is saved? Every religion has its perspective on human problems and seeks a way to attain salvation from them. In Christianity, the redemption that Jesus Christ provides is solely initiated by God, which makes it unique from all other religions and philosophies. All other religions and philosophies rely on human actions to achieve redemption. So, as B. B. Warfield states, there are basically only two doctrines of salvation: God's salvation and salvation from ourselves. The first is the doctrine of sin and salvation in Christ, and the second is the salvation from troubles of our own making by ourselves.[2]

Wikipedia defines salvation in Christianity as follows: "In Christianity, salvation (also called deliverance or redemption) is the saving of human beings from sin and its consequences—which include death and separation from God—by Christ's death and resurrection, and the justification entailed by this salvation."[3]

Wikipedia's definition is simple and captures three essential points in understanding salvation. It specifies what believers are saved from (sin), how they are saved from these things (Christ's death and resurrection), and what they are saved for (justification). In his book *Concise Theology: A Guide to Historic Christian Beliefs*, J. I. Packer states, "Salvation is a picture-word of wide application that expresses the idea of rescue from jeopardy and misery into a state of safety."[4] He also organizes his discussion of salvation into three main questions: Saved from what? Saved by what? Saved for what?

Salvation in Christianity is a vast topic that covers the entirety of God's saving work. To explore this concept, we can ask three closely related questions: What are we saved from? We are saved from sin, God's wrath, judgment, the dominion of sin, and the power of death (Rom 1:18, 3:9, 5:21). How are believers saved? Through Christ's death and resurrection, and in Christ. What are we saved for? Wikipedia lists justification as the goal of salvation, but it goes beyond justification and involves all the benefits of salvation from being united with Christ.

Finding accurate answers to these questions is crucial, as incorrect answers can have eternal consequences. Scripture offers distinct answers, and we aim to provide clear and concise biblical answers, particularly from the perspective of Reformed traditions.

2. Warfield, *Plan of Salvation*.
3. Wikipedia, "Salvation in Christianity."
4. Packer, *Concise Theology*, 146.

To begin with, we may restate R. C. Sproul's experience, which is reported in his well-known book *Essential Truths of the Christian Faith* under the chapter titled "Salvation":

> I was once confronted by a young man in Philadelphia who asked me, "Are you saved?" My reply to him was, "Saved from what?" He was taken aback by my question. He obviously hadn't thought much about the meaning of the question he was asking people. The question of being saved is the supreme question of the Bible. The subject matter of the sacred Scriptures is the subject of salvation.[5]

One can imagine the scene where the noted theologian and an eager but naïve young man conversed with important questions on salvation. Can you sense almost palpably a minor irritation felt by R. C. Sproul by being interrupted by an uncalled and unexpected question by the young man in a busy street in Philadelphia, and the young man's embarrassment at R. C. Sproul's probing question, "Saved from what?" The young man might have expected a simple answer to a simple question. Still, R. C. Sproul's well-meant and teasing question was intended to encourage and challenge him to think deeply about the context of such an important question with serious implications. According to the Bible, God saves believers from sin, the power of sin, death, and God's wrath and judgment, with the last two as the main consequences of sin.

At this point, however, it is also important to recognize that the question "Saved from what?" presupposes a human condition as a situation from which we need to be saved. Going further, this question also presupposes an ideal creation by God (Gen 1–2), the entrance of sin by human rebellion (Gen 3), and the whole ensuing biblical narrative. In other words, the grand story of how God has acted from the protoevangelium of Gen 3:15 to Rev 22:2 is in the background when we use the words "salvation" or "save." John Calvin provides classic answers in the Reformed tradition in the first three chapters of book 2 of the *Institutes of the Christian Religion*, and we will attempt to summarize the key points.

The question "Saved from what?" is only the first part of three necessary questions to ask when we want to gain and grasp a working knowledge of salvation in Christianity, a comprehensive and complex subject. After raising the first question, there are at least two more equally

---

5. Sproul, *Essential Truths*, 159.

important questions to ask.[6] First, we need to ask, "Saved by what?" This question refers to the ways and means by which salvation is achieved, and it involves the works of Christ. A well-known OT verse in Jon 2:9, "Salvation is of the Lord" (NKJV) or "Salvation belongs to the Lord!" (ESV), succinctly captures the answer to the question. Peter's sermon before the Jewish council finds an equally well-known NT verse on the centrality of Jesus in God's salvation: "This Jesus is the stone that was rejected by you, the builders, which has become the cornerstone. And there is salvation in no one else, for there is no other name under heaven given among men by which we must be saved" (Acts 4:11–12). This powerful word from Peter captures one of the five *solas* of the Reformed doctrine of salvation—namely, "Christ alone." After raising the first question, "Saved from what?," and the second question, "Saved by what?," we need to ask one more and final question, "Saved for what?" This question relates to the goal and purpose of salvation and its results and benefits.

As is well-known, salvation in Christianity is not only the central subject but also a comprehensive and complex concept; thus, it is challenging to comprehend it well. Toward our goal of providing concise but thorough knowledge on salvation in Christianity, our approach is to divide the subject matter of salvation into these three related questions and provide satisfactory answers.

In carrying out our task, we rely primarily on three sets of well-established resources for their reliability and wide acceptance among biblical scholars in the study of salvation in Christianity. First, we rely partly on relevant portions of classic teachings from John Calvin's *Institutes of Christian Religion* and Herman Bavinck's *Sin and Salvation in Christ*, both of which were cited earlier. Secondly, the fourth volume of the *ISBE* and the *Dictionary of Paul and His Letters* are very helpful for the brevity of the discussions on the subject.[7] Third and finally, Bruce Demarest's book *The Cross and Salvation: The Doctrine of Salvation* and Herman Ridderbos's classic book on Pauline theology, *Paul: An Outline of His Theology*, provide valuable insights on the NT perspective on salvation.[8]

---

6. By narrowing down our discussion of salvation to just three fundamental questions—what we are saved from, what we are saved by, and what we are saved for—we are essentially leaving aside the doctrines of grace and election. By doing so, we emphasize the need for salvation, the ways and methods of salvation, and the ultimate objective of salvation.

7. Hawthorne et al., *Dictionary of Paul*.

8. Demarest, *Cross and Salvation*; Ridderbos, *Paul*.

Word Study of Salvation

It is safe and reasonable to include a brief word study on the pertinent subject of "salvation" or "save."[9] Let us first note that "salvation" or "saving" is used with different emphases with respect to promise and fulfillment. Specifically, the Old Testament views and presents salvation as a provisional and promise-based approach. In comparison, the New Testament views salvation as being accomplished through the events of Jesus, which include his coming, death, resurrection, and ascension. The Hebrew words for salvation clarify the meaning of this important theological concept. The root *ys* means "be broad" or "spacious," suggesting freedom from powers restricting holistic personal development. In the OT, the Hebrew verb *yasha'* and its derivatives appear 353 times. In the Niphal, the passive counterpart of the active Qal, it bears the meaning "be saved" or "be delivered," while in the Hiphil, which often denotes causation of a verbal action by someone, it means to "deliver," or "give victory," or "save."[10] Physical deliverance is seen in that Noah built an ark so that God would provide "deliverance of his family" (Heb 11:7), Moses failed to see that God brings "deliverance" from Egypt (Acts 7:25). The Hebrew nouns *yeshuʾah* (appearing seventy-eight times), *yeshaʾ* (thirty-one times), and *teshuʾah* (appearing thirty-four times) mean "help," "deliverance," and "salvation."[11] In sum, the preceding verbs and nouns are mostly used in the general sense of deliverance from danger, distress, or bondage.

In the NT, the verb *sozo* (appearing more than one hundred times) means to "rescue," "deliver," or "save."[12] The noun *soteria* (appearing forty-nine times) can be used to denote deliverance from physical danger. The personal noun *soter* (twenty-four times) means "redeemer," "deliverer," and "savior." This word group generally connotes rescue or deliverance from danger, diseases, enemies, or bondage. But in the NT, the personal, spiritual, and ethical dimensions become publicly known. This Greek word group then carries the theological meaning of deliverance from sin, death, and judgment of God. In the NT, God is the Savior in that the divine Father planned the gift of salvation and sent his only

---

9. This discussion draws from Liefield, "Salvation."

10. Bromiley, "*Sozo* (To Save), *Soteria* (Salvation)," *TDNTA* 1132–40. Hebrew verbs use "simple" and "causative" tenses. In "simple" tense, there are two types: Qal (active—"he loved") and Niphal (passive—"he was loved"). The "causative" tense has two types: Hiphil (active—"he caused to love") and Hophal (passive—"he was caused to love").

11. Longman and Strauss, "Save, Savior," *BED* 704.

12. Longman and Strauss, "Save, Savior," *BED* 704–6.

Son into the world on a rescue mission. Jesus Christ is the Savior because his life, death, and resurrection purpose was to save sinners from their lost condition. Therefore, the salvation Jesus brought is primarily personal and spiritual. It is helpful to note that Jesus, *Iesous*, is a transliteration of the Greek form of the Hebrew name *Yeshua*, which means, "Yahweh is salvation." Christians are, at a minimum, those who believe in and commit themselves to Jesus as Savior.

Misunderstandings of Salvation

1. Getting saved is about being forgiven of sin and going to heaven when one dies.

This is a common oversimplification of salvation in Christianity. Salvation includes the forgiveness of sin and entering heaven, but it is far more than that. Forgiveness is a complex and multifaceted concept. At its core, salvation involves being rescued from danger or calamity. In a more specific sense, salvation refers to the redemption of humanity from sin and its consequences and the restoration of our relationship with God. The question of salvation is central to the Bible and its teachings. To fully understand salvation in Christianity, we must grasp what we are saved from, how (the way and means of salvation), and for what purpose we are saved. The forgiveness of sin assumes that humanity is in a lost and miserable condition from which we need to be saved and that our salvation comes as a gift from God through faith in the redemptive works of Jesus Christ. Ultimately, the goal of salvation is to ensure that we can enter heaven to be with God after reconciliation and praise him for our salvation.

2. Good deeds and works earn salvation.

There are different beliefs about how one can attain salvation. Some believe that good deeds or religious rituals can earn it or that one's good or bad deeds will determine the future state of one's existence. However, mainstream Christian theology teaches that salvation is a gift from God that can only be received through faith in Jesus Christ. Romans 3:23–24 states that all have sinned and fall short of God's glory, and all Christian traditions agree. However, there are differences in the emphasis between the Roman Catholic and Eastern Orthodox traditions, which emphasize good works required for salvation, and the Reformed view, which emphasizes faith alone. The issue concerns the relative importance placed on faith or good works. The Reformed view holds that faith comes first and good deeds follow, while other Christian traditions believe that good deeds are necessary for salvation. Romans 3:28 seems more in line with the Reformed view by stating that a person is justified by faith apart from observing the law.

3. We are saved by saying or doing the right things.

The common misconception is that we can be saved by saying or doing something. Romans 10:9–11 states that confessing with your mouth that "Jesus is Lord" and believing in your heart that God raised him from the dead will lead to salvation. This means that what you say with your mouth and what you believe in your heart saves you. However, it's essential to recognize that making a public confession or statement of faith and belief in your heart alone does not save people. It is interesting to note from the text that confessing with your mouth comes first, followed by believing in your heart. However, our words and actions as outward expressions often reflect what's already in our minds and hearts. Therefore, it's important to recognize that a public confession is not always the best evidence of what they believe in their heart. That is why going forward during an evangelistic or revival rally or raising your hand and making a public statement of faith doesn't automatically guarantee salvation. We have witnessed many publicly confessing their faith fall back into old sinful life habits. True salvation by faith happens in the heart and is evidenced by a transformed life. This includes a desire for God's word, a hunger for prayer and praise, obedience to God's commands, repentance of sin, and service to others. In other words, true salvation requires genuine conversion of the heart through faith, not just an outward act of saying or doing the right things. In short, it's not just what we say that matters, but what's in our hearts, evidenced by changed life, that counts.

4. Once saved, always saved.

Many Christians believe salvation is a one-time event that cannot be lost, regardless of subsequent behavior. However, most Christian traditions recognize that falling away from faith or rejecting salvation is possible and does occur. Some individuals claim to have been saved since childhood, often pointing to a moment when they attended a Bible camp and responded to a gospel invitation. However, if there has been no change in their lives since then, it may not be a true conversion. A genuine Christian conversion produces the fruit of salvation, such as a changed heart, evidenced by an interest in God, a desire to read and study the Bible, and a willingness to praise, pray, and serve him.

5. Salvation is universal.

This is a belief that everyone will eventually be saved, regardless of their faith or actions. While some Christian denominations adhere to universalist views, most Christians believe in the necessity of personal faith in Jesus Christ for salvation.

Saved from Sin, the Power of Sin, Death, and the Wrath and Judgment of God

The phrase "saved from" or "salvation from" does not appear verbatim in the Bible. However, the Bible teaches that we are saved from sin and the power of sin; we are also saved from the consequences of sin—namely, death and the wrath and judgment of God.

Let's examine each of them more closely. Let's begin by examining the meaning and significance of salvation from sin. What does it mean to be saved from sin?

In our earlier discussion of sin, from which we need to be saved, we focused on its origin, nature, and dynamic aspects in detail. One of the important insights we gained about the effects of sin is that it is a corrupting force, like spiritual AIDS. It attacks our spiritual immune system, making life progressively miserable. Once we learn to view the corrupting influences of sin on us, we begin to think about several important implications of mankind falling into sin—a subject not covered in our earlier discussion of sin—especially as taught by Paul, concerning the effects of sin, in Rom 5–8.

In understanding Paul's view of the meaning and significance of mankind falling into sin, we must note Paul's unique ways of viewing sin. First, Paul often conceptualizes and personifies sin and death as power, like a demon or monster. As discussed earlier, sin is not a standalone entity but a parasite that lives off its host. The parasitic existence of sin was explained by its ability to cling to what is good and destroy the good host. Secondly, Paul often thinks of sin not as a separate entity but as part of closely linked notions of sin, death, law, and life. Paul used these terms in diverse contexts with different meanings, but they are synecdochic in that when one is mentioned, the rest of the terms are in the foreground.

Sin, now as the personified entity, does many things in Rom 5–8: "*Sin* came into the world through one man, and death through *sin*, and so death spread to all men" (5:12); "Let not *sin* therefore reign in your mortal body" (6:12); "For *sin* will have no dominion over you, since you are not under law but under grace" (6:14); "For *sin*, seizing an opportunity through the commandment, deceived me and through it killed me" (7:11); "So now it is no longer I who do it, but *sin* that dwells in me . . . that is, in my flesh" (7:17–18).[13] When we say that we are saved from sin, we affirm that we are saved first from all these destructive influences of sin on us.

Secondly, the Bible teaches us that we are saved from the power of sin. Herman Bavinck, in his *Dogmatics*, makes a succinct statement about the dynamic aspect of the sin of Adam and all his descendants: "Sin gives birth to sin,"[14] meaning that a sinful state follows a sinful act. In other words, every sinful act of the will arises from antecedent impulses and desires, and every act of sin retroactively impacts and reinforces the impulse and desire. It is in this way that sin becomes a habit. Those who commit sins become servants of sin. Sin was originally not an independent entity, but it now lives like a parasite with domineering and reigning power; it cajoles, lures, enslaves, and destroys the host.

In Rom 7:11 and 7:13, Paul explains that he believes sin is a powerful force that caused his death. This idea of sin as a powerful, active force is a recurring theme throughout Rom 5–7, as seen in verses 5:21 and 6:6, 11, 12, and 14. Paul emphasizes the seriousness of sin by stating that sinners are slaves to sin, in Rom 6:17 and 6:20. However, through the redemptive work of Jesus Christ, the power of sin can be broken, and humanity can be restored to God. Once we are saved from the power of sin, we will be free from its destructive force.

---

13. Emphasis mine throughout.
14. Bavinck, *Sin and Salvation*, 77.

Third, the Bible teaches us that we are saved from death. What does this mean? Relating death as a consequence of sin, two verses come to our minds—Gen 2:17b and Rom 6:23a. Let's examine Gen 2:17b, which says, "for in the day that you eat of it you shall surely die." The phrase "in the day" suggests a definite certainty rather than an immediate consequence. Next, God's warning, "You shall surely die," requires some explanation—what kind of "death" does this refer to? The Hebrew word here can refer to physical, spiritual, or a combination of the two.

To understand the type of death referenced here, we must continue to read the text and see what happens in Gen 3 and thereafter. Assuming that both Adam and Eve were present during the temptation, they would have been aware that death was the consequence of disobeying God's prohibition. When the serpent declared, "You will not surely die" (Gen 3:4), he spoke a half-truth, making grand promises but delivering little. It's important to note that the snake cast doubt on God's trustworthiness when he asked, "Did God actually say, 'You shall not eat of any tree in the garden'?" (Gen 3:1). Now, he further casts doubt on the truthfulness of God's word by asserting that they will not surely die. Genesis 3:19 does not convey the full execution of the threatened punishment but modifies and postpones it.

The next verse, Rom 6:23, says, "For the wages of sin is death." To understand the consequences of sin and why death is the penalty in Paul's teaching, it is essential to analyze the concepts of life and death together and understand their respective roles.[15] Paul uses the terms "life" and "death" in various contexts with multiple meanings. Paul uses two Greek words to refer to life. The first word is *bios*, meaning daily life or material existence. The second and more frequently used word is *zoe*, which refers to a unique quality of life through faith in Christ. It is often combined with the word *aionios* (meaning "eternal") to mean "eternal life." This type of life is qualitatively different from life as we know it today and is bestowed by God as part of the age to come.

Death can refer to the end of physical, earthly, and human life. However, it often describes the spiritual-physical state of humanity "in Adam," which originally came about due to Adam's sin (Rom 5:12–21; 1 Cor 15:21–22). Paul uses "death" and "sin" and then "flesh" and "sin" in close association, particularly in Rom 5–7 where he contrasts life in Adam with life in Christ. Death and sin work together as a joint power,

---

15. Scott, "Life and Death."

with death coming as the consequence of sin. Paul teaches then that sin increased with the coming of the law, which enslaved humanity to sin and death. As a personified entity, death is the "last enemy" (1 Cor 15:26); when we are saved, we are saved from death as the last enemy.

Fourth, we are saved from the wrath of God and forthcoming judgment. The term "wrath" or "the wrath of God" is mentioned two hundred times in the Bible. In Romans, the concept is extensively explained where God's wrath is directed towards human wickedness and unrighteousness (Rom 1:18, 2:5–8, 5:9). The primary idea is that the wrath of God will be entirely and ultimately revealed on the eschatological "day of wrath" (Rom 2:5; 1 Thess 1:10; 5:9).

To understand the eschatological nature of the wrath of God, we need to look at the OT concept of the wrath of God. In the OT, the wrath of God is not seen as an essential part of God's character but rather as a response to the sinful and rebellious nature of mankind throughout history. The wrath is an expression of God's holiness, omnipotence, sovereignty, and kingly rule, exercised against a nation's rebellion when it fails to live up to the terms of the covenant. This context helps us understand that the wrath of God is the inevitable result or consequence of human sin before a holy God. Therefore, it is essential to remember that the underlying meaning of wrath, or the wrath of God, must exclude any notion of malicious, capricious, or vindictive anger on the part of God.

As per Paul's teachings, all people are affected by sin; therefore, no one is righteous. Consequently, everyone is liable to God's wrath. Paul sees the wrath of God as both a present reality and a future expectation. Romans 1:18 reveals that the wrath of God is against all ungodliness and unrighteousness of men. Romans 2:5 and 1 Thess 1:10 and 5:9 also warn about the coming wrath. However, believers can escape this eschatological wrath through God's redemptive action in Christ Jesus (Rom 5:8–9). This action involves the death of Christ, which will be discussed in the next section.

Finally, we wish to examine salvation *from* futility, which is probably the best description of the most serious human plight. So far, we have examined four things we need to be saved from: sin, the power of sin, and the two major consequences of sin (death and God's wrath/judgment). According to Paul, sin did not exist in God's original creation, and it is not a part of original human nature. God did not create a flawed world. However, when Adam and Eve disobeyed God's command, sin entered the world, and the world became flawed. We can describe the existing human condition as a flawed creation, resulting in futility. A feeling of futility is the sense you feel when you can't see the point in even trying, the sense that no matter how much you work at it, nothing good will happen, so you might as well give up. Paul's teachings on sin suggest that all human attempts to save ourselves, find lasting satisfaction, meaning, and purpose in life, or have positive thoughts on our own are futile because of the fallen nature of humanity. When Adam sinned, the entire created world became subject to futility.

In Paul's letters, the most prominent terms used to convey the general idea of futility, uselessness, or lack of purpose are *kenos* (adjective), *mataios* (adjective), *mataiotes* (noun), and *mataioomai* (verb). Paul's use of *mataiotes* ("futility") was probably influenced by the LXX, especially Ecclesiastes (1:2, 14; 2:1, 11, 15, 17). The book of Ecclesiastes and Rom 8:20–21 both describe a sense of hopelessness. Romans 8:20–21 states that "the creation was subjected to futility, not willingly, but because of him who subjected it, in hope that the creation itself will be set free from its bondage to corruption and obtain the freedom of the glory of the children of God." In this passage, Paul personifies "the creation" and describes it as being in bondage to corruption.

The apostle discusses the state of creation in futility by making three statements about its past, present, and future. Firstly, he mentions that creation was subjected to futility (8:20a). This refers to God's judgment that affected the natural order after Adam's disobedience. Using *mataiotes* ("futility"), Paul sums up the result of God's curse. In the passage, the apostle talks about how the creation is subject to futility, not by its own choice but by the will of someone who hoped for it. This someone is none other than God, who is both Judge and Savior. As John Stott often emphasizes the paradox of human sin and salvation, only God save the world he cursed as the result of the fall.[16]

Furthermore, the creation will be set free from its bondage to corruption. The key word here is "hope," which points to a future where creation will be liberated from its past curse. Currently, nature is trapped in an unending cycle of decline, decay, death, and decomposition. But in the future, creation will be freed into the glorious freedom of the children of God. God's creation will share in the glory of his children, who in turn share in the glory of Christ. Those who are saved will be fellow heirs with Christ, which is truly remarkable.

---

16. Stott, *Cross of Christ*.

The *Pactum Salutis* and the Person of Christ

How Christ's work procures our salvation through his death, resurrection, and ascension is at the heart of the doctrine of salvation. As mentioned earlier, the heart of the doctrine of salvation in the Reformed tradition is the works of Christ in the Trinitarian framework. To understand the doctrine of salvation in the Reformed tradition, we need to have some basic background of covenant theology. It is well-known that covenant theology adequately understands the works of Christ in this framework; one needs to have background knowledge of the role of Christ as the mediator between God and man. This, in turn, requires a working knowledge of the covenant of redemption (the *pactum salutis*). It describes an inter-Trinitarian covenant between the Father and the Son to redeem sinners through the substitutionary death of the incarnate Son (Eph 1:3–14). This covenant of redemption—the *pactum salutis* in Latin—is a central doctrine of Reformed dogmatics. In addition, we also require a knowledge of the person of Christ as the Son of God, God himself in the flesh. The *pactum salutis* and the person of Christ describe the role of Christ as the mediator between God and humanity, and they are presuppositions and necessary preparation for understanding Christ's work of redemption. For this reason, Calvin and Bavinck first discuss Christ's role as the mediator between God and humanity before discussing Christ's redemptive works.

Calvin writes in chapters 12–14 of book 2 in the *Institutes* on Christ's office as the Mediator, Christ's two natures, and Christ's offices of Prophet, King, and Priest before he explains how Christ performed the role of redeemer through his death, resurrection, and ascension in chapter 16. In his *Sin and Salvation in Christ*, Herman Bavinck analyzes these topics more thoroughly. He discusses the covenant of grace in chapter 5 and the person of Christ in chapter 6 in anticipation of the works of Christ in part 3.

Let us first discuss the *pactum salutis* in God's eternal counsel before we discuss the works of salvation as actually carrying out the *pactum salutis*. We do this by drawing mainly from the writings of Calvin and Bavinck, and DeYoung, among others.

DeYoung has probably the most succinct explanation of the meaning of *pactum salutis* and its role in theology, and the following is a quotation from his work:

> In simple terms, the covenant of redemption—or in Latin, the pactum salutis—refers to the eternal agreement between the Father and the Son to save a people chosen in Christ before the ages began. . . . In traditional Reformed theology, the *pactum* has been a critically important doctrine, helping to make sense of . . . election in Christ, God's activity in history, and the intratrinitarian love of God.[17]

The work of Christ for salvation is "an undertaking of the one God in three persons in which all cooperate, and each one performs a special task. It is the triune God—Father, Son, and Spirit—who together conceive, determine, carry out, and complete the entire work of salvation."[18] Bavinck continues to discuss the benefit of this *pactum* to believers in that the covenant of grace in the form of the *pactum* for our salvation rests on an eternal, unchanging foundation, the counsel of the Triune God. In this regard, the *pactum* has also been a pastoral teaching because it gives the believer confidence that because our covenantal relationship with God has its origin in the covenantal relationship with the Son before the ages, we do not have to merit our salvation but can rest secure in Christ, our guarantor.

However, it should be noted that the *pactum* has often been criticized—both within and without the Reformed tradition. Without going further into the details of these criticisms, there is an excellent book by J. V. Fesko, *The Trinity and the Covenant of Redemption*, which addresses these criticisms.[19] The most crucial question for us is whether there is good supporting evidence in Scripture for the notion of the *pactum*. The answer is definitely yes, as evidenced by several biblical references. Some of them are John 6:38–40 ("I have come down from heaven, not to do my own will but the will of him who sent me"); 5:30, 43; 17:4–12; as well as in Ps 2:7–8; Ps 110 ("Sit at my right hand"); Zech 6:13 ("counsel of peace"); and Luke 22:29 ("I assign to you, as my Father assigned to me, a kingdom").

Let's shift our focus to the second topic, the person of Christ. Calvin offers four reasons why it was "necessary, not absolutely, but by divine decree, that the Mediator should be God, and become man."[20] Firstly, by divine decree the Mediator should be God and become a man. Secondly,

---

17. DeYoung, "Theological Primer."
18. Bavinck, *Sin and Salvation*, 194.
19. Fesko, *Trinity*.
20. Calvin, *Institutes*, §2.12.1.

it was necessary for the Mediator to be God and man in order to convert those sinners who were heirs of hell into children of God. Thirdly, in our flesh the Mediator could yield perfect obedience, satisfy divine justice, and pay the penalty of sin. The perfect obedience of our Mediator and his sacrificial death is fit to satisfy God's justice and pay the penalty for our sin; our salvation entirely relies on them. Finally, the fourth reason the Mediator was God and man was to provide consolation and confirmation for the whole church. As to why it had to be the sacrificial death of the Mediator, the Son of God, John Murray points to the reality and gravity of sin, requiring and making expiation by the Mediator indispensable. He continues to write, "The precise nature of Christ's priestly offering and the efficacy of his sacrifice are bound up with the constitution of his person."[21] This demonstrates Christ's unique role as the Mediator in his redemption work as the Christ.

How does the Bible explain that Jesus Christ came to this world as the Mediator? Galatians 4:4–5 provides an answer: "When the fullness of time had come, God sent forth his Son, born of woman, born under the law, to redeem those who were under the law, so that we might receive adoption as sons." This verse first teaches us that God sent his unique Son at the right time in human history. God's providential guidance of the events of the world had prepared people and nations for the coming of Christ and the spreading of the gospel. Secondly, this verse also teaches us that Jesus Christ is the royal Son of God, the one whom the Father loved and sent as his emissary for a rescue mission. As the Son who alone knows the Father and is known by the Father, Jesus exercises his unique authority to forgive sins and reveal the Father's will. This Jesus is God's unique Son, himself born in the flesh to redeem sinners to be adopted as children of God. The glorious truth of the incarnation through which the second person in the Godhead became a human being is too rich and deep for the human mind to comprehend and reproduce in a precise formula. The early church's history was full of heresy (Ebionism, Docetism, Arianism, and Gnosticism) until the Nicene Creed (AD 381) and the Chalcedonian Creed (AD 451) on Christology settled the matter.

It is important to note that God's incarnation is linked to the creation of humans, who are made in God's image. This creation is a supposition and preparation for the incarnation. Hence, we know that the world was created perfectly and could be restored when it fell. A mediator had to

---

21. Murray, *Redemption Accomplished*, 15.

come between humanity and the divine to achieve the restoration. According to the Scriptures, the incarnation takes place through a virgin birth. In this way, the Son of God became a true and complete human person. This doctrine, too, has been challenged and attacked throughout the church's history. However, the doctrine has been part of Christian confession from the earliest church, and all Gospels consistently portray Jesus as the eternal Son of God and the Son of David. So, in this way, the Son of God became a true and complete human person.

Several theories about Christ's two natures exist, especially in modern times. But the Reformed theologians insisted that it was the person of the Son who became flesh. At the same time, there were several theories about the real historical Jesus. On this question, Bavinck closed the debate: "The conclusion of the matter is that the historical Jesus of the Gospel is the same as the confessed Christ of Paul, John, and the early church."[22]

The Work of Christ: Death, Resurrection, and Ascension

Now, we focus on the heart of the doctrine of salvation: how Christ's work procures our salvation through his death, resurrection, and ascension. Calvin discusses this topic in the first chapter of book 3 in his venerable *Institutes*. Herman Bavinck discusses this topic under "Salvation in Christ," part 4 of *Sin and Salvation in Christ*. However, Saint Paul provides a fuller discussion of salvation in Christ with the idea of being "in Christ" as the primary goal of salvation. Paul uses the phrase "in Christ" 165 times in his letters. This topic of new life in Christ as a benefit of salvation is often treated as a union with Christ, and there are several good books on it.[23]

Theologians in the Reformed tradition divide the doctrine of salvation into two main subjects: Christ's death on the cross as Christ's humiliation, and the resurrection and ascension as Christ's exultation.

---

22. Bavinck, *Sin and Salvation*, 235.

23. Bavinck, *Sin and Salvation*, 235; Smedes, *Union with Christ*; Billings, *Union with Christ*; Wilbourne, *Union With Christ*; Ferguson, *In Christ Alone*. For the most comprehensive work on Paul and union with Christ, see Campbell, *Paul and Union*.

The Cross and Salvation

Let us first take up and examine the death of Christ. The redemptive work of Christ on the cross is summarized in 1 Tim 2:5-6: "For there is one God, and there is one mediator between God and men, the man Christ Jesus, who gave himself as a ransom for all, which is the testimony given at the proper time." J. I. Packer describes the roles of the mediator: First, the mediator brings together two parties, the God of holiness and righteousness and sinful humanity, who are alienated, estranged, and at war with each other. Second, the mediator must have links with both sides to identify with and maintain both interests. To bring the needed reconciliation between the two parties, however, the wrath of God at our sin somehow has to be absorbed and satisfied. In his mercy and grace, God, the angry Judge, sent his Son into the world to bring about the needed reconciliation. First Timothy 2:5-6 emphasizes that Jesus, God's incarnate Son, Israel's Messiah, is the one and only Mediator, the only way to salvation (Acts 4:12). The verse in 1 Tim 2:4 also highlights the importance of this knowledge for all who need to be saved: "to come to the knowledge of the truth."

In 1 Tim 2:5-6, "the man Christ Jesus" is described as "who gave himself as a ransom for all, which is the testimony given at the proper time." "Ransom" refers to purchasing someone's release and describes Pauline and NT understandings of Christ's work as redemptive and the "ransom" (Matt 20:28). This phrase also reminds us of Jesus' own words: "For even the Son of Man came not to be served but to serve, and to give his life as a ransom for many" (Mark 10:45). Since Jesus gave himself as the "ransom," the substitution (dying on behalf of sinners) is also included.

So far, in our explanation of Christ's work in securing our salvation in his death, we have used closely related terms and ideas, like atonement, expiation (it's closely related term, propitiation, will be discussed momentarily), and redemption. The Scripture uses these closely related terms to emphasize how Christ's works secure our salvation, each with a different emphasis. What follows is a brief explanation of the terms. These various terms collectively illustrate the multifaceted aspects of Christ's work for the salvation of humanity in Christian theology.

Atonement means making amends, blotting out the offense, and giving satisfaction for the wrong done, thus reconciling God to humanity. The key ideas in the atonement involve substitution and satisfaction in restoring a broken relationship through paying a price, often symbolized by the shedding of blood in sacrificial offerings. NT references to the blood of Christ mean that Christ's death was God's act of reconciling us to himself, overcoming his hostility to us that our sins provoked. The first representative for the notion of atonement is Rom 3:21–25, which says, "But now the righteousness of God has been manifested apart from the law, although the Law and the Prophets bear witness to it—the righteousness of God through faith in Jesus Christ for all who believe. For there is no distinction: for all have sinned and fall short of the glory of God, and are justified by his grace as a gift, through the redemption that is in Christ Jesus, whom God put forward as a propitiation by his blood, to be received by faith." The second verse is Rom 5:8–9, which says, "But God shows his love for us in that while we were still sinners, Christ died for us. Since, therefore, we have now been justified by his blood, much more shall we be saved by him from the wrath of God."

"Expiation" and "propitiation" are the most closely related terms. They are two translations, each having different connotations of one Greek word, *hilasterion*. Paul uses it in Rom 3:25, which says, "whom God put forward as a [*hilasterion*] by his blood, to be received by faith. This was to show God's righteousness, because in his divine forbearance he had passed over former sins." Regarding the crucified Christ whom God put forth, some translate it as "propitiation," others as "expiation," and others (such as the NLT) as a "sacrifice." Expiation implies the erasing or wiping out of sin through atoning death; propitiation implies that Christ's death appeases divine wrath caused by sin. So, the key idea behind expiation is the removal or cleansing of sin through shedding blood or offering sacrifices. It emphasizes the idea of covering sin and purifying the individual from guilt. Leviticus 17:11 says, "For the life of the flesh is in the blood, and I have given it for you on the altar to make atonement for your souls, for it is the blood that makes atonement by the life," and describes it. Propitiation involves the appeasement of God's wrath through a sacrificial act. The Bible signifies that God's justice is satisfied through offering a substitute, often involving the shedding of blood.

Redemption in the Bible is a broad and overarching term that explains salvation through the works of Christ, and it refers to buying back or liberating from bondage by paying a ransom. It signifies the deliverance of believers from the slavery of sin through the sacrifice of Jesus Christ. Paul sees salvation as a process of redemption. Redemption in the historic Reformed tradition is always "definite" or "limited" redemption because Christ did not die for everyone but only for those called. John 10:14–15 says, "I am the good shepherd. I know my own, and my own know me, just as the Father knows me and I know the Father; and I lay down my life for the sheep." Ephesians 1:7 also says, "In him we have redemption through his blood, the forgiveness of our trespasses, according to the riches of [God's] grace."

Scripture emphasizes that the Mediator must suffer many things and die to achieve our salvation. Christ, who knew why he had to die, did not die as a helpless victim. Instead, he freely embraced his Father's purpose for the redemption of sinners, as revealed in the Scriptures. In this regard, the death of Jesus Christ was not an accident, but rather it was by God's set plan. Act 2:23 speaks to the point, which says, "This Jesus, delivered up according to the definite plan and foreknowledge of God, you crucified and killed by the hands of lawless men."

Finally, we must not forget that Christ's complete obedience in his life and death achieves his exaltation and, through it, salvation of his own. On this point, Herman Bavinck emphasizes that Christ's entire life and work, from his conception to his death, was an act of self-denial, an offering presented to the Father as head of the new humanity. Bavinck further argues that the redemption Christ obtained for us is comprehensive and includes the complete redemption of the whole person, including body and soul. The renewal of all creations results from his obedience, and the new creation in the Scripture storyline is the Bible's overriding theme.

Resurrection and Ascension of Christ

With regard to the efficacy of Christ's death and resurrection in accomplishing salvation, Calvin says, "Next follows the resurrection from the dead, without which all that has hitherto been said [referring to the death of Christ] would be defective."[24] Much has been accomplished by the death of Christ on the cross: we are reconciled to God, satisfaction is given to his justice, and the curse and penalty of sin are removed. But it is through the resurrection that we were first raised for justification. Romans 4:25 describes the redemptive acts of Jesus our Lord as "who was delivered up [to die] for our trespasses and raised for our justification." This verse clearly shows that Jesus Christ's death and resurrection are necessary for forgiveness of sin and justification. "Raised [resurrected] for

---

24. Calvin, *Institutes*, §2.16.13.

our justification" points to our justified standing. Verses 24–25 together explain two important truths. First, when God the Father raised Christ from the dead, it was a demonstration that he accepted Christ's suffering and death as full payment for sin and that the Father's favor, no longer his wrath against sin, was directed toward Christ, and through Christ toward to those who believe. Since Paul sees Christians as united with Christ in his death and resurrection (Rom 6:6, 8–11; Eph 2:6; Col 2:12; 3:11), God's approval of Christ at the resurrection results in God's approval also of all who are united to Christ, and in this way results in their "justification." For this reason, our justification is always "alien justification," Christ's justification applied to us in faith. By Christ's death, sin and its consequences are taken away; righteousness and hope are renewed and restored by his resurrection. First Peter 1:3–4 states, "According to his great mercy, he has caused us to be born again to a living hope through the resurrection of Jesus Christ from the dead, to an inheritance that is imperishable, undefiled, and unfading, kept in heaven for you."

Resurrection is the first step in Christ's exaltation. Jesus' appearance and the apostles' witnesses and testimony attest to the historical reality of resurrection. The ascension into heaven naturally follows the resurrection. By his resurrection, Christ "was declared to be the Son of God . . . according to the Spirit of holiness" (Rom 1:4), yet it is only by his ascension to heaven that his reign truly commenced. Ephesians 4:10 says, "He who descended is the one who also ascended far above all the heavens, that he might fill all things." Bavinck summarized Christ's work of salvation: "As our mediator, he has obtained the full benefits of our whole salvation, beginning with an objective atonement for our sins. Refusal to acknowledge propitiation as the heart of his death and resurrection results from a misunderstanding of God's love. It is God's love that is the basis for his providing Christ as the means of propitiation. Through Christ's Sacrifice, a new relationship of reconciliation and peace has been accomplished between God and humanity. The benefit of this work of Christ is unrestricted; it covers every dimension of experience; it extends to all creations."[25]

---

25. Bavinck, *Sin and Salvation*, 419.

The Goal of Salvation in Christ

Throughout our study of Christ's redemptive work by his death and resurrection, we have covered a lot of ground. However, we must not stop here. We must address the third and final question: Saved for what? This question deals with the application of benefits and the purpose of salvation. John Murray's well-known book *Redemption Accomplished and Applied* accurately summarizes the two main aspects of the Christian doctrine of salvation: accomplishment and application.

Let us now focus on the application by focusing on the goal and purpose of salvation, procured and accomplished by Christ's death and resurrection. A traditional way to examine the application is to treat it under the title of the order of salvation (the *ordo salutis* in Latin), as is the case with Herman Bavinck and John Murray. The key idea behind the order of salvation is that the application of benefits of redemption does not comprise one act but a series of acts and processes. Specifically, we have (effectual) calling, regeneration, justification, adoption, sanctification, and glorification.

A succinct summary of the order of salvation follows, drawn largely from Murray's classic work, *Redemption Accomplished and Applied*. Among several verses relating to the order of salvation, Rom 8:29-30 sheds the most light on this. In these two verses, Paul elaborates on what he means by God's purpose from verse 28, in which he works out all things for our good. He maps out God's saving purpose through five stages, from its beginning to its consummation. These stages he names foreknowing, predestination, calling, justification, and glorification. First comes foreknowledge, which means knowing something beforehand in advance of its happening. Secondly, those God foreknew, "he also predestined to be conformed to the image of his Son" (8:29). Then we come to Paul's third affirmation: those he predestined, he also called (v. 30a). Fourthly, those he called, he also justified (v. 30b). Fifthly, those he justified, he also glorified (v. 30c). One may notice that the stage of sanctification between justification and glorification is omitted in verse 30. One may argue that glorification is included implicitly in "predestined to be conformed to the image of his Son," the glorified Lord. So, Rom 8:30 provides us with a broad outline of the order in the application of salvation, and that order is calling, justification, and glorification.

As we review these verses, we can see that these five stages are intended as the order of logical arrangement and progression. There are some debates on whether or not the order of salvation described above should include more steps (repentance, faith, regeneration, conversion, justification, sanctification, and perseverance), and the proper sequence among various stages if we expand the list. Yet, it is reasonable to conclude that the verse in Rom 8:30 provides a broad outline of the order in applying redemption—calling, justification, and glorification, especially when we are called to repentance, faith, regeneration, and conversion. Among calling, justification, and glorification, it is straightforward to see that glorification comes at the last stage. Therefore, the real question of the order of salvation is whether calling precedes justification or vice versa.

Since we already know that we are justified by faith alone, we need to discuss the relationship between faith and justification. Some argue that justification comes before faith, while others say it's the reverse. However, in answering the question, we must consider the context of justification that has already been accomplished by Christ's work in the application of redemption. Therefore, we must rephrase the question. Which comes first: justification as part of the benefit of redemption, or faith? Scripture clearly states that we are justified by and through faith (Rom 1:17; 3:22, 26). By incorporating the role of faith into justification, we expand the broad order of salvation: calling, faith, justification, and glorification. It is important to note that every step of man's salvation, from calling to glorification, depends entirely on God, in Christ, through the power and working of the Holy Spirit. In summary, God alone determines, purchases, applies, and secures salvation.

So far, we have reviewed a traditional way to examine the application of salvation procured by Christ's death and resurrection, which is to treat it under the title of the order of salvation (*ordo salutis*), as is the case with John Murray. In his *Redemption Accomplished and Applied*, however, Murray devotes a whole chapter to the union with Christ, not only in its application but also as the central truth in the entire doctrine of salvation. The union with Christ is frequently described as our being "in Christ." When Paul affirms spiritual blessings in one long sentence in the original Greek in Eph 1:3–14, he repeatedly uses "in Christ," "in him," and "through Jesus Christ" in choosing, predestining, and redeeming us. He did all those acts (calling, justification, and glorification) included in the order of salvation, to the praise of glorious grace (v. 6). Parallel to this is another emphasis—Christ is "in" the believers (Rom 8:10, Gal 2:20, Col 1:27). The sweeping scope of the union with Christ is immense: Eternal election of the Father is in Christ (Eph 1:3–4). The people of God were represented in Christ when he gave his life (death), resurrected, and ascended. It is in Christ that the people of God are created new. And it is in Christ that believers die. Finally, it is in Christ that the people of God will be resurrected.

It is this recognition that the theme of union with Christ applies not only to the application of salvation but to the whole spectrum of salvation, and it links all aspects of salvation together in one harmonious whole. Consequently, the theme of union with Christ has become prominent and widely accepted in the twentieth century, as its breadth and significance in the doctrine of salvation are increasingly being recognized, especially among Protestant traditions.

In his *Redemption Accomplished and Applied*, John Murray discusses the nature of this union with Christ.[26] First, it is spiritual in that the bond of this union is the Holy Spirit himself. How Christ dwells in his people and his people dwell in him is beyond our ability to understand. Still, the spiritual relationship is in harmony and agreement with the nature and work of the Holy Spirit. Second, it is mystical, not in the sense that it is completely unintelligible and we cannot understand, but in the sense that it was kept secret thus far but is revealed now (Rom 16:25–26). Sinclair Ferguson explained the "mystical union" for us in his book *The Christian Life: A Doctrinal Introduction*.[27] First, it is a federal union, not in the sense of a form of government, but in the covenant between God and his people. The main idea behind this is that what Christ does becomes ours by our union with him. In other words, Christ's righteousness through his obedience becomes ours based on this covenant. Secondly, it is a carnal or flesh union. By incarnation, the Son of God became one with us. By incarnation, he thus established this bridge between God and us in our flesh, by which he might come into contact with our sin and being "made sin" for us (2 Cor 5:21). By this, he shares in the weakness of our flesh and became truly our brother for us. Third, it is a faith union. We are brought to the union with Christ by faith and faith alone. Believers are often called into the fellowship of Christ. In the language of the union with Christ, the prepositional phrase "in Christ" is used along with "into Christ," "with Christ," and "through Christ," depending on the context. So, the life of faith is the intimate and living union with living Christ. The best analogy

---

26. See Murray's classical book on redemption, *Redemption Accomplished and Applied*, 165–73.

27. Ferguson, *Christian Life*, 100–103.

for this life is that of the vine and the branches (John 15:1). For the intimate and living communion with Christ, we need to be grafted into the vine to depend entirely upon its nourishment.

You may recall my friend's question at the close of the Bible study of sin and salvation, mentioned at the beginning of this book: "What is salvation, anyway?" This question triggered a flood of thoughts about the whole doctrine of salvation. It begins with the perfect creation of God, later marred by Adam and Eve's original sin, which necessitated the need for salvation. This, in turn, leads to thoughts about the things we are saved from, followed by Christ's redemptive work and its significance. As my thoughts finally turned to the many wonderful benefits of salvation through the union with Christ, my friend interrupted me with another simple request: "Would you please explain the salvation in Christianity in a few words?" I smiled back at him and answered, "It is too wonderful to explain it in just a few words." And I told him to look up Eph 1:3–14, which sums up salvation in Christianity well, not in a few words but in one long sentence in the original Greek.

CHAPTER 5

The Kingdom of God

The term "kingdom of God" is often cited in the Gospels and thus familiar among Christians. Our Lord's first sermon at the beginning of his ministry proclaims, "The time is fulfilled, and the kingdom of God is at hand; repent and believe in the gospel" (Mark 1:15). This verse summarizes Jesus' preaching ministry with the good news of the presence of the kingdom of God, demonstrating the fulfillment of God's promise announced by the prophets. The meaning of "at hand" may be interpreted in several ways. Still, the clear meaning of this verse is that the kingdom of God, God's rule over his people and their lives, is now being established by Jesus the Messiah, demonstrating that the kingdom of God is a present reality.

The familiarity among Christians with the term "the kingdom of God" is enhanced by repeated recitations of the Lord's Prayer, which begins in Matt 6:9–10: "Our Father in heaven, hallowed be your name. Your kingdom come, your will be done, on earth as it is in heaven." Many of us have prayed these words for years, but do we understand what this prayer is all about? Have you ever wondered why and how the kingdom of God is a present reality, as emphasized above, while at the same time something to be realized in the future, as emphasized in the Lord's Prayer? What are the implications of these seemingly contradictory teachings for Christian living?

When we ask fellow Christians, "*What* is the kingdom of God?" we usually receive no immediate answer because many are unprepared to give one. On occasion, we may get different interpretations of the kingdom of God. Some may say it refers to God's sovereign rule or reign over the world. Others may say it refers to a specific realm or territory where God's rule is exercised, and some may even say it is the people of God. Assuming these answers explain the different aspects of the kingdom of God, how do we make sense of them?

Thus far, we have raised two questions on whether the kingdom of God is a present reality or a future event (*when*) and *what* the kingdom of God is. But they are just the beginning of closely related questions surrounding the kingdom of God. There are other important questions. For instance, *where* can the kingdom of God be found: Is it within us, among us, or an external reality? The most difficult question regarding the kingdom of God is *how* it comes. Is it going to be a new state of things suddenly to be realized in external forms, similar to the current Jewish expectations? Or will it be a spiritual creation gradually and invisibly realizing itself? Or would it be a spiritual kingdom within hearts and minds, or an earthly triumph of the kingdom, as some millennialists believe it to be?

Considering the what, when, where, and how of these questions about the kingdom of God, we would readily agree that the subject of the kingdom of God is both broad and complex. It is broad because the ideas of the reign and realm of the kingdom of God are prevalent in both the Old and New Testaments. The notion of the kingdom of God is prevalent throughout the Scriptures, from Genesis to Revelation, encompassing the whole history of biblical redemption. It is complex for two reasons: First, the concept of the kingdom of God has evolved with different emphases over time. Secondly, the Scriptures are full of diverse descriptions of the kingdom of God, especially in the teachings of Jesus.

In the NT, the kingdom of God and closely related terms—like the kingdom of heaven, the kingdom of Christ, and the kingdom—appear many times, especially in the Synoptic Gospels.[1] Still, no word of explanation is ever offered or defined clearly.[2] Instead, they are described

---

1. The total number of times the term "kingdom of God" and related phrases appear in the Synoptic Gospels is 108. The distribution is as follows: fifty times in Matthew, fourteen times in Mark, thirty-nine times in Luke, and five times in John. Caragounis, "Kingdom of God," 417–30.

2. When dealing with the kingdom of God, the lines between definition and meaning can get blurry. However, the definition provides a foundation and framework for interpreting the meaning within specific contexts, and the meaning delves deeper into the significance and impact of the kingdom of God.

in Jesus' teachings, which took the form of parabolic teaching methods on the kingdom of God. Specifically, the kingdom of God is like seeds growing in different soils, a sower of seeds, a mustard seed, leaven, and a hidden treasure. Why were there no clear definitions or explanations? It's possible that Jesus and the people who listened to his message were already familiar with the kingdom of God, so he did not need to define or explain it further. Another possible reason is that the idea of the kingdom of God pertains to a heavenly reality that is very different from our earthly experiences, making it difficult to put into words. This is why Jesus used parables to teach about it.

Given the broad scope and complexity of the kingdom of God idea and the lack of background knowledge on the part of many Christians, it would be beneficial and necessary to briefly review and summarize the key elements of the historical development of the kingdom of God in the three periods involved: the Old Testament, intertestamental Judaism, and the New Testament.

To begin with, it is proper to state that the biblical idea of the kingdom of God is grounded in the faith that one eternal, living God has revealed his will and purpose over the world and Israel. Interestingly, as mentioned earlier, the exact term "the kingdom of God" is not found in the OT. Nevertheless, God is often represented as the King of the universe and the King of Israel in a redemptive sense. For instance, in the Song of Moses, after the deliverance from Egypt, Yahweh's reign is declared: "The Lord will reign forever and ever" (Exod 15:18). And Yahweh's role as the Lord of the covenant (Exod 19:4–6) is also proclaimed. Yahweh exercised the functions of king in Israel, and his rule or reign in the OT meant an ever-present, close relationship between God and his people. In brief, the kingdom of God, God's rule over his people in the OT, was an ever-present reality. It was not something to be realized in the distant future.

When human kings were installed and served as vice-regent of God, it became apparent that the perfect realization of the kingdom of God could not be realized as a present reality but would have to be realized in the future. The book of Daniel points to the future kingdom as God's supernatural, universal, and everlasting reign.

In the Jewish Rabbinic literature, the kingdom of God is represented as both the already existing reign of God over the world and Israel, and to be extended and enforced in the messianic era in the future. It should be noted that the phrase "the kingdom of God" appears for the first time in intertestamental Judaism. However, the Jews were primarily interested in the material enjoyment that the kingdom of God was supposed to bring; they were not interested in what the messianic age would bring (Amos 9:13–15, Isa 65:17–25).

As the NT narrative opens, the theme of fulfillment appears (Matt 1:22; 2:15, 17, 23). And then, suddenly, John the Baptist showed up and cried out, "Repent, for the kingdom of heaven is at hand" (Matt 3:2). As Jesus begins his ministry right after the temptation with his first sermon, he says, "Repent, for the kingdom of heaven is at hand" (Matt 4:17). As is well-known, the kingdom of heaven in Matthew's Gospel can be substituted with the kingdom of God and the kingdom of Christ. As we study the kingdom of God in the NT, we need to emphasize the central role of Jesus Christ in the coming of the kingdom of God. In announcing it, we also know that the kingdom of God is the central message of Jesus' ministry. How should we then interpret and understand the kingdom of God at hand? What does the Scripture teach us about the kingdom of God as it teaches us *what* the kingdom of God is, *when*, and *how* God's kingdom comes? Does the *how* part of the question deal with in what manner, or the way, that the kingdom of God comes? What follows is a brief but thorough survey of the critical issues and difficulties on this topic and the answers to most of these questions in comprehending the concept of the kingdom of God, mainly based on readily available resources.[3]

Misunderstandings of the Kingdom of God

Given the broadness and complexity of the kingdom of God, it is not surprising that there are many common misunderstandings about it. Here are a few examples.

1. The kingdom of God is primarily the spiritual realm with God as King, as some translations say that the kingdom is "within you" (Luke 17:21 NKJV).

This means that it is in the hearts of believers, indicating a spiritual reality. This translation is hardly correct; a possibly better translation is, "The kingdom of God is *in the midst* of you" (Luke 17:21 ESV, emphasis mine), meaning that it is in those who follow Jesus, among whom the reign

---

3. Ladd, *Theology*; Ladd, *Gospel of the Kingdom*; Ladd, "Kingdom of God"; Bright, *Kingdom of God*; Vos, "Kingdom of God"; Caragounis, "Kingdom of God."

of God is manifested. The rule of God is broad enough to include not only the spiritual realm but also the whole creation, including material well-being. An even better translation could be, "The kingdom of God is *within your reach*." An application of this interpretation is then, "The kingdom of God is here; be sure not to miss it."

2. The kingdom of God is a social gospel.

Jesus spent a significant portion of his ministry teaching about ethical behavior, love, forgiveness, justice for the poor, and helping others. Based on Jesus' teaching, the kingdom of God calls for social reform and ethical living by promoting justice, compassion, love, and peace, working for a better world, and demonstrating God's presence and values. However, focusing solely on man's social reform and ethics is too limited. The order of things ("the way that life and the world are organized and intended to be" as defined by *Longman Dictionary of Contemporary English*[4]) introduced by Jesus is called the kingdom of God because in it as a whole, God is the actor and enforcer.

3. The kingdom of God is a physical kingdom that will be established on earth politically or geographically.

The statement is a perspective that some Christian denominations hold because they believe in a millennial reign of Christ, where he will rule over a restored Earth for a thousand years. Most other Christians interpret the kingdom of God as the presence of God's rule in the hearts of believers, or a spiritual reality that coexists with the current world rather than replacing it. This perspective emphasizes living according to God's will now rather than waiting for a future physical kingdom. The kingdom of God is a present reality and will be fully realized in the future.

---

4. *Longman Dictionary of Contemporary English*, s.v. "order of things." https://www.ldoceonline.com/dictionary/the-order-of-things.

4. The kingdom of God is mainly an internal, individual experience.

The kingdom of God has a communal dimension, too. We experience it through our relationships with others, fellowship and service, and building a just and loving society together.

5. The kingdom of God is a Jewish political and nationalistic ideology and agenda.

This is a simplification of a complex concept. The kingdom of God is a central concept in Judaism and Christianity. It refers to God's rule or reign over the world and creation, where justice, peace, and God's will prevail. The kingdom of God has social and political implications, yet it is not purely a nationalistic or political agenda. Christians believe the kingdom of God has implications for all areas of life; they do not equate it with Jewish political or nationalistic agenda.

Word Study: The Kingdom of God

"Kingdom of God" or "kingdom of heaven" refers to God's sovereign, dynamic, and eschatological rule or reign. To grasp the term more fully, we can examine the terminology of the first word, "kingdom." According to the *Baker Expository Dictionary*, this important NT word, the "kingdom" (*basileia* in Greek, *malkut* in Hebrew), is most commonly used regarding the spiritual kingdom whose ruler is God.[5] This kingdom is always expressed in Matthew's Gospel as "the kingdom of heaven" and elsewhere in the Gospels as the "kingdom of God." However, this term expresses a broad range of ideas and spiritual reality about the nature and characteristics of the kingdom of God.

The *Baker Expository Dictionary* lists four major characteristics. First, it is a spiritual kingdom (1 Cor 15:50). Thus, "the kingdom of God is not a matter of eating and drinking but of righteousness and peace and joy in the Holy Spirit" (Rom 14:17). Second, it is to be contrasted with the kingdom of this present world (Matt 12:22–28). Third, it has arrived but has not yet reached its fulfillment or culmination (Matt 10:7; 13:31–33; Luke 11:20). Fourth, it is both inclusive and exclusive. It will include every tribe, language, and nation (Rev 5:9–10), but at the same

---

5. This word study draws from Longman and Strauss, "Kingdom," *BED* 457.

time, not all will enter it (Matt 13:1–23; 18:3–4; 19:23–24; 25:31–46; Luke 9:62). Finally, understanding the true nature of the kingdom of God will bring comfort and encouragement to believers because that is their ultimate destination. Paul triumphantly expresses his confidence in 2 Tim 4:18, which says, "The Lord will rescue me from every evil deed and bring me safely into his heavenly kingdom."

Moving onto the second word, "God." The noun *elohim* is the most commonly used word to refer to God in the OT. It is regularly used in conjunction with the divine name and translated as "Lord God." The "Lord God" belief is grounded in the faithful confidence that one eternal, living God has revealed himself to mankind and has a purpose for the human race, which he has chosen to accomplish through Israel.

The *Baker Dictionary* notes that the first action of God in the OT is the creation of the world and electing a people for himself. Some important descriptions of God include God as holy, jealous, king, refuge, savior, shepherd, the true God, and the God of heaven and earth.

The Kingdom of God in the Old Testament

Let's begin by pointing out that there is no exact phrase "kingdom of God" in the OT canonical books, although "kingdom of the Lord" appears in 2 Chr 13:8.[6] However, the concept of kingship or God's rule is present throughout the OT. We also note that there is no formal definition of it in the OT and the teaching of Jesus. How do we account for this? It was probably because the term was well-known to the Israelites, and its definition would not have been needed. Vos puts it this way: "It is *the* kingdom, the well-known kingdom, with which He [Jesus] presupposes familiarity, not merely on His part but also the part of His hearers. Our Lord did not come to found a new religion but to usher in the fulfillment of something promised long beforehand."[7]

That is why Jesus declares that the kingdom of God was "near" (Matt 3:2). We can easily surmise that he assumed that his listeners had some understanding of what he meant, even though they did not fully

---

6. The following discussion on the kingdom of God in the Old and New Testaments draw heavily from Caragounis, "Kingdom of God" and Bright, *Kingdom of God*. For further reading, I would recommend a series of articles: Morgan, "Kingdom of God"; Dunson, "Kingship and Creation"; Dunson, "From Abraham to Israel"; Dunson, "Prophetic Hope."

7. Vos, "Kingdom of God," 304.

comprehend it. Unfortunately, modern-day Christians lack the necessary background from the OT to grasp what his listeners understood upon hearing the term "kingdom of God." Therefore, it would be helpful to briefly review the concept of the kingdom of God in the OT here at the outset. In doing so, we can conveniently divide the discussion into three subject areas: (1) the kingdom of God at creation; (2) the kingdom of God during the early period, from the call of Abraham through the divided monarchy to the fall of Jerusalem; and (3) the kingdom of God in prophetic hopes. It would be especially beneficial for us to pay close attention to the progressive nature of the historical revelation of the OT portrayal of the kingdom of God.

Kingship and Creation

Let us examine the kingdom of God at creation. Right after the account of the creation of man in Gen 1, God blesses and commissions Adam with the command, "Be fruitful and multiply and fill the earth and subdue it, and have dominion over the fish of the sea . . . and over every living thing that moves on the earth" (Gen 1:28). We should first note that the phrase in this command, "subdue and have dominion" means to rule; the object of this rule is the earth. So, in a sense, God commissioned Adam as a kingly human figure to rule over the earth. This verse teaches us several important truths about the kingdom of God in the OT. They are that (1) God is the supreme king over all creation (Ps 10:16), (2) God commissions or appoints a human king as vice-regent to rule, and finally, (3) God is the king of Israel in a special redemptive sense, as most prominently exemplified in the exodus from Egypt.

What follows God's commissioning of Adam in Gen 1:28 covers the broad scope of the creation over which Adam is commanded to rule. They include every plant yielding seed and every tree (v. 29), every beast of the earth, every bird of the heavens, everything that creeps, every living thing that has breath, and every green thing (v. 30). In short, Adam is to rule over the whole world as a subordinate king underneath God, who is the true King over all. Even though Genesis is silent about it, we can speculate that God's commissioning of Adam to rule was intended to go beyond the garden of Eden to extend the rule of God over the farthest reaches of the earth. Adam rebels against God's will to pursue his autonomy to be like God and fails to subdue and have dominion over the whole as a subordinate king under God. As a result, God's rule or reign over the earth through Adam failed.

From Abraham to the Fall of Israel and Judah

The biblical narrative of the descendants of Adam tells the story of the increasing corruption on earth, as illustrated in Gen 6. The Scripture states, "The wickedness of man was great in the earth, and every intention of the thoughts of his heart was only evil" (Gen 6:5–6). God thus brings judgment by flood over the earth but saves Noah and his descendants. After the flood, God established a covenant with Noah and his descendants and blessed them with the commandments to rule the earth. However, Noah's descendants continued to follow the path of evil and corruption until we come to the story of the Tower of Babel in Gen 11. As people came together to build the Tower of Babel, they said, "Come, let us build ourselves a city and a tower with its top in the heavens, and let us make a name for ourselves, lest we be dispersed over the face of the whole earth" (Gen 11:4). This statement probably best illustrates the desire for human autonomy, an attempt to escape the rule of God.

Despite the failures of Adam and Noah and their descendants to rule the earth, God calls Abraham and his descendants to carry on his redemptive works from the patriarchs and judges through to the united monarchy, and from divided monarchies to exile. The divine speech in this call, which came suddenly and unexpectedly, sets the agenda for what God continues to do, as recorded in Gen 12:1–3: "Now the Lord said to Abram, 'Go from your country and your kindred and your father's house to the land that I will show you. And I will make of you a great nation, and I will bless you and make your name great, so that you will be a blessing. . . . And in you all the families of the earth shall be blessed.'"

With the call of Abraham, God continues to exercise his rule over "all the families of the earth" (Gen 12:3), now through Abraham and his descendants. In the narrative of the United Monarchy, Saul, Israel's first king, did not rule according to the Lord's commands and was eventually removed from his throne. After Saul, David was anointed king of Judah (1 Sam 16:18), and God was with him (2 Sam 5:10); thus, his kingship brought about the most prosperous period in Israel's history. For our purpose, God's covenant with David comes with God's promise that his house and kingdom shall be established forever before God (2 Sam 7:16).

This points to Solomon, who built the house of the Lord, and eventually to Jesus, the Messiah who would sit on the throne eternally. So, God's promise to David of establishing the eternal kingdom is to be realized through the establishment and rule of a messianic kingdom.

In the early stage of the OT, God was often depicted as the King of the universe and the deliverer of redemption from Egypt. The kingdom of God, as portrayed in the OT, was a present and real relationship between God and his people rather than something to be realized in the future. However, as human kings were installed and failed, it became clear that the perfect realization of the kingdom of God could only be realized in the future. The Lord God made a covenant with Israel, which affirmed Yahweh's suzerainty over his people. The OT emphasizes the rule of God as Creator, Deliverer, and covenant Lord, particularly during the time of the judges.

One may recall that toward the end of the period of judges, the Israelites wanted earthly kings like those of their neighboring nations. When they asked for the earthly king, the prophet Samuel rebuked them with a warning in 1 Sam 12. Samuel's objection to Israel's request for the earthly king was not about their request for the king himself. Rather, it was objected to because Israel's desire for a powerful king was motivated by fear and earthly mindedness (1 Sam 8:4–9). Deuteronomy 17:14–20 reports laws concerning Israel's kings. In them, God says, "you [Israelites] may indeed set a king over you whom the Lord your God will choose" (Deut 17:15)."

However, the history of the United Monarchy (ca. 1050–931 BC) and the divided monarchy until exile (931–586 BC) was mostly the record of the corruption and failures of their kings, with only a few exceptions. They failed to make Israel a "kingdom of priests and a holy nation" (Exod 19:6) and "a light for the nations" (Isa 42:6, 49:6). Consequently, God's will and intention in his promise that Israel would be a blessing to the nations (Gen 12:1–3) did not materialize and was even at risk of being forfeited when both Israel and Judah fell and were taken into exile.

The Prophets of Hope

When the two kingdoms and their people went into exile, the kingdom of God and his rule through an Israelite king and the hope of God's rule to reach the farthest of the earth seemed to end. But God raised Israel's prophets to tell them that he did not abandon his intention to rule over his people and the world through a Davidic king during the waning days of the two kingdoms and even in exile.

Among several unifying themes in the prophetic books, we wish to call attention to the two important prophetic messages relevant to the issue of the kingdom of God. First, the exile is purifying judgment, after which the return of his people and the restoration of the rule of God are promised. Second, the only hope for establishing an enduring and faithful kingdom in Israel is a future work of redemption. As the history of the record of Israel's kings and leaders shows, the human heart is too corrupted to carry out God's redemptive purpose. God needed to give his people a new heart under a new covenant.

Among all the prophets, Isaiah is best known for the richest prophecy of the return of God's people (Isa 35:1–4, 8–10), a future Savior, and for God's kingdom to be reestablished (Isa 40:9–11). Likewise, Jeremiah is well-known for his prophecy of the new heart under a new covenant (Jer 31:31–34). The realization of the hope for the required restoration and renewal lies beyond the day of punishment that has occurred already in history and the coming day that will bring history as we know it to a close.

The book of Daniel is another important OT book closely related to the kingdom of God. Even though this book is difficult to understand, with strange visions, the central theme of the book of Daniel is God's sovereignty over history and empires because he sets up and removes kings as he pleases (Dan 2:21, 4:34–37). All of this world's kingdoms will end and be replaced by the Lord's kingdom, which will never pass away (2:44, 7:27). His kingdom is supernatural, universal, and everlasting. This kingdom will be ruled by "one like a son of man" who comes "with the clouds," a figure who combines the distinctive traits of humanity and divinity (7:13). The book is especially important for understanding how the idea of God's kingdom changed over time. You may recall that in the early stage of the OT, it was seen as an earthly, political kingdom that was present and led by a Davidic king. Under the new situation, it becomes clear in Daniel that the kingdom is a heavenly one, ruled by the kingdom's agent. Daniel 7 describes this agent as "one like a son of man" who has power over earthly kings. These ideas greatly impacted Jewish messianic thought and the teachings of Jesus.

The Kingdom of God in Jesus' Life, Death, and Resurrection

As previously mentioned, the Gospel features over one hundred references to the kingdom of God and similar terms like the kingdom of Heaven and the kingdom.[8] These references describe and depict various aspects of the kingdom.[9] However, fully explaining the kingdom of God within Jesus' teachings and ministry is beyond the scope of this work. Is there a way to summarize it succinctly?

One approach is to organize the references to the kingdom of God into two broad categories: (1) sayings of Jesus in his teaching regarding the nearness and the future revelation of the kingdom of God and (2) the kingdom of God in the death, resurrection, and the coming kingdom of God in the Parousia of Jesus.

The Kingdom of God in the Teaching of Jesus

The first group of references, of the time having been completed and the kingdom of God drawing near, is found in Mark 1:14–15: "Jesus came into Galilee, proclaiming the gospel of God, and saying, 'The time is fulfilled, and the kingdom of God is at hand; repent and believe in the gospel.'" There are a couple of things to be noted here. First, this is not only his first sermon but also a summary of his message. Second, this verse echoes the language and tone of God's coming for his people's redemption, as in Isa 40:9 and 52:7. The time of waiting for the coming of God's messiah is finished; he has come, and the kingdom of God is close "at hand," meaning that God's rule over people's hearts and lives is now being established, and people should repent and believe in the gospel. There are several competing interpretations of "at hand" (*engiken* in Greek) through the influences of Albert Schweitzer, C. H. Dodd, and others. But Jesus referred to the beginning of God's sovereign action that brought salvation.

The second group of Jesus' sayings focuses on the theme of the fulfillment of the promises of OT prophets. In this connection, it is worth noting that Matthew repeats Mark's summary of Jesus' first message. However, Luke's account of Jesus' ministry starts with visiting the

---

8. Beasley-Murray, "Kingdom of God," 19–30; Henry, "Reflections."
9. For a book-length treatment of the kingdom of God in the teachings and ministry of Jesus, see Ladd, *Gospel of the Kingdom*. For an in-depth treatment of the kingdom of God, see also Vos, "Kingdom of God."

synagogue on the Sabbath day and reading from the book of Isaiah (Luke 4:14–21). He read from Isa 61: "The Spirit of the Lord is upon me, because he has anointed me to proclaim good news to the poor. He has sent me to proclaim liberty to the captives and recovering of sight to the blind, to set at liberty those who are oppressed, to proclaim the year of the Lord's favor" (Luke 4:18–19). Jesus told the people, "Today this Scripture has been fulfilled in your hearing"(Luke 4:21). The meaning of these passages is plain: God is fulfilling his works of the kingdom in and through Jesus. These passages also answer John's question when he sends his disciples to Jesus asking, "Are you the one who is to come, or shall we look for another?" (Luke 7:20). Jesus is God's representative, the Messiah through whom the kingdom comes (Luke 7:18–22).

Thirdly, a group of sayings of Jesus portrays the manner or the way the kingdom of God arrives. The kingdom of God breaks in powerfully in the teachings, healings, and miracles Jesus performs in his ministry. Mark 3:27 talks about plundering the strong man's house by binding, and this verse also echoes the language of Isa 49:24–25, which says, "Can the prey be taken from the mighty, or the captives of a tyrant be rescued? . . . 'Even the captives of the mighty shall be taken, and the prey of the tyrant be rescued, for I will contend with those who contend with you, and I will save your children.'" The parabolic teaching tells us that Jesus has defeated Satan, "the strong man," by the power of God and has released his captives. When Jesus casts out demons, as in Matt 12:28, he says, "But if it is by the Spirit of God that I cast out demons, then the kingdom of God has come upon you."

Fourth and finally is a group of sayings of Jesus that deals with the location of the presence of the kingdom of God. The main point here is that the kingdom of God is present and manifested not only in the words and deeds of Jesus but in his person. Luke 17:20–21 contains the Pharisees' question of when the kingdom of God would come, and Jesus' two-part answer: "The kingdom of God is not coming in ways that can be observed . . . for the kingdom of God is in the midst of you." As mentioned earlier, several translations of the last phrase are possible: "within you" (NKJV), "in the midst of you" (ESV), and "within your reach" (my suggested rephrase).[10] The context of Jesus' saying requires that the object of "within you" means the Pharisees, but it is obvious that this does not mean that the kingdom of God is within unbelieving

---

10. Beasley-Murray lists several citations of this translation in "Kingdom of God," 23.

Pharisees. So, some understand "within you" to mean our hearts and minds, mainly as a spiritual realm, which is also too limited. The second translation, "in the midst of you," is quite possible because the kingdom of God is among believers. The third translation, "within your reach," makes the most sense because it means that the kingdom of God lies in your power to receive it. Applying this understanding means embracing it now and not missing it.

Thus far, we have examined four groups of sayings of Jesus by concentrating on the kingdom of God as a near or present reality. But Jesus has as many sayings about the future realization of the kingdom of God. The Lord's Prayer beginning in Matt 6:9–10 contains the best-known passage for this: "Our Father in heaven, hallowed be your name. Your kingdom come, your will be done, on earth as it is in heaven."

One should note that this prayer consists of the initial invocation of calling God our Father in heaven, and then six petitions. Praying to God as "our Father" conveys the authority, warmth, and intimacy of a loving father's care. By calling God "our Father," Jesus also invites his disciples and believers into the intimacy of God the Son with his Father. "In heaven" reminds his disciples and believers of God's sovereign rule over all things. Praying "hallowed be your name" is the petition to treat God with the highest honor and set him apart as holy.

Verse 10 of the Lord's Prayer lists two requests that directly affect our comprehension of the kingdom of God. To understand the intended meaning, it's helpful to recite each request with the refrain "on earth as it is in heaven." So, we first pray that the kingdom of God, God's powerful saving rule, will pass on earth, just as it already exists in heaven. Similarly, we continue to pray that his will, plan, and purpose at the time of creation may be realized on earth as it is already in heaven.

The Beatitudes (meaning "blessings") Jesus gives in Matt 5:2–12 primarily concern the future kingdom when God will bless the redeemed community of believers.

> Blessed are the poor in spirit, for theirs is the kingdom of heaven.
> Blessed are those who mourn, for they shall be comforted.
> Blessed are the meek, for they shall inherit the earth.
> Blessed are those who hunger and thirst for righteousness, for they shall be satisfied.
> Blessed are the merciful, for they shall receive mercy.
> Blessed are the pure in heart, for they shall see God.
> Blessed are the peacemakers, for they shall be called sons of God.

> Blessed are those who are persecuted for righteousness sake, for theirs is the kingdom of heaven.
> Blessed are you when others revile you and persecute you and utter all kinds of evil against you falsely on my account. Rejoice and be glad, for your reward is great in heaven, for so they persecuted the prophets who were before you. (Matt 5:3–12)

One can readily recognize the present tense in the first and the last two blessings, while in the rest, the tense is the future. This shows that the blessings of the kingdom of heaven are experienced in the present, but they will also be known and experienced fully in the future.

The Kingdom of God in the Death, Resurrection, and Parousia

The central message of Jesus' teaching is the kingdom of God. He demonstrated this through his ministry of healing and miracles and embodied the kingdom itself. As the King, Jesus reigns over the kingdom of God. He is also known as the Messiah, the long-awaited Savior of Israel who fulfilled God's promises. Jesus fulfilled his atonement and, in his dying declaration on the cross, proclaimed, "It is finished." This declaration signifies the triumph of our salvation. Thus, Jesus unites the kingdom and the cross.

When Jesus died on the cross through his self-sacrifice and self-substitution, he achieved not only the salvation of sinners but also the revelation of God and the conquest of evil. To examine the relationship between the kingdom of God and the cross, resurrection, and parousia, we must focus on the theme of the victory and conquest of evil through Jesus' death on the cross and subsequent resurrection. This view of atonement was introduced in an influential book, *Christus Victor* (initially published in 1930), by Gustaf Aulén, who demonstrated that this concept of atonement as a victory over sin, death, and the devil was the dominant view of the NT.[11] A succinct summary of what we glean from John Stott's *Cross of Christ* and other sources follows.[12]

The victory of Christ achieved through death on the cross may look counterintuitive. How can Jesus' death on the Roman cross be victory?

---

11. Aulén, *Christus Victor*.

12. In his book, John Stott lists three subjects (the "Salvation of Sinners," "Revelation of God," and "Conquest of Evil") in the third part, "The Achievement of the Cross." Chapter 9, "The Conquest of Evil," is relevant to our discussion here. Stott, *Cross of Christ*, 165–251.

His death on the cross might look like the failure of Christ's kingdom mission. Nevertheless, it was, indeed, the victory of Christ the King. To understand this, we must consider the full array of royal imagery in Mark 15. His robe was a purple cloak, his head was adorned with a crown of thorns, and Roman soldiers saluted him—"Hail, King of the Jews!"—and kneeled in homage to mistreat and mock him. When Jesus was delivered to Pilate for questioning and judgment to die on the cross, the title of the King of the Jews was repeated four times. When the chief priests and scribes mocked and ridiculed him to come down from the cross and save himself, they called him "the King of the Jews." He stayed and died on the cross for others. He was, indeed, the King, but a different kind of king.

How did God win the victory over evil through Christ's death on the cross? John Stott answers this question by showing how the Scripture unfolds the conquest of evil in six stages. In the first stage, the defeat of Satan and the conquest of evil was predicted in Gen 3:15 as part of God's judgment on the serpent. Many OT texts declare God's present and future rules and the ultimate crushing of Satan (1 Chr 29:11, Isa 9:6–7). In the second stage, the conquest of evil began in the ministry of Jesus. Recognizing Jesus as his future conqueror, Satan made many attempts—through Herod's murder of the Bethlehem children in his birth, through wilderness temptation—to avoid the way of the cross. But Jesus was determined to fulfill his mission. He announced that through him, God's kingdom had come and that his mighty works were evidence of the presence of the kingdom of God. As Jesus' ministry expanded, Satan retreated before it, demons were dismissed, and sickness was healed.[13] When the seventy-two returned with joy in Luke 10:17–20, saying, "Lord, even the demons are subject to us in your name!" Jesus said to them, "I saw Satan fall like lightning from heaven."

In the third and decisive stage, evil was conquered at the cross, achieving Christ's victory. According to John's Gospel, Jesus mentioned the ruler (or prince) of this world three times as the hour of his death approached. This shows that at the time of his death, Jesus understood that the final contest would take place in which the powers of darkness would be beaten. Hebrews 2:14–15 contains verses of Christ's victory. Jesus became man and died on the cross so that "through death he might destroy the one who has the power of death, that is, the devil." Perhaps the best-known NT verse of the victory of Christ on the cross is found in

---

13. For example, see Mark 1:24 (demons), Matt 3:23 (sickness), and Mark 4:39 (nature).

Col 2:14–15, regarding how God forgave us "by canceling the record of debt that stood against us with its legal demands. This he set aside, nailing it to the cross. He disarmed the rulers and authorities and put them to open shame, by triumphing over them in him."

John Stott beautifully explains the irony of Christ's seemingly powerless death, yet achieving the decisive conquest of evil and Christ's victory.

> He was "crucified in weakness" though the weakness of God was stronger than human strength. Thus, he refused either to disobey God, to hate his enemies, or to imitate the world's use of power. By his obedience, his love and his meekness he won a great moral victory over the powers of evil. He remained free, uncontaminated, uncompromised. The devil could gain no hold on him and had to concede defeat.[14]

We have examined the first three stages through which the victory of Christ unfolds in the Scriptures: first, by predicting the defeat of Satan right after the fall; second, by the public ministry of Jesus; and third, by a decisive conquering of evil won at the cross. Now we come to the fourth stage, the resurrection of Jesus, which confirms, announces, endorses, proclaims, and demonstrates the conquest of evil and the victory of Christ. According to Acts 2:24, "God raised him up, loosing the pangs of death, because it was not possible for him to be held by it." The reason was that death had already been defeated.

In the remaining two stages, the victory of Christ, which was decisively won at the cross and publicly confirmed and demonstrated at the resurrection, continues to unfold until it is finally fully realized. In the fifth stage, the conquest and victory of Christ is extended as the church goes out in its mission, in the power of the Spirit, to preach the gospel of Christ crucified, as the Lord summons his people in the Great Commission.[15] The term "church" has multiple meanings. It can refer to a specific local gathering of Christians, a group of Christians within a certain geographical region without specifying one particular congregation, or the church in a more universal sense. In the universal sense, it refers to the entire church, which is triumphant because Jesus Christ, its head, is triumphant.

---

14. Stott, *Cross of Christ*, 235.

15. For an excellent article on the church's growth and the expansion of the kingdom of God, see McLaughlin, "Church Militant."

THE KINGDOM OF GOD 91

The church is also referred to as the militant church because "God has mobilized his people as soldiers in his army, commanding us to expand the borders of his kingdom by conquering and annexing enemy territory. This is primarily a spiritual battle fought on spiritual grounds against spiritual enemies. However, because God's spiritual enemies include unredeemed human beings, the spiritual battle necessarily engages the unbelieving human world."[16]

In the sixth and last stage, we are waiting for the conquest of evil to be consummated and for Christ's victory to be fully realized at the parousia. Jesus Christ, the Lord's Anointed, is already reigning, but he is also waiting until his enemies become his footstool for his feet. On that day, the defeat of Satan is to be finalized (Rev 20:10)—God highly exalting Jesus, entrusting him with the rule of the cosmos and giving him the name that is above every name "so that at the name of Jesus every knee should bow, in heaven and on earth and under the earth, and every tongue confess that Jesus Christ is Lord, to the glory of God the Father" (Phil 2:10–11). First Corinthians 15:24–26 describes the end of the whole story of salvation: "Then comes the end, when he delivers the kingdom to God the Father after destroying every rule and every authority and power."[17]

Potential Misconceptions and Fundamental Aspects of the Kingdom of God

We have gone through a well-known story of redemption by highlighting significant events in both the Old and New Testaments, focusing on the kingdom of God. However, the topic of the kingdom of God is complex and broad, as pointed out earlier, and it's easy to misunderstand it while grappling with difficult questions: What is the kingdom of God? When does it come? Where is it? How does it come? So what? In other words, how should we then live?[18] In 1900, Geerhardus Vos addressed some of these questions and provided deep insights into understanding the

---

16. McLaughlin, "Church Militant," 15.

17. On the reign of Christ and the subjection of all things under his feet, see also Pss 8:6 and 110:1; Eph 1:20–21; Col 2:15; Heb 2:5–9 and 12:2; 1 Pet 3:18–22.

18. This section contains some difficult issues on the kingdom of God, and it is all right for those interested in simply grasping the basics of the subject to skip this section. This section is primarily based on Vos, "Kingdom of God."

nature of the kingdom of God with warnings against misconceptions. Here's a summary of what we can learn from his article.

Vos notes that our Lord presupposes familiarity with the kingdom of God, not just on his part but also on the part of his listeners. He did not intend to establish a new religion but to fulfill God's long-standing promises. As we have discussed earlier, the kingdom of God in the OT refers to a present and genuine relationship between God and his people rather than a future event. In intertestamental Judaism, which is between the Old and New Testaments, the kingdom of God referred to the existing reign of God over Israel and the world, as well as the future extension and enforcement of this reign in the Messianic era. However, when Lord Jesus uses the term "the kingdom of God," he never uses it in the sense of OT theocracy; instead, he always means "the new form," which God's reign is to assume in the near or distant future.[19]

In the absence of a clear definition of the kingdom of God in the Scripture, there has been a debate among scholars about its definition (known as *basileia tou theou* in Greek and *malkut* in Hebrew). Some believe it should be viewed as an abstract sense of rule or reign, while others argue it should be seen as a concrete realm. You may recall from our word study at the outset that the kingdom of God refers to God's sovereign, dynamic, and eschatological rule and reign. Vos explains that the Hebrew term for the kingdom of God in the OT refers to the royal authority that God exercises, which is an abstract concept. The abstract meaning was also sufficient when the Gospel proclaimed that the kingdom of God was at hand. However, the Gospel also speaks about having a meal, eating bread in the kingdom of God, or inviting people into the kingdom of God. It also speaks of being fit or worthy of the kingdom of God, being shut out or cast out from it, and of the kingdom being sought, possessed, received, inherited, or taken away. In these instances, the sense and meaning of the kingdom is not abstract but concrete. Considering these thoughts together, it is clear that both meanings will be recognized in our Lord's teachings. In his recent article on the subject, George Eldon Ladd came to the same conclusion.[20]

Scholars have debated seriously about how the kingdom of God will arrive. Some believe it will come suddenly as a new order or state of things in external forms, as the Jewish expectation states. Others believe

---

19. Vos, "Kingdom of God," 305.
20. Ladd, "Reign or Realm?," 230–38.

it will gradually become a spiritual creation, realizing itself invisibly. Vos distinguished these two beliefs and named them "the eschatological and spiritual-organic conceptions."[21] After carefully reviewing the evidence, Vos concludes that both conceptions of the kingdom of God are present in our Lord's teachings.

Vos then offers two helpful insights into the nature of the kingdom of God. Firstly, the kingdom of God is a state of things that lies beyond the sphere of earthly and natural life. It is so different from the natural condition that it could not evolve from the latter by any gradual process. (Matt 8:11; 13:43; Mark 14:25; Luke 13:20, 29; 22:16, 29, 30). Secondly, Jesus was aware of revealing a relatively new thought in his kingdom parables. He designates it as "the mystery of the kingdom" (Mark 4:11 NKJV). It is fitly called a mystery because this new idea that the kingdom is realized gradually, without being detected, and spiritually is so novel and startling compared to the Jewish exclusively eschatological expectations.

These insights offered by Vos help guard us from two misconceptions about the nature of the kingdom of God, which we discussed at the outset. First, the kingdom of God as an eschatological kingdom must not be confounded with the ordinary Jewish expectations of the coming age. In Jesus' mind, God's kingdom is never any political power, be it Rome or others, but it is always a supernatural power, viz., that of Satan. Second, some translations (like the NKJV) say that the kingdom is "within you" (Luke 17:21), meaning that it is in the internal sphere, indicating a spiritual reality. But this does not imply that purely natural processes are at work, nor is the spiritual side of the kingdom confounded with the purely ethical, as is often done in modern interpretations of the subject. The scope of the coming kingdom of God is broader than that of the Christian's ethical activity or the inner life of the soul.

Vos saves the best part of his discussion of the kingdom of God for the last part of the article, written in 1900. To bring some final insights into the kingdom of God, he contrasts the conception of the kingdom of God and the content of the idea from a material point of view. Vos first recognizes that the content of our Lord's teaching materials, which can be subsumed under the kingdom of God as its organizing principle, deals with "the order of things." He then raises an important question, "Why does he introduce the order of things, announced by Jesus, under this

---

21. Vos, "Kingdom of God," 308–10.

name of the Kingdom of God?"[22] The point of the question is this: the notion of the kingdom of God was current among the people of his days and is intimately associated with their false political expectations. Why did our Lord insist on making it the central teaching theme despite the strong possibility of being misinterpreted? We must safely conclude that he must have ascribed to it a profound significance. Vos suggests that we must also ask, "What concrete, historical associations were connected with the name (i.e., the kingdom of God) in the mind of Jesus?"[23]

Vos repeats the phrase "the order of things" four times and rephrases it as "the order of the divine kingdom" without explaining its meaning.[24] The *Longman Dictionary of Contemporary English* defines it as "the way that life and the world are organized and intended."[25] So, it would be reasonable to understand it to mean the way the divine kingdom is organized/structured and ruled/governed.[26] With that understanding, let us now turn to four fundamental aspects of the kingdom of God, which constantly recur in Jesus' teachings despite the great variety of illustrations. Learning these basic facts would help us answer the questions raised above.

First, the order of things introduced by Jesus is known as the kingdom of God because God is supreme in every aspect. Under the term "kingdom of God," Jesus explained how life and the world are organized, governed, and intended to be. Simply put, the way to achieve this is by prioritizing God in everything because he is supreme. Vos emphasizes that the concept of the kingdom of God is theocentric, incomprehensible to any worldview that elevates man above God. This highlights how modern interpretations of the kingdom concept, which focus exclusively on the ethical relationships among people, are flawed and one-dimensional.

---

22. Vos, "Kingdom of God," 310.

23. Vos, "Kingdom of God," 310.

24. Vos, "Kingdom of God." The "order of things" is repeated from pages 310–12, and the rephrase, "the order of the divine kingdom," occurs on page 313.

25. *Longman Dictionary of Contemporary English*, s.v. "order of things." https://www.ldoceonline.com/dictionary/the-order-of-things.

26. This phrase is mainly associated with French philosopher Michel Foucault's book *The Order of Things*. Here, it refers to the underlying assumptions and the ways of thinking that shape how a particular culture understands knowledge and truth. Foucault argues that these assumptions change throughout history, meaning what is considered normal or true can vary depending on the time period. So, if someone says, "That's just the order of things," he or she might mean something is inevitable or just how things are done.

The understanding of the kingdom is deeply religious, mirroring the central teachings of our Lord. The kingdom of God signifies submitting all temporal matters, ethical actions, and spiritual experiences to a transcendent life-purpose centered on God.

The idea of placing God first and foremost is best articulated in the opening and closing lines of the Lord's Prayer: "Your kingdom come," and "Thine is the kingdom and power and glory forever." Thus, the concept of God's messianic kingdom lies at the core of the Lord's Prayer. It is a kingdom to be ruled by God's chosen Messiah, serving as the Redeemer of God's people and their King. Since the kingdom of God is focused on himself and his glory, it can be viewed as the highest goal intended and planned by God, which people should aspire to. Jesus taught that disciples must seek first the kingdom of God and his righteousness (Matt 6:33), while those who do not follow him chase after worldly things.

Secondly, the new order of things, the kingdom of God, represents the domain where God demonstrates his supreme and royal power. Yahweh's supreme and royal power has been evident throughout history, especially in the book of Daniel, which emphasizes God's sovereignty over history and empires. The Jews interpreted this feature in a national and political sense, but Jesus elevated the idea to a higher spiritual level. He battled and conquered Satan, sin, and death, which were his enemies. Our Lord speaks of the kingdom as real and present, consisting of the power that overcomes Satan. For instance, he states, "But if it is by the Spirit of God that I cast out demons, then the kingdom of God has come upon you" (Matt 12:28). Our Lord ascribes the Holy Spirit as the source of all power to establish the kingdom.

Third, Jesus spoke of establishing the kingdom of God, the realm where God is recognized as the Supreme Ruler and Judge and where his will is carried out with righteousness and justice. According to Vos, the structure of this divine kingdom includes the functions of kingship (rule) and legislative and judicial roles. This idea is supported by Matt 6:33, where Jesus advises us to prioritize seeking God's kingdom and righteousness and assures us that all other necessary things will be provided.

Fourth and finally, the new order of things that Jesus proclaimed is called the kingdom of God. This is because all the blessings that come with it are gifts given graciously and sovereignly by God. The king is the source of grace and blessings for all his subjects. In the OT, the kingship and fatherhood of God are intertwined. Therefore, it is reasonable to assume that the idea of God's fatherhood is a part of our Lord's teaching of the kingdom of God.

Vos finally turns his attention to the church's role as it relates to the kingdom of God. While recognizing that the kingdom of God rests upon the abstract conception of the divine rule exercised and carried out through the work of salvation, Vos concludes that the primary meaning and the goal of the name ("the kingdom of God") is not church as an organization but as organism. He argues that it is plain that the principles and forces considered must inevitably result in establishing a spiritual, ethical, and social organism—namely the church.[27] Then the church's main responsibility and purpose for its existence is to make the invisible kingdom of God visible. This is achieved by living in a way that testifies to the reality of Christ's kingship in every aspect of our lives, including our jobs, families, schools, and even our finances. We must recognize that God in Christ is the King of every sphere of life. If we want to witness the manifestation of the kingdom of God in this world before Christ's second coming, it is up to us to demonstrate it by living as citizens of heaven and subjects of the King.

---

27. The church is a divine organism, a living, vibrant, spiritual body (Eph 2:19–22; 4:11–16; 5:23–33; 1 Cor 12:12–27). As such, it is also arranged or organized and exists as a unit; so, it is a divine organization. Therefore, the church is both an organism and an organization.

CHAPTER 6

Election and Predestination

THE CONCEPT OF GOD choosing individuals or groups for salvation or specific tasks is common in both the Old and New Testaments. In the OT, the idea of election is first seen in the selection of Abraham when God called him to go to Canaan. The concept of election becomes clearer as the story continues with Abraham's descendants: Isaac, Esau, and Jacob (Gen 25:23b). In the NT, the idea of election continues, fulfilling the OT concept and developing more fully in Paul's teachings. The biblical doctrine of election holds that God chose specific individuals from the human race before creation, foreseeing them as fallen but to be called, brought to faith, justified, and glorified through Jesus Christ (Rom 8:28–39, Eph 1:3–14, 2 Thess 2:13–14, 2 Tim 1:9–10). This doctrine teaches that all salvation is based on God's eternal election in Jesus Christ, which stems entirely from God's sovereign freedom. Predestination is similar to election, emphasizing the final destiny of those chosen to be saved even before birth and highlighting that our ultimate destiny is in God's hands, not dependent on us. Essentially, the terms *election* and *predestination* are synonymous, and the doctrine of election and predestination refers to the same concept with slightly different emphasis.

The doctrines of election and predestination are admittedly complex and can be challenging to comprehend fully. As a result, common misunderstandings abound, and some oppose them for various reasons, ranging from God's perceived unfairness in the doctrine, concerns about human free will, and implications for evangelism. However, a clear understanding of what these doctrines actually teach would at least alleviate or refute many of these objections. Their complexity comes partly from the fact that these doctrines involve the sovereignty and will of God, human sinfulness and free will, and the role of Jesus Christ as the Messiah and Savior. Therefore, it must be emphasized that they should be viewed in their proper biblical context and framework of reference.[1]

Like many other truths about God, the doctrines of election and predestination involve mystery. However, it is a pastoral doctrine that encourages Christians to recognize the wonders of God's grace in salvation. It leads us to humility, gratefulness, praise, faithfulness, and holiness as we embrace it. Paul's hymn of praise at the beginning of Eph 1—"Blessed be the God and Father of our Lord Jesus Christ, who has blessed us in Christ with every spiritual blessing in the heavenly places, even as he chose us in him before the foundation of the world"—demonstrates this principle.

The doctrine of election and predestination is a controversial and thought-provoking topic. Nevertheless, this doctrine provides comfort and assurance for those among the elect because election depends on God, not on us. However, what about those who are not chosen? Reprobation is the term given to God's eternal decision regarding those sinners whom he has not selected for life. God chose not to change them and to leave them in their sinful conditions, in which their hearts desire to remain, and finally to judge them as they deserve for what they have done.

We often hear the term "double predestination" with the doctrine of election and predestination. However, this term can be confusing because it can have different meanings depending on what it refers to.

In Reformed theology, God is believed to have elected some for salvation and left others in their sinful conditions, leading to damnation. Therefore, in the Reformed view, there are two outcomes: the elect and the reprobate. In this sense, the Reformed view teaches double predestination.

However, if double predestination refers to the symmetrical way/mode of how divine power works in election and reprobation, we must reject it. In election and predestination, God actively works to bring faith to the elect. Some have inferred from certain passages (notably, Rom 9:22, 1 Tim 2:4, and 1 Pet 2:8) a symmetrical parallel in how God works in election and reprobation. In other words, they argue that God worked

---

1. For two helpful essays on predestination, see Letham, "Predestination" and Hyde, "What Does Predestination Mean."

actively in the election to bring faith to the elect, and he also worked actively in reprobation to prevent them from entering into faith. Then, they ask whether double predestination, in this sense, is biblically supported. However, a strict parallelism in the mode of God's outworking must be denied without a doubt. This point will be discussed in more detail later when we examine the Canons of Dort.[2]

An interesting question is how one can know if they have been chosen or elected. The answer can only be found by observing the results of one's life, much like how we identify a tree by examining its fruit. J. I. Packer wisely emphasizes that we should regard everyone we encounter as potentially being among the chosen ones.[3]

The doctrines of election and predestination are influenced by the doctrine of God (especially the sovereignty of God and the Trinity), the doctrine of man (especially human sinfulness), and the doctrine of salvation (especially the role of Jesus Christ as the Messiah and Savior). Therefore, the appropriate framework for studying these doctrines requires, at the very least, consideration of God's sovereignty, human sinfulness, and Jesus Christ as the Lord and Savior of the world.

Given the broad scope and complexity of the doctrines of election and predestination, it can be challenging to comprehend them fully, and they must be handled carefully. Not surprisingly, many misunderstandings surround this doctrine. Despite its complexity, this doctrine is essential in all Christian churches since it is clearly outlined in the Holy Scriptures. However, it is also important to note that churches have different interpretations. For example, the Methodist, Lutheran, and Presbyterian views all differ. Each church is attempting to grapple with the complexities of this doctrine.

Misunderstandings of Election and Predestination

It is important to note that many misunderstandings surround the doctrines of election and predestination and their implications. Some of these misunderstandings stem from severe distortions of these doctrines. Therefore, addressing common misconceptions about the Christian doctrines of election and predestination is necessary. These misconceptions

---

2. For more details on the question of double predestination, see Sproul, "Is Double Predestination Biblical?" See also Piper, "Is Double Predestination Biblical?"

3. See "Election" in Packer, *Concise Theology*, 151.

must be clarified, corrected, and debunked before presenting historic Christian beliefs on election and predestination.

1. If God ordains all things, electing some for salvation and eternal life and rejecting others, he is an arbitrary God.

This perspective mistakenly assumes that God's choice in the election is random or arbitrary without reason. In truth, while God's election is unconditional and not based on human merit, it arises from his sovereign will and purpose. Therefore, his election is not arbitrary. God chooses his people "according to the purpose of his will" (Eph 1:5) for reasons known to him.

2. If God elected some for salvation and rejected others, he is an unfair God.

Fairness is about treating everyone the same. God's sovereignty refers to his right and authority to rule over his creation. Romans 9:15 says, "For he says to Moses, 'I will have mercy on whom I have mercy, and I will have compassion on whom I have compassion.'" This tells us that while all sinners deserve condemnation, God can choose to bestow grace on some and withhold it from others. In his most recent book, Kevin DeYoung provides detailed answers to the question, "Is predestination fair?" based on an exposition of Rom 9.[4]

By sovereignty, God is neither obligated to save anyone nor to show equal mercy to all. When he chooses to save some, it is an act of mercy, not unfairness. We need to be careful not to go beyond what Scripture teaches or accuse God of unfairness, recognizing the limits of our understanding. The appropriate response is to trust God's goodness and justice, even when we cannot fully comprehend his ways.

3. God chose some for salvation while leaving others for punishment for their sins (reprobation). God's decision in the election is, therefore, unjust.

This statement oversimplifies complex theological questions about God's sovereignty, justice, and the nature of salvation. The doctrine of

---

4. DeYoung, *Daily Doctrine*, 80–81.

divine election—that God chose some for salvation while leaving others for reprobation—does not necessarily imply injustice on God's part for several reasons.

First, all humans are sinful and deserving of judgment. Salvation is an act of grace, not something earned or deserved. Second, God's ways and thoughts are beyond our comprehension, and we cannot fully understand or judge his actions based on human reasoning. In explaining God's sovereign choice in Rom 9, Paul raises a pertinent question and answers it: "Is there injustice on God's part? By no means!" (Rom 9:14). Thirdly, justice means giving people what they deserve. Since all have sinned, justice would mean condemnation for all. God chose some to be saved by his grace. In the election, the chosen ones would receive what they do not deserve, while in reprobation, those not chosen are justly condemned.

4. Predestination negates human will and responsibility.

Some people mistakenly believe that if God predestines, humans have no real choice or accountability. God's sovereignty does not negate human responsibility. People are still accountable for their choices and actions. The Bible affirms God's sovereignty and human responsibility as a paradox beyond complete human comprehension. We are called to choose and believe, even as God works out his eternal purpose. God is not capricious; he is an almighty God and gracious Father.

While we can affirm both God's absolute sovereignty and our human responsibility, fully reconciling them is beyond our finite understanding (Rom 9:20). However, it is important to note that in typical Reformed theology, reprobation has two parts: preterition (the determination to pass by some) and condemnation (the determination to punish those who are passed by). This distinction allows us to affirm both God's absolute sovereignty and human responsibility. We will return to this issue when we thoroughly examine the Reformed view of election and predestination. So, we must approach such matters with humility, recognizing the limits of our knowledge. It is noteworthy that Paul ends his lengthy discussion of God's sovereign choice, the grafting-in of the gentiles, and the remnant of Israel with a doxology, starting in Rom 11:33, which reads, "Oh, the depth of the riches and wisdom and knowledge of God! How unsearchable are his judgments and how inscrutable his ways!"

5. The double predestination is a terrifying and harsh theological belief.

To evaluate this statement, let us recognize that the qualifying term *double* has been confusing in the discussions concerning predestination. The doctrines of election and predestination affirm that God elects some people for salvation while others are not chosen. One of the significant passages supporting the doctrine of predestination is Rom 8:29–30, which says that for those whom he (God the Father) foreknew, he predestined; those whom he predestined, he called; those whom he called, he justified; and those whom he justified, he also glorified. This passage gives the idea of God positively and actively working out his plan of salvation for those elected.

Some erroneously derive a logical conclusion from the doctrines of election and predestination in the opposite direction and apply it to reprobation. In other words, God actively and positively pursues his actions to carry out his justice and prevent those who were nonelected from receiving salvation. However, such a view of "double predestination" would be a caricature and a severe distortion of the Reformed doctrine of predestination. The logical error in the distorted view of double predestination lies in its symmetrical view of predestination. The Reformed view holds that predestination is double in that it involves both election and reprobation but is not symmetrical for the mode of divine activity. The Bible does not contain the doctrine of double predestination, although a few isolated passages come close to it. Often cited verses and passages are Rom 9:22; 1 Tim 2:4; and 1 Pet 2:8.

6. John Calvin invented the doctrine of double predestination out of his head.

Though John Calvin (1509–1564) has been so closely identified with the doctrine of election, this misunderstanding is an old caricature. Instead, it is clear from extensive commentaries on Romans, among others on Genesis, Ephesians, and more, that Calvin was driven to this doctrine by his careful and thorough reading of the Scriptures.[5] Additionally, he delivered two sermons on Ephesians (in 1558). In the second sermon, he provided a clear answer to the general question of how not all hear the gospel, or

---

5. Clark, "Election and Predestination."

not all who hear it believe.⁶ Beginning with Paul's doxology, he moves on to rejoicing in the gospel, which has been made known so that it is within every man's power to believe. Some receive God's grace and others refuse it. To exclude human merit in salvation, Paul writes, " For by grace you have been saved through faith. And this is not our own doing; it is the gift of God" (Eph 2:8–9). One may also recall that Paul writes, "Blessed be the God and Father of our Lord Jesus, who has blessed us in Christ with every spiritual blessing in the heavenly places, even as he chose us in him before the foundation of the world" (Eph 1:3–4).

Calvin's doctrines of election and predestination result from his exegetical, homiletical, and pastoral teaching. He presented the doctrines as good news for sinners and a source of encouragement to believers.

Word Studies⁷

In the Old Testament, the verb *bachar* describes selecting one of several options. The Lord chooses an individual or a nation to bless and chooses Israel's king and prophet to fulfill specific purposes. The story of David's selection, passing by his brothers, illustrates the divine choice well. Another well-known use of *bachar* occurs in the covenantal choice that Moses sets before Israel: "I have set before you life and death, blessing and curse. Therefore choose life" (Deut 30:19). Finally, in choosing Abraham God chose his descendants.

In the NT, Paul uses three cognate terms when discussing the election: the verb *eklegomai*, the noun *ekloge*, and the adjective *eklektos*. Paul uses the verb *eklegomai* four times (1 Cor 1:27 [twice], 28; Eph 1:4), and it means "choose," either by selecting someone or something from among other items or giving preference to someone or something. One good example of selecting someone includes Jesus' selecting the twelve disciples from a large group of Jesus' followers. Another well-known example is that believers are chosen out from among the world.

More often, the verb *eklegomai* signifies a choice or preference. When Jesus visited the house of two sisters, Mary and Martha, Martha asked Jesus to tell Mary to help her. Jesus pointed out that Mary had chosen best by sitting and listening to his teaching (Luke 10:38–42). In the examination

---

6. Clark, "Election and Predestination," 116–20.

7. This section is based largely on two entries from the *Baker Expository Dictionary*: Longman and Strauss, "Choose, Chosen," *BED* 149–51, and "Predestine," *BED* 621.

of the election, this verb is central. Jesus uses the verb to indicate his choice of followers with the phrase "I chose you," in John 6:70, 13:18, and 15:16. The last verse is emphatic: "You did not choose me, but I chose you and appointed you that you should go and bear fruit."

While the verb *eklegomai* is the primary Greek word in the doctrine of election, Paul also uses its cognate adjective *eklektos* (chosen, selected, privileged, especially beloved) six times (Rom 8:33; 16:33; Col 3:12; 1 Tim 5:21; 2 Tim 2:10; Titus 1:1), and it means basically "picked out" or "selected." Finally, Paul uses the noun *ekloge* five times, meaning someone or something as chosen or elected. The elect is the people of God selected from out of the world for his redemptive purpose. The elect enjoy a special relationship with God because God justifies them by grace through the works of Christ (Rom 8:33-34). The people of God are described as "a chosen race, a royal priesthood, a holy nation, a people for his own possession" (1 Pet 2:9), all phrases adapted from the OT.

Additionally, two significant Greek words in the doctrines of election and predestination are the verb *proorizo* (predestine) and *proginosko* (foreknow). The former signifies determining something in advance, and the latter means to know beforehand. This word also takes on a strong Hebraic sense of the word "know" (Rom 8:29; 11:2; 1 Pet 1:20), which means intimate knowledge and communion with a person rather than mere knowledge. Note that these two words are attributed only to God, who aligns individuals and events with his purpose and plan. The object of the verb includes the crucifixion and believers. The Roman soldiers carried out the crucifixion, but it was foreordained by God (Acts 4:28). A well-known NT verse with this verb *proorizo* is Rom 8:29: "For those whom he foreknew he also predestined to be conformed to the image of his Son." In verse 30, a series of five words (predestined, called, justified, and glorified) are used sequentially to explain the process of salvation.

Election and Predestination in the Scriptures

Election in the Old Testament: God's Chosen People

When man first sinned, his fellowship with God was broken. Nevertheless, God, by his grace, introduced the revelation of the redemption plan into history (Gen 3:15). From chapter 4 of Genesis and on, there is a people of God who live in righteousness and truth while the increasing corruption on earth continues.

The first clear statement of the election starts with God's call of Abraham (Gen 12:1). Within two generations of Abraham, the idea of the election had become clear with the birth story of Esau and Jacob, God's promise to Isaac, and God's continued blessings on Jacob. In all narratives of divine election and blessings to Abraham and his descendants, God always took the initiative to bring his elect into a covenantal relationship with himself.

God elected Abraham and his descendants, and consequently, Israel became God's elect nation (Deut 4:37, 7:6, 10:15, 14:2). For this reason, God entered into a covenantal relationship with the Israelites after he delivered them from Egypt (Exod 19:3). By this covenant, Israel became a nation separated from all others for God's revelation for the world. A pertinent question is, Why did God choose Israelites as his people? It was because of his love, not their merit. Deuteronomy 7 emphasizes this: Israelites were chosen to be a people for his treasured possession because of his love for them (Deut 7:6-8, 14:2).

However, Israel's election did not mean that every Israelite trusted God's promise and faithfully served him. Throughout history, the nation's obedience to its covenant Lord greatly varied. Only some faithfully believing remnants in Israel were the people of God.

Election and Predestination in the New Testament

Like many other aspects of God's revelation, the NT continues and fulfills the OT concept of election, and expands the scope of the election. First, in the NT God continues and fulfills it by choosing a people for his purpose in the church. In this plan, Jesus is the ultimate fulfillment of God's election, the "Chosen One" who carries out God's salvific purpose. Second, the NT expands the scope beyond national Israel. While the OT focused primarily on the election of Israel as a nation, the NT broadens this to include gentiles. The apostle Paul wrestles with how God's election of Israel relates to including gentiles in Rom 9–11.

The NT has three new developments regarding the concept of election. First, there is a shift in the focus of the election. While Israel's election in the OT was so that they would serve as a light to the nations, the NT emphasizes election for salvation and being incorporated into Christ's body, the church. So, the focus of the election has evolved. Second, the NT centers its election on Christ. Jesus is presented as the ultimate elect one, through whom all the others' election is mediated. Believers are described as chosen "in Christ" (Eph 1:4), linking individual election to Christ's election. Third, the News Testament maintains the election's individual and corporate aspects. While the OT emphasizes the election of Israel, the NT balances this with a focus on the individual's election to salvation. At the same time, the corporate aspect remains essential, with the church being described as God's chosen people.

Jesus taught the doctrine of election. His teaching on election centers upon the covenant of which Christ is the head and is based on a plan and purpose. His teachings contain many references to the elect and to God's action in choosing and calling them to himself in and through Christ (Matt 24:22; Mark 13:20; Luke 18:7; John 6:37, 65; 10:15). While on earth his ministry focused on teaching Israelites, after his ascension Jesus Christ led the church to see that God had also chosen gentiles to become members of his household (Acts 15:5, Gal 2:11). The same truths come out even more forcefully in John's Gospel. Jesus shares his deep discernment of the Father's predestined plan and purpose for his own life. He lives by the will of the Father (John 4:34, 5:30, 6:38–40). Jesus is also declared as the Savior of the world. The idea of the election is probably most powerfully presented in John 6:35–40, which reads, "Jesus said to them, 'I am the bread of life; whoever comes to me shall not hunger, and whoever believes in me shall never thirst. . . . All that the Father gives me will come to me, and whoever comes to me I will never cast out" (vv. 35, 37).

The presentation of the concept of election in Acts, 1 Peter, and Hebrews mostly parallels what we find in the Gospels and Pauline literature. Some of the highlights in these later NT books may be summarized: (1) God determines events and dates (Acts 1:7, 17:26, 15:7), (2) God elects or appoints individuals (Acts 1:2, 24; 10:41–42; 13:17), (3) God chooses or appoints Christ (Acts 3:20, 1 Pet 1:20), and (4) God elects people to salvation (1 Pet 2:9–10, Acts 2:39, 15:17).

Among all other disciples, Paul taught the doctrine of election in its fullness. Paul's teachings of election and predestination are extensive and complex, but a succinct summary presented by W. A. Elwell can be found in the *DPL*:

> The closely related ideas of election and predestination are crucial and integral to his extensive theology. A good way to comprehend his teachings on election and predestination is to recognize that in all of God's dealings with His creation,

He works out of a predetermined overall plan for a purpose according to His will to His glory. One distinct feature of his teachings on election and predestination is emphasizing the three key phrases: God's plan, purpose, and will. They pervade in his letters, especially in Romans, 1 Corinthians, and Ephesians. God's plan has a definite goal: to sum up all things in Christ (Eph. 1:10). The plan encompasses the objects, means, and ends. The main objects include human beings and Israel; the means include the election and predestination of specific human beings, the works of Christ, and the proclamation of the Gospel. The ends are redemptive, and the ultimate end is the praise of God's glory (Eph. 1:5, 11).[8]

While Paul's teachings on election and predestination are scattered around his letters, three subject areas are critical.

1. The Electing God and His Purpose

It was God who elected and predestined. Ephesians 1:4 says, "He [God the Father] chose us in him [Jesus Christ] before the foundation of the world, that we should be holy and blameless before him." Ephesians 1:10 says it was "as a plan for the fullness of time, to unite all things in him [Jesus Christ], things in heaven and things on earth." Finally, 1 Thess 1:4b says, "He [God the Father] has chosen you." Salvation depends first on God, not on human beings. The gospel's good news is that humans do not need to strive to earn God's favor. As Rom 3:24 says, God's grace is given freely.

2. The Election of God

Paul speaks of the election of God in two different ways: first, the election of persons, especially groups of people (Rom 8:33, Eph 1:4, Col 3:2, 1 Thess 1:4, 2 Tim 2:10, Titus 1:1), and second, the election of Israel.

Two prominent passages regarding the election of persons are Rom 8:28–29 and Eph 1:3–5. First, Rom 8:28 says that God weaves everything together for the good of his children. Verses 29–30 explain why those who believe in Christ can be assured that all things work together for good. The complex reasoning runs like this: those who were foreknown

---

8. Elwell, "Election and Predestination," 225.

with God's covenantal affection are predestined, those who are predestined are called, those who are called are justified, and those who are justified are glorified. The chain of salvation cannot break but continues. Because of this, no one can charge God's elect with guilt.

Secondly, Eph 1:3–5 is part of Paul's list of spiritual blessings in Christ (Eph 1:3–14), and the passage qualifies the idea of election ("as he chose us") in four different ways. First, the election is in Christ, emphasizing the mediation of Christ for all God's blessings, including the election. Second, the election is before "the foundation of the world" (v. 4), meaning it is above the temporal or cosmic time. Third, the purpose of the election is to make us "holy and blameless before him" (v. 4), indicating redemptive and moral intent. Fourth, the election is an act of love. The word *predestination* enters in verse 5, which is synonymous with election. The goal of the predestination is adoption into God's family.

Paul also speaks of Israel's election in Rom 9–11 in general, and specifically in Rom 9:11; 11:5, 7, and 28. Paul struggles here with the question of how and why the election of Israel is somehow set aside. He solves this difficulty by finding a deeper meaning to election in the purpose of God through the idea of Israel's remnants. This is a complex subject for us, as we marvel when he breaks forth into his doxology, saying, "Oh, the depth of the riches and wisdom and knowledge of God! How unsearchable are his judgments and how inscrutable his ways!" (Rom 11:33).

3. Contours and Characteristics of Election

Ephesians 1 is a marvelous chapter that provides the contours and characteristics of the doctrine of election. Election—like every blessing in Christ—is in and through Jesus Christ before the foundation of the world, emphasizing Christ's mediator role. We have redemption through his blood, the forgiveness of our trespasses according to the riches of his grace. Election is also according to his purpose and will, which he (God the Father) outlined in Christ "as a plan for the fullness of time, to unite all things in him, things in heaven and things on earth" (Eph 1:10). The purpose of the election is for us to be holy and blameless before him. Finally, the basis of election is his free love, just as the basis of the election of the Israelites in the OT was his love.

Unconditional Election: Reformed View of Election and Predestination[9]

We have briefly reviewed what the Scriptures tell us about election and predestination. As our brief review of scriptural passages, especially Pauline teachings, demonstrates, this doctrine is closely related to and based on other key Christian doctrines, such as the doctrines of God, sin, grace, justification, Christ, and the church. Therefore, it must be viewed and studied with them. Studying this doctrine can be challenging, given its broad scope, complexity, and difficulty. To fix our thoughts on the essential teaching of the doctrines, let us state clearly what the doctrine of election is at the outset before we delve into a reformed view of election and predestination.

The doctrines of elections and predestination can be summarized in two parts: First, God elected a certain number of individuals from the human race before creation for salvation in Christ and reprobated others. Second, God's elections must be traced finally to God's unquestionable and inscrutable will. The first part describes the contents of God's sovereign election, and the second part explains the basis of God's sovereign decision.

The reformed doctrine is generally known as "unconditional election." The word *election* is a biblical word (Matt 24:22–31; Rom 8:33; 9–11; 2 Tim 2:10; Titus 1:1; 1 Pet 1:1; 2 Pet 1:10). Therefore, Christian believers from various backgrounds or affiliations believe in election. However, this does not mean that their theology of election is the same. As mentioned earlier, churches have different interpretations. For example, the Methodist, Lutheran, and Presbyterian views all differ. Each church is attempting to grapple with the complexities of this doctrine.

The term *unconditional* can be confusing and requires some explanation. Breaking it down, we have the prefix "un-," meaning "not," and the word *conditional*, meaning "dependent on something." Combined, they form an adjective describing something that holds without any attached conditions. The meaning of *unconditional election* from this word analysis says that God will save people unconditionally, i.e., no matter whether they come to faith or not. The true and intended meaning of unconditional election in the Reformed tradition is that salvation

---

9. There are voluminous works on this topic. See Calvin, *Institutes*, §§3.24.1–17; Clark, "Election and Predestination," 90–122; and "The Divine Counsel" in Bavinck, *God and Creation*, 337–405.

comes to the sinner because, from all eternity, God elected a people to be his own without considering the merits of individuals. In other words, salvation is entirely of and from the Lord and does not depend on us. Like other truths about God, the doctrine of election entails mystery and sometimes stirs controversy. However, this doctrine is a pastoral doctrine to help Christians see how great is the grace that saves them, to exclude human merit, and to teach us that everything comes from God's pure goodness and grace.

Reformed theology has taught unconditional election, its "U" in the well-known acronym TULIP, which encapsulates the five points of Calvinism or doctrines of grace.[10] To understand the proper context of God's unconditional election, we need to be reminded from our brief review of the Scriptures that this doctrine of election depends on the doctrines of God, sin, grace, justification, Christ, and the church.

A foundational theological principle in the Reformed theology of the doctrine of God is the belief that God is a living and true God. Herman Bavinck, in his book *The Wonderful Works of God*, teaches us that "As the living God he is at the same time *operative* God. He cannot do otherwise other than work. He works always."[11] Two foundational theological principles—God's sovereignty and the whole counsel of God (often expressed as God's plan, purpose, and will)—undergird Reformed theology in understanding God's work.

The belief in God's sovereignty in creation, providence, and grace is fundamental to biblical faith and worship. The Scriptures often portray God on his throne, signifying his sovereign rule. God's rule and dominion are carried out as he chooses and carries out all that he wills. Nothing and no one can prevent or thwart his plans. For our immediate purpose, God is sovereign, and he elects to carry out his wonderful works according to his whole counsel of God, often expressed as his plan, purpose, and will. One can see from the above discussions that the election is a subset of teaching on the sovereignty of God in the salvation of his people.

The doctrine of election next depends on the prior doctrine of sin, total depravity, represented by the "T" in TULIP. Sin has its roots in pride and enmity against God. The original creation was "very good,"

---

10. See *TableTalk* magazine's Dec. 2023 issue, which presents excellent articles on TULIP (total depravity, unconditional election, limited atonement, irresistible grace, and perseverance of the saints) and brief discussions on the Canons of Dort. Archived issues of the magazine can be found at https://tabletalkmagazine.com/.

11. Bavinck, *Wonderful Works*, 144.

but Adam and his wife, Eve, sinned by disobeying God's command, which led to their estrangement from God and affected their offspring. This resulted in sinful distortion, which we refer to as depravity. Drawing on the root, *pravus* ("crooked"), the Latin word *depravare* means "to distort or disfigure."[12] The term "depravity" vividly illustrates the Bible's teaching about the destructive and condemning effects of sin. Depravity affects everyone (Gen 6:5, Rom 3:10–12), and we are all "dead in the trespasses and sins" (Eph 2:1).

Total depravity does not mean the highest possible degree of depravity, like "utter depravity," but rather corruption in the entirety of our being. In other words, every part of us—our mind, will, and body—is affected by evil. The result is our inability to hear the gospel; even if we hear it, we refuse to accept it unless God first chooses us and does prior regenerating work in us.

We have discussed God's sovereignty and man's sin, which are closely related to the doctrines of election and predestination. Now, we will focus on the role of God's sovereignty and man's free will in salvation. An important question that arose in early Christian history is why some individuals accept the gospel for salvation while others do not. Different theories of election play a key role in answering this question. The orthodox and Reformed view, supported by the apostle Paul, Augustine, Luther, and Calvin, emphasized God's sovereign election, while others stressed human choice.

The controversy as to the basis of God's sovereign election flared up in Europe in the late sixteenth century between the Reformed view and the Arminian view. The name of the person who is at the center of the controversy is James Hermanson (ca. 1559–1609), known to us as Jacob Arminius. Arminius taught that God elects those whom he foreknew would believe. So, he retains God's foreknowledge, but God's election is conditioned upon man's will to believe. His errant teaching may be called "conditional election," conditional on man's decision by free will. After he died in 1609, the Arminians (those who followed Arminius) published a remonstrance, a forceful protest, against the Reformed church. They outlined five objections to the Reformed doctrine as early as 1610. The Canons of Dort is the document then produced by the Synod of Dort (in Dordrecht, the Netherlands) in response to the Five Articles of

---

12. *Latdict*, s.v. "pravus, prava, pravum." https://latin-dictionary.net/definition/31537/pravus-prava-pravum. See also *Latdict*, s.v. "depravare."

Remonstrance, point by point.[13] Five points are closely associated with TULIP, but in a different order. We will only present the first point on election and predestination here for our immediate purpose.

The first point in the canons is encapsulated by "unconditional election," which represents the Reformed view of election and predestination. This point provides the answer to the question raised earlier: Why do some believe and repent at the preaching of the gospel, but others remain in their sins and under the just condemnation of God? The answer to this question is presented in the sixth article of the Canons of Dort and quoted below:

> That some receive the gift of faith from God and others do not receive it proceeds from God's eternal decree, for "known unto God are all His works from the beginning of the world" (Acts 15:18). "Who worketh all things after the counsel of His own will" (Eph. 1:11). According to which decree, He graciously softens the hearts of the elect, however obstinate, and inclines them to believe, while He leaves the non-elect in His just judgment to their own wickedness and obduracy. And herein is especially displayed the profound, the merciful, and at the same time the righteous discrimination between men, equally involved in ruin; or that decree of election and reprobation revealed in the Word of God, which though men of perverse, impure and unstable minds wrest to their own destruction, yet to holy and pious souls affords unspeakable consolation.[14]

The sixth article teaches us several important truths about God's election and predestination.

1. It affirms that God's eternal, sovereign, and gracious decision is the source of faith.

2. It supports God's foreknowledge and sovereign will by citing Acts 15:18 and Eph 1:11.

3. It affirms the concept of election (those chosen to receive salvation by faith) and reprobation (those not chosen).

4. It highlights the *active* work of God that "graciously softens the hearts of the elect and inclines them to believe." This reminds us of the passage Rom 8:29–30, which explains the chain of the process

---

13. Venema, "Why Five Points?"

14. Puritan Reformed Theological Seminary, *Canons of Dort*. Another great modern translation is available in Van Dixhoorn, *Creeds*, 137.

for salvation: for those whom he foreknew, he also predestined; for those whom he predestined, he also called; those whom he called, he justified; and those whom he justified, he glorifies. In contrast, one should note the passive tone and voice in God's decision for those not chosen. The article says, "He leaves the non-elect in his judgment to their own wickedness and obduracy."

5. It highlights God's mercy toward the elect and justice toward the non-elect. To ask why God works that way is beyond what we know and remains a mystery.
6. It acknowledges that grasping this doctrine is complex and can be misunderstood while it provides comfort to others.

Combining the truths in items 3 and 4 above, predestination is double in the sense of including both election and reprobation. However, the mode or the way of God's works in election and reprobation is not symmetrical. The truths in items 5 and 6 are then based on items 3 and 4.

Earlier, we noted that in typical Reformed theology, reprobation has two parts: preterition (God's sovereign decision to pass over some, not electing them to salvation) and condemnation (God's judgment against sin in those passed over). In connection with this distinction, as in the fourth item above, we should note that the Reformed theology emphasizes that in the election, God actively works to bring about the salvation of those elected through foreknowing, predestination, and ensuing stages. In contrast, preterition is viewed as a passive act—God simply does not extend saving grace to some, rather than actively working their condemnation. Condemnation is based on the person's own sin and guilt, not an arbitrary decision by God. This distinction also allows us to maintain God's sovereign election and human responsibility for sin and unbelief. Finally, it should be noted that while Calvin did not use the terms *preterition* and *condemnation*, he laid the groundwork for this distinction. Francis Turretin, a seventeenth-century Reformed theologian, explicitly developed the distinction. Well-known theologians, like Charles Hodge and Louis Berkhof, continued to hold the distinction. More recently, R. C. Sproul also discussed preterition and condemnation in his writings on predestination.

Difficulties About Election and Predestination

The doctrines of election and predestination are considered difficult to understand and controversial. Their complexity stems partly from the involvement of God's sovereignty and will, human sinfulness and free will, and the role of Jesus Christ as the Messiah and Savior. Some oppose these doctrines due to potential conflicts between God's sovereignty and human free will and their implications for evangelism.

God's Sovereignty and Man's Free Will

The Scriptures teach that God is sovereign. God's sovereignty refers to his absolute power in creation, providence, and grace in carrying out the works of God. God's sovereignty means that God ordains everything, including electing some for salvation and rejecting others. The Scriptures also teach about man's free and responsible agency, which indicates that an intelligent person acts with rational self-determination. So, there appears to be a conflict between God's sovereignty and human free agency. A general question arises: How can a person be a free and responsible agent if God's sovereignty preordained his actions? Specifically, with the doctrines of election and predestination, how can we say that man has free will and agency if the sovereign God preordained salvation for some and others for reprobation? Are the two teachings of the Scriptures in conflict, or at least in tension? Various responses to this controversial question reflect long-standing philosophical and theological debates.

Some argue that the teachings about God's sovereignty and man's free will contradict each other, but readily recognize that finite human minds cannot fully comprehend how they relate. Therefore, one has to either accept them without understanding how they relate to each other or reject them on rational grounds. Others point out correctly that we do not fully understand how these two truths work together, but this does not necessarily mean they are contradictory. The two truths, that God is sovereign and we have a responsibility as rational beings, can hold together for reasons unknown, and they remain mysterious to us. Still, others believe God's sovereignty includes allowing humans to make free choices within certain limits. God remains in ultimate control, and we are responsible for what God ordains us to be responsible for, as free agents to make moral choices and correct decisions. These diverse views on the relationship between God's sovereignty and man's responsibility show this is a complex theological issue.

Understanding the nature of the debate on God's sovereignty and man's free will would be enhanced by understanding the meaning and significance of the two terms, God's sovereignty and man's free will. Toward that goal, we can benefit from studying God's sovereignty from Bavinck's two well-known works, the *Reformed Dogmatics* and *Wonderful Works of God*. His books provide valuable insights into God's sovereignty in Christian theology. The Scripture declares God as the living and true God. As a living God, he always works (John 5:17). The Holy Scripture also declares that God brings everything into being according to his will. Some passages say the counsel of God and his purpose does this; in other passages, it is by decree, ordination, or good pleasure of God.

However, the doctrine of God in Christian theology takes its point of departure in God's nature, not his will. Christian theology maintains that the world was brought into being by an act of God's free and sovereign will, and God has his mind and reason. However, God's nature is reflected in God's free and sovereign will, which is wise, just, holy, and merciful. In other words, his will is one with his being, wisdom, goodness, and all other perfections. On the nature of his free and sovereign will, Bavinck writes that "God's sovereignty is one of unlimited power, but not of blind fate, incalculable choice, or dark force of nature. Rather, it is the will of an almighty God and gracious father."[15]

Bavinck lists many biblical passages to support God's free and necessary will. A few representative passages are Ps 115:3, "Our God is in the heavens; he does all that he pleases"; Job 9:12, "Who will say to him, 'What are you doing?'"; Job 33:13, "Why do you contend against him, saying, 'He will answer none of man's words'?"; Isa 45:9, "Does the clay say to him who forms it, 'What are you making?'"; Matt 20:15, "Am I not allowed to do what I choose with what belongs to me?"; and Rev 4:11, "For you created all things, and by your will they existed and were created." Bavinck concludes that election and reprobation demonstrate God's freedom even more clearly. Though they remain a mystery and difficult to comprehend, God's decision rests alone in God's sovereign good pleasure.

Let us focus on man's free will, sometimes called "human free agency." We are responsible creatures with reason, who make moral choices and

---

15. Bavinck, *God and Creation*, 181.

correct decisions. However, our sinfulness is a limiting factor, and consequently, we have only limited free agency in making moral choices and decisions. Does not the limited agency call for humility when we recognize our capacity for ethical reasoning and our tendency for error?

Collecting these thoughts together, I contend that our tendency to perceive a conflict between God's sovereignty and man's free will is best attributable to our unwillingness or inability to accept God's sovereignty and free will, which is wise, just, holy, and merciful. Remembering that it is the will of an almighty God and gracious Father will significantly reduce the contentious complaints against God's sovereignty. Paul clearly states that God "chose us in[Christ] before the foundation of the world, that we should be holy and blameless before him. In love he predestined us for adoption . . . through Jesus Christ, according to purpose of his will, to the praise of his glorious grace, with which he blessed us in the Beloved" (Eph 1:4–6). Paul's teaching shows that the purpose of election is for our holiness and being free of guilt; the sole basis of God's predestination of us is his love.

God's Sovereignty and Evangelism

A reformed view of election is called *unconditional election* because this election is not based on anything good or meritorious in the chosen ones. Instead, it expresses God's free and sovereign will. According to the doctrine of election, God had ordained some for salvation before their birth but left others for reprobation. Evangelism means spreading the gospel of Jesus Christ through preaching and teaching. Christ calls us to be his witness, and evangelism is the means to the end of gospelizing the world. When we consider God's sovereignty and evangelism together, many find it difficult to reconcile them and begin to question the need for evangelism. If God preordained those who will be saved, does it not exclude the activity of evangelism? Why do we need to evangelize if the outcome is already determined?

To counter this argument, we need first to note that the need for evangelism is emphasized in Matthew in two passages. Matthew 13:23 says, "As for what was sown on good soil, this is the one who hears the word and understands it. He indeed bears fruit and yields." The word of God has to be spread by the hard work of evangelism, just like the seed has to be sown on good soil. Matthew 28:19–20, known as the Great

Commission, also says, "Go therefore and make disciples of all nations, baptizing them in the name of the Father and of the Son and of the Holy Spirit, teaching them to observe all that I have commanded you." Works described in this verse are all the hard work of discipleship, part of evangelism. Similarly, Paul also emphasizes the need for calling upon Christ, believing in him, and preaching, in Rom 10:14–15: "How then will they call on him in whom they have not believed? And how are they to believe in him, of whom they have never heard? And how are they to hear without someone preaching? And how are they to preach unless they are sent?"

Regarding the possible dilemma between God's sovereignty and evangelism, we should also note that the Bible has no problem joining the two. Jesus taught that all those the Father gave him would come to him (John 6:44), but this did not prevent him from offering a genuine gospel (John 6:35). Paul, who obviously believed in the sovereignty of God and suffered so much for sharing the gospel, said to Timothy, "I endure everything for the sake of the elect" (2 Tim 2:10).

Kevin DeYoung presents another powerful argument: many of the greatest evangelists and missionaries in the modern era have been Calvinists.[16] They all believed in God's sovereign election of those to be saved, but they focused their efforts on missions and evangelism.

Combining these passages and gathering our thoughts, we understand that God's sovereignty and evangelism's hard work are not in conflict; instead, they are cooperative efforts. In other words, a firm belief in the election is instead the reason for the evangelistic hope to reach those who need to hear the gospel through missions.

---

16. DeYoung, *Daily Doctrine*, 86.

CHAPTER 7

Repentance

WHEN JOHN THE BAPTIST, a herald for Jesus, preached his message in the wilderness of Judea, he said, "Repent, for the kingdom of heaven is at hand" (Matt 3:2). When people hear that message, in Jesus' time or today, many would understand it as a call to feel sorry for their misdeeds and change their behavior. However, the NT word for repentance means changing one's mind so that one's views, values, goals, and ways are to be changed, resulting in a different way of living one's life. Repentance involves the idea of turning from one way of thinking and living to a different way. We often hear of "true repentance," which assumes the existence of false repentance, a spurious kind of repentance. It involves being sorry, often caused by a fear of punishment or a loss of blessing. Given its importance in regeneration and conversion and its pervasive use in the Scripture, we must understand repentance's real meaning, significance, and nature.

In the Old Testament, to "repent" was to call for Israelites to turn from unrighteousness (Jer 1:11, Ezek 18:21, Zech 1:4) and to turn to (2 Chr 15:4) or return to God (Isa 55:7). This involved a radical change in one's way of life. What made repentance possible for them was the prior assurance that God desired to forgive (Joel 2:13, Exod 34:6). In the NT, the call to repent was the first and the urgent call in the preaching of John the Baptist (Matt 3:2), Jesus (Matt 4:17), the twelve disciples (Mark 6:12), Peter at Pentecost (Acts 2:38), Paul to the gentiles (Acts 17:30, 26:20), and the glorified Christ to churches in Asia (Rev 2:5, 16, 22; 3:3, 19).

The term "repentance" is commonly and frequently used both in the church and outside, but we often get confused about it partly because of its seemingly paradoxical nature. On the one hand, repentance is turning from sin, a constitutive part of the Christian conversion. It is believers who must repent in regeneration. On the other hand, regeneration is a divine act where God and the Holy Spirit supernaturally create a spiritual rebirth, changing a person's inner being from spiritually dead to alive. So, repentance is not meritorious but the gift of God, provided in his love and grace. Next, on the one hand repentance must occur at the initial stage of regeneration. The result of regeneration is conversion, where we are turned around and move in a different direction. On the other hand, as Martin Luther wrote in the *Ninety-Five Theses*, repentance is a lifelong activity.[1] So, repentance must occur in the early stage of regeneration, but at the same time, it continues throughout the entire Christian life. Finally, the Greek term *metanoia* is commonly translated in English to "repentance," but whose literal meaning is "change of mind."[2] So, on the one hand, repentance involves reversing an earlier mental view of sin and God. On the other hand, we also know that repentance is far more than just a shifting intellectual outlook. It encompasses the whole person's intellect, heart, will, soul, and body.

Another source of confusion and potential misunderstanding stems from the close relationships among the related terms of regeneration, repentance, conversion, and sanctification. Each of these terms is closely related to each other and an inseparable part of the process of salvation, and it can be difficult to distinguish between them and understand the true meaning and significance of each of these terms.

Given the paradoxical and inseparable nature of these closely related terms, it is necessary to examine first the Bible and traditional confessional documents, such as the Westminster Confession of Faith and the Westminster Shorter Catechism (WSC). Both of these two documents define "repentance unto life." This phrase again assumes the existence of a repentance which does not lead to life. Additionally, we must take time to examine traditional doctrinal classics on repentance by Calvin and Bavinck and other reliable resources that will help us dig deeper into the truth about repentance.[3] In 2 Cor 7:10, Saint Paul

---

1. The first thesis states, "Our Lord and Master Jesus Christ, when He said 'Repent,' willed that the whole life of believers should be repentance." Mark, "95 Theses."

2. Longman and Strauss, "*Metanoia*," *BED* 670.

3. Calvin, *Institutes*, §§3.3.17–18; Bavinck, *Holy Spirit*; Beeke, "Appropriating

distinguishes between two types of grief and the resulting repentance: "For godly grief produces a repentance that leads to salvation without regret, whereas worldly grief produces death." True and genuine repentance results from godly grief, which leads to salvation. These examples tell us that true repentance is far more than remorse or regret. Cain (Gen 4:12), Esau (Heb 12:17), and Judas (Matt 27:3) provide examples of carnal and worldly grief, which do not lead to life. Several common misunderstandings of repentance are listed below.

Misunderstandings of Repentance

1. Repentance is the confession of past misdeeds.

Confession of past wrongful deeds is part of repentance but falls short of capturing its full meaning and process. Repentance involves acknowledgment that one has done something wrong or sinful, remorse, confession, commitment to change, and action to carry out change through obedience. This fuller understanding of repentance recognizes its transformative nature and the necessity of resulting behavioral change.

2. Repentance is seen as a one-time event at a conversion.

Repentance is a crucial and decisive part of the initial conversion, but it does not stop there. For believers, ongoing repentance is necessary even after initial justification. This continuous repentance is part of maintaining a healthy relationship with God. Repentance is not about repeatedly getting saved but about living out one's salvation by turning continually from sin to God.

3. Repentance means completely stopping all sinning before coming to Christ.

The cessation of sinful deeds is not a requirement for repentance but rather an outcome and proof of conversion. Conversion is the result of regeneration, a process in which God and the Holy Spirit supernaturally change the disposition of the soul from spiritual death to spiritual life.

Salvation," 270–300.

This shows that salvation is the work of God and the Holy Spirit and that repentance is an ongoing process of Christian life.

4. Repentance is a human effort, relying on willpower to change behavior.

This is incorrect. Repentance is not about changing behavior through human effort but responding favorably to the gospel message. True repentance involves a fundamental change of mind, heart, disposition, and attitude toward sin and God. And this comes about through the works of the Holy Spirit. Though people may want to change their behavior by relying on their willpower, they usually fail because they lack the capacity to change their hearts and minds. This often leads to frustration and failure. The biblical view of repentance is God-centered. It is to turn towards God, not just to improve oneself by human effort. It involves recognizing our need for Christ and relying on him rather than our own efforts.

5. Repentance involves seeking God's forgiveness to avoid facing his judgment.

While repentance is necessary for God's forgiveness and salvation, it is not the cause of the forgiveness. Forgiveness comes from God's free grace in Christ.

6. True repentance is turning away from sin and toward God.

Repentance involves more than just turning away from sin and moving toward God. Before making this turn, it requires a genuine awareness of one's sinfulness and offensiveness to God and an understanding of God's mercy in Christ, accompanied by grief and hatred for one's sins. After these initial steps, turning away from sin and moving toward God naturally follows. After that, sincere and serious efforts to obey God's commandments come into play to live a new life.

Word Study of Repentance

The word "repent" in modern English can have two meanings.[4] It can refer to feeling regret in thought, attitude, or action, or it can more commonly involve regretting and changing from one attitude or allegiance to another. To fully grasp the exact meaning of this very important word in the Bible, it's necessary to examine the original Hebrew and Greek terms that are translated as "repent."[5]

Repentance in the Old Testament

In the OT, the words "repent" and "repentance" are mentioned twenty-three times. It's important to note that "repentance" is described more as an action rather than a feeling like contrition. Two Hebrew words are used when discussing repentance in the OT: *nacham* and *shub*. Though both of these words are often translated as "repent," *nacham* should not be confused with *shub*, which often includes an aspect of remorse for wrongdoing and carries with it a sense of turning back to God. This turning, or returning as the prophets often call it, has three facets: (1) obedience to the will of God, (2) trusting in God and rejecting all human help and all false gods, and (3) turning aside from everything ungodly.

The Hebrew verb *nacham* indicates a decision to change the course of action. The subject of *nacham* can be people. For example Gods says the people may "change their minds when they see war and return to Egypt" (Exod 13:17), people are seen turning away from righteousness (Jer 1:11; Ezek 18:21; Zech 1:4), and sometime they turn to God (2 Chr 15:4) or return to God (Isa 55:7). In all the rest of the cases, the subject of *nacham* is God. In those cases, *nacham* can describe God experiencing regret and even changing his course. For example, when Israel sins by worshiping the golden calf, God tells Moses that he is going to destroy them and start over with Moses (Exod 32:7–10). With Moses imploring God to turn from his fierce anger and relent concerning this disaster planned for the people (v. 12), God relented concerning the disaster he had said he would bring on his people (v. 14). Jeremiah 18:7–8 also reported the same "relenting" and changing of God's intended course of action. However, as the *Baker Expository Dictionary* points out, God does not *nacham*

---

4. See "Repentance" in DeYoung, *Daily Doctrine*, 247–48.
5. The following discussions draw from Longman and Strauss,"Repent, Repentance," *BED* 669–70.

in the same way as humans do. The Lord "regrets" or "changes the mind" of the intended punishment while people repent their own wickedness. It should be pointed out that God's ability to change his course is connected to his sovereignty and grace. This demonstrates that a prophetic judgment of destruction is designed to bring repentance; God wants to change his course from bringing punishment.

In the OT, repentance wasn't just about feeling sorry; it also involved specific actions like fasting, wearing sackcloth, and performing rituals to show a genuine commitment to change and to restore one's relationship with God. The prophets often called for this kind of repentance, encouraging people to return to God with sincere hearts and obedient lives.

Repentance in the New Testament

In the NT, repentance is conveyed primarily by the noun *metanoia* and the related verb *metanoeo*. Etymologically, this verb suggests a change of mind (*meta* + *noeo*). But in a religious context, it means "repent" by rejecting evil and turning to God, signifying the complete reorientation of one's whole being to God. So, the NT's use of "repent" is deeply influenced by the OT's notion of "turning" to God (*shub*) as a reversal or turnaround, a change in the direction, and a return to covenant fidelity. Repentance thus involves far more than intellectual change or remorse; it entails a new or renewed relationship with God that transforms all the dimensions of one's life, including conduct, and is akin to conversion.

The term "repentance" is prominently featured in the Synoptic Gospels, Acts, and Revelation, but not in John's Gospel and letters. John the Baptist and Jesus began their ministries with the same prophetic call for repentance. In Matthew and Mark, repentance is the keynote of Jesus' inaugural preaching. Matthew records Jesus' preaching: "Repent, for the kingdom of heaven is at hand" (Matt 4:17b). Mark 1:15 records his sermon in full: "The time is fulfilled, and the kingdom of God is at hand; repent and believe in the gospel."

Jesus' first sermon recorded in Mark's Gospel consists of two indicative statements ("the time is fulfilled" and "the kingdom of God is at hand"), a command ("repent"), and a call ("believe in the gospel"). The first clause indicates that the divinely measured time (*kairos*) of expectation has ended; the old era has now passed away. The second clause announces the dawn of the new era, meaning that the kingdom's time must have started. These two parallel statements explain the basis for the ensuing command ("repent") and a call to believe in the gospel. What must people do in response to the two crucial events in human history? Jesus singles out two appropriate responses: repent and believe in the gospel.

Faith and Repentance

In Christian understanding, repentance is a fruit of faith, which is itself a fruit of regeneration. In turn, faith is strengthened by repentance. Therefore, repentance and faith are so closely related that it is impossible to separate one from another. However, as Calvin emphasizes, they are different concepts and must be distinguished. Regarding their close relationship, the NT consistently presents faith and repentance as the appropriate responses to hearing the gospel message.

A summary of what Herman Bavinck teaches about the relationship between faith and repentance follows.[6] One must be born again or from above (John 3:6–8). In the fundamental sense, being born of God is always a divine act through which a person is transformed and inwardly renewed. A regeneration, a birth from God, must logically precede faith. In regeneration, God grants the new believer faith and repentance. The repentance is a turning away from sin and to God in faith. Faith is grasping God's grace offered in the gospel, accompanied by repentance that involves a hatred of sin, from which the new believer flees. Therefore, faith is essential for repentance, which in turn strengthens faith and thus completes the inseparable relationship between faith and repentance.

In elucidating the inseparable relationship between faith and repentance, Herman Bavinck states,

> We should not dare to turn around towards God if we did not trust inwardly in our souls through the Holy Spirit that as a Father He will accept our confession of sins and forgive us. True repentance stands in inseparable connections with the true, saving faith.[7]

In Christianity, faith is the means by which God unites the elect with Jesus Christ and makes them recipients of the blessings of salvation secured by his death and resurrection. A genuine desire to repent is evidence of faith. Therefore, true faith is repentant faith. True repentance

---

6. Bavinck, *Holy Spirit*, 29–33, 96–98.
7. Quoted in Garriott, "True Repentance," 64–65.

begins in the heart through the work of the Holy Spirit and extends to the whole person, manifested in thoughts, attitudes, and actions.

Doctrine of Repentance: The Shorter Catechism and the Westminster Confession of Faith

The Westminster Shorter Catechism provides a concise answer to the question, "What is repentance unto life?"

> Repentance unto life is a saving grace by which a sinner, being truly aware of his sinfulness, understands the mercy of God in Christ, grieves for and hates his sins, and turns from them to God, fully intending and striving for new obedience.[8]

The catechism defines repentance as a saving grace. It is a grace, a merciful gift from God in Christ, not a human effort, and it is saving because it leads to salvation. It then adds two additional elements: the true sense of sin with a feeling of deep sorrow, and the sequence of aversion to sin, turning away from sinful behavior, turning to God, and envisioning a transformed life through obedience.

Although the WSC provides a comprehensive and theologically rich definition of repentance, some may say that it can be strengthened by making what is implicit explicit. One can add the necessity of continuing and ongoing aspects of repentance and the inseparable relationship between repentance and faith.

The Westminster Confession chapter 15, "Repentance Leading to Life," describes repentance in six paragraphs. We will focus on the first three, for the final three deal with other issues not directly relevant here.

15.1 Repentance which leads to life is the blessed product of the gospel working in believer's lives. Along with the doctrine of faith in Christ, it is a doctrine to be preached by every minister of the gospel.

15.2 In this repentance, the sinner is able to see his sins as God sees them, as filthy and hateful, and as involving great danger to the sinner, because they are completely contrary to the holy nature and righteous law of God. Understanding that God in Christ is merciful to those who repent, the sinner suffers deep sorrow for

---

8. WSC 87 in Rollinson, *Westminster Confession*, 159.

and hates his sins, and so he determines to turn away from all of them. And turning to God, he tries to walk with him according to all his commands.

15.3 Although repentance is not any satisfaction for sin and does not cause the forgiveness of sin (since forgiveness is an act of God's voluntary grace in Christ), yet it is necessary to all sinners, and no one may expect to be forgiven without it.[9]

The Westminster Confession describes the nature of repentance by stating first that it is the product of the gospel, the fruit of the Holy Spirit's work in hearts and minds in the process of regeneration upon hearing the gospel message. But being born again or from above is always the work of God by which a person is inwardly changed and renewed. Therefore, regeneration must precede faith, which is closely related to repentance, thus emphasizing the inseparability of faith and repentance.

After delineating the nature of repentance, the Westminster Confession highlights the required elements of repentance: (1) contrition, demonstrating deep remorse and penitence of sin; (2) believing and accepting God's pardon to forgive in Christ; and (3) the determination to turn away from sin and to God, demonstrated by living an obedient life. Psalm 51 illustrates what is involved in David's heart in his full and genuine repentance of sin.

Though people's experiences and depth of emotion will differ, the Westminster Confession describes its true nature and what's involved. This is full and true and consistent with Calvin, Bavinck, and modern writers' classical doctrines of repentance.

The Doctrine of Repentance in Calvin and Bavinck[10]

John Calvin's View of Repentance

Calvin defines repentance as follows in his *Institutes*:

> A real conversion of our life unto God, proceeding from sincere and serious fear of God; and consisting in the mortification of our flesh and the old man, and the quickening of the Spirit.[11]

---

9. Rollinson, *Westminster Confession*, 31.
10. Calvin, *Institutes*, §§3.3.1–25; Beeke, "Appropriating Salvation," 270–300.
11. Calvin, *Institutes*, §3.3.5.

Calvin defines repentance as a "real conversion," the true turning of our lives to God that arises from a heartfelt fear and reverence of him. It consists of mortifying the flesh and sin and quickening the Spirit. So, repentance has four required components: turning from self to God from the heart, genuine fear of God, dying to self and sin, and vivifying new life in Christ through the Holy Spirit.

Turning to God: Repentance is withdrawing from ourselves and turning to God, laying aside the flesh and the old nature, and putting on a new mind. It is viewed not only as inward change but also as the redirection and transformation of a believer's entire being from sin to righteousness. Unlike the Roman Catholic Church, which emphasizes the outward aspects of repentance, Calvin underscores the inward aspects and pays less attention to its external dimensions.

Fear of God: Repentance proceeds from a sincere fear of God, arising from reverent awe of his holiness, power, and anger about sin and to give him complete reverence and honor him as God. Without a pure, earnest fear of God, a person will not be aware of the heinousness and foulness of sin.

Mortification: For Calvin, repentance is turning to God from heartfelt fear and reverence of him, and it consists of two parts: the mortification of the flesh and the quickening of the Spirit.[12] Though Christians are brought to faith and new life in Christ, they are never free from sin in this life. Therefore, they must engage in a lifelong battle against the sinful tendencies that remain in them. Romans 7:14–25 shows that mortification is a lifelong, arduous work and process in which slow and gradual progress is made, through Christ, to completion.

For Calvin, mortification is "grief of soul and terror, produced by a conviction of sin and a sense of the divine judgment." When a man is brought to a true knowledge of sin, he begins to hate sin, disappoint himself, and confess that he is lost and wishes he were different from what he is. This is the first part of repentance, often called "contrition."[13]

Vivification: Mortifying sinful desires and tendencies is only a required preparation for making a new life in Christ come alive through the quickening of the Spirit. Vivification involves three stages. What follows the mortification is, first, the sense of comfort produced by faith when believers look up, begin to breathe, take courage, and pass, as it

---

12. Calvin, *Institutes*, §3.3.8.
13. Calvin, *Institutes*, §3.3.3.

were, from death unto life. Then comes the joy that the soul feels after being calmed from anxiety and fear, which is followed finally by the desire for pious and holy living that springs from the new birth.[14]

Lastly, how do believers achieve mortification and vivification, the two major phases in repentance? Calvin teaches that we experience them by union with Christ, often described as our being in Christ. In turn, union with Christ is accomplished by us participating in Christ's death and resurrection by faith. Then Calvin recaps the exposition of repentance by saying, "In one word, then, by repentance, I understand regeneration, the only aim of which is to form in us anew the image of God, which was sullied and all but effaced by the transgression of Adam."[15]

For Calvin, repentance is "regeneration," a more inclusive and broader term that refers to not only conversion but also renewal, signifying the total transformation of a person. This will become more transparent when we briefly review Herman Bavinck's narrow view of repentance.

Herman Bavinck's View of Repentance

From John's baptism through Jesus' preaching and into the apostolic teaching, the consistent message was a call to repent, a radical turnabout for anyone to enter the kingdom of heaven. One must be born again, born from above. A birth from God, regeneration, is "always a work of God by which a person is changed inwardly and renewed." Bavinck defines the term *regeneration* in two ways.[16] In a broad and full sense, "regeneration refers to the total transformation of a person." In contrast, in the narrow and restricted sense, it refers to "the implantation of new life that then leads to conversion and further sanctification."[17] In this view, the conversion is the outcome of regeneration.

Bavinck recognizes that soteriology, a doctrine of salvation, is as difficult as the doctrines of the Trinity and Christ's two natures. One of the main reasons for the difficulties lies in the close relationships among the terms regeneration, repentance, conversion, and sanctification. Each of these terms represents a distinct theological stage or action in the believer's journey. Therefore, presenting a brief summary of understandings distilled from classical doctrinal studies by Calvin, Bavinck, and others would be beneficial.

14. Calvin, *Institutes*, §3.3.3.
15. Calvin, *Institutes*, §3.3.9.
16. Bavinck, *Holy Spirit*, 29–95, 96–175.
17 Bavinck, *Holy Spirit*, 32.

Regeneration: It is the act of God whereby he imparts new spiritual life to a person. It is often called being "born again" or "born from above." This process is solely the work of the Holy Spirit, who revives a person from spiritual death to life in Christ. This is why Sinclair calls the Holy Spirit the "Spiritus Recreator," also a chapter title of his excellent book on the Holy Spirit.[18] John 3:3–8 and Titus 3:5 are scriptural references for this.

Repentance: It involves a change of mind and heart, turning away from sin and toward God. It is a conscious decision to reject sin and embrace faith in Jesus Christ. Repentance is often seen as a necessary component of conversion, as it reflects a genuine acknowledgment of one's sin and a desire to be reconciled with God. The cause of repentance is not something that originates from human effort alone but is primarily attributable to the work of God. Acts 26:20 and Luke 13:3 are good scriptural references.

Conversion: It is the human response to the work of regeneration, involving both repentance and faith. It is the act of turning to God and trusting in Jesus Christ for salvation. While regeneration is God's work, conversion is the believer's response to that work. Conversion includes both a negative aspect (repentance and turning from sin) and a positive aspect (turning to God through faith in Christ). Acts 3:19 and 26:18 are two scriptural references for this.

Sanctification: It is the process by which believers are progressively made holy, becoming more like Christ in their character and conduct. Unlike regeneration, which is a one-time event, sanctification is an ongoing process involving divine action and human cooperation. It begins at conversion and continues throughout the believer's life. Sanctification involves the work of the Holy Spirit, in transforming the believer's life, and the believer's active pursuit of holiness. First Thessalonians 4:3 and 2 Tim 2:21 are two good scriptural references.

After understanding regeneration, repentance, conversion, and sanctification, we can now delve into Herman Bavinck's perspective on repentance. According to Bavinck, the new life implanted in regeneration yields, on the one hand, faith, knowledge, and wisdom with the intellect and, on the other hand, conversion and repentance with the will. Bavinck's view emphasizes that regeneration is a work of the Holy Spirit, transforming both a person's intellect and will.

Bavinck argues that regeneration affects the intellect by instilling faith, which is seen as a gift from God and the beginning of a new life in

---

18. See Ferguson, *Holy Spirit*, 115–38.

Christ. The knowledge gained is not just theoretical but experiential, as it involves a relationship with God. Wisdom, in this context, is the practical application of this knowledge in one's life, guided by faith.

Bavinck describes regeneration as producing conversion and repentance in relation to the will. As you may recall, the two Hebrew words in the OT are *nacham* and *shub*. Bavinck understood the second word, *shub*, as being "always used for what we in dogmatics call repentance or conversions."[19] For Bavinck, "repentance" and "conversion" refer to the same stage or action in the process of regeneration. While this is true, one can make a fine distinction between them: while conversion is a turning away from sin and a turning towards God, which is a fundamental change in the direction of one's life, repentance is the ongoing process of continuing to confess sin, leading to a continuous renewal of the will.

Comparing the views of repentance given by the two most prominent Reformed theologians, one can see that Bavinck took a narrow and restricted view, as discussed above. In contrast, Calvin's view of repentance is "regeneration," a more inclusive and broader term, referring to not only conversion but also renewal, signifying the total transformation of a person.

Spurgeon's Sermon: "The Repentance unto Life"

On September 23, 1855, Charles Spurgeon preached a sermon titled "The Repentance unto Life," mirroring the title of chapter 15 of the Westminster Confession of Faith.[20] Here is a brief summary of the sermon.

He first defines "the repentance unto life" as a repentance accompanied by spiritual life in the soul, ensuring eternal life for everyone who possesses it. After defining this, he moves on to the first focus of his sermon, which is false repentance. First, "trembling beneath the sound of the gospel is not 'repentance.'"[21] Hearers of the gospel can be exceedingly stirred and moved by it. Some may be very disturbed by the preaching of the gospel, but they do not necessarily experience "repentance unto life."

Spurgeon illustrates his point by using three biblical figures: King Agrippa in hearing from Paul's defense (Acts 26), King Ahab stealing Naboth's choice vineyard (1 Kgs 21), and Judas in the betrayal. Agrippa was almost persuaded to become a Christian, but he never proceeded beyond the "almost" stage and remained there without actually repenting. Next,

---

19. Bavinck, *Holy Spirit*, 135.
20. Spurgeon, "Repentance unto Life."
21. Spurgeon, "Repentance unto Life," 2.

after putting Naboth to death and taking possession of the vineyard from him, the Lord condemned Ahab. Upon hearing the Lord's condemnation, King Ahab tore his clothes, put sackcloth on his flesh, fasted, and went about dejectedly. So, God granted some mercy. But he rebelled, and in a battle, he died. His repentance was not repentance unto life. We know Judas's story well. He had sinned, confessed his wrong, and returned the gold; still, he was a castaway after all that. These are well-known examples of false repentance and should be a warning.

Spurgeon moves on to the second focus of the sermon, which is on the marks and signs of true repentance.[22] He first dispelled the idea that a deep, horrible, and awful display of emotions must accompany true repentance. People go through various repenting experiences; some easily open their hearts to God, while others struggle to get there. As long as it is sincere and genuine, the degree of emotion in repentance does not matter either. Some may erroneously think that repentance needs to be perfect. But we must remember that repentance is grace. It is not a condition of salvation because it is grace, and God only gives it to those to whom he will.

What, then, would be signs of true repentance? There must be genuine sorrow for sin. Additionally, there must be a visible result of repentance. Those who are truly penitent will bring forth works of repentance, visible evidence of practical repentance. Finally, it would show a lasting effect on living in righteousness and holiness.

He comes to a conclusion and third focus of the sermon on "the blessed beneficence of God," i.e., repentance being the gift of God. The marvel of divine mercy is that he not only invites men to receive grace as a way of salvation but also positively makes man willing to be saved. God punished his Son, Jesus, for our sins and thus provided salvation for all his lost children and sent his ministers as messengers. He prepared feasts and invited guests; some came but others refused. His stupendous mercy is that he actually makes them willing by sweet spiritual suasion. Spurgeon says, "The Holy Ghost then brings home the Word of God to the consciences of His children in so blessed manner that they can no longer refuse to love Jesus."[23]

The last part of his sermon focuses on achieving true repentance, which is the best part. Some people might say, "I have been trying to repent for a long time. I have been praying and trying to believe and doing all I can during pains and afflictions." Spurgeon explains that this

---

22. Spurgeon, "Repentance unto Life," 4–6.
23. Spurgeon, "Repentance unto Life," 7.

approach is not the path to true repentance. He shares the story of two travelers to illustrate his point. One man remarks to the other, "I don't know how you do it, but you always seem to remember your wife and family and everything they are doing at home. You connect all things around you with them, but I always try to bring them to my mind, and yet I can never do it." The other man replies, "That's the problem—because you are trying. If you could connect them with every little thing you encounter, you would easily remember them. I think of them at different times—when they are waking up, praying, and having breakfast. This way, I always have them in my thoughts." Spurgeon draws a parallel with repentance, suggesting that if a man says, "I want to believe," and tries to force himself into repentance through mechanical means, he will never achieve it. Instead, he explains that the path to repentance is through God's grace, by believing in Jesus and thinking of him, especially his sufferings and agonizing pains of death on the cross.[24]

Spurgeon emphatically confessed, "I have never known a man who has thought upon and taken a view of the cross, who has not found that it begat 'repentance' and begat faith." His conclusion follows:

> If you want faith, remember He gives it. If you want repentance, He gives it! If you want everlasting life, He gives it liberally. He can force you to feel your great sin and cause you to repent by the sight of Calvary's cross, and the sound of the greatest, deepest death shriek . . . "My God! my God! why have Thou forsaken me?" That will beget "repentance." It will make you weep and say, "Alas! and did my Savior bleed? And did my Sovereign die for me?" Then, beloved, if you would have "repentance," this is my best advice to you—look to Jesus.[25]

Do I humbly let God do his work through me? How many times did I look to Jesus today, this week? The quality of our Christian life depends on our answers to these questions.

---

24. Spurgeon, "Repentance unto Life," 7–8.
25. Spurgeon, "Repentance unto Life," 8.

CHAPTER 8

Death and Afterlife

DYING AND DEATH RAISE disquieting thoughts and disturbing emotions. That is why most people do not want to talk about them. Intellectually, we all know that they are unavoidable. In real life, however, we think and act as if death is something we do not need to deal with. We recognize that death is a profound mystery that has perplexed humanity throughout history. There is plenty that we do not know about death: the true nature of death, the finality of death, the conundrum between physical and metaphysical aspects, and the potential conflict between naturalistic versus supernaturalistic explanations of it with the consequent meaning and significance of life and death.

Death is also known to be humankind's most profound problem, and yet it remains the most neglected subject. Unlike in past cultures, the vast majority die in hospitals and care homes today, away from the eyes of others. It is common for many people not to watch anyone die or even see a corpse except in the brief glance of an open coffin at a funeral. So, the hiddenness of dying and death in modern society helps us not to confront but rather conveniently ignore the unavoidability of our own mortality. But Ps 90:12 says, "So teach us to number our days that we may get a heart of wisdom," which teaches us that our attempt to repress deep thoughts about death is not wise. Even a moment's serious reflection will convince us of its grave importance, regardless of our belief system, especially in the Christian life. As Sinclair Ferguson points out, "'death' does have a place in the Christian life, and in fact marks one of the great crises and transition points in its development."[1] In his well-known work, the *Reformed Dogmatics*, Herman Bavinck also teaches that as Christ's death and resurrection restore life, "death is no longer the end but a passage into eternal life," especially for those saved through Christ's work.[2]

One must also recognize that death is a complex and multifaceted subject. Thanatology is the study of death and the losses it brings about. Many seem to have a growing interest in it, which seems to attest to the enduring importance of the subject. The amazing advances in medical science and technology during the recent decades have raised difficult, practical, and ethical issues and questions as to the point of death. However, we know that though science and technology may help extend our lives to some extent, they do not offer any real solution. What about philosophy? Famous philosophers, starting from Socrates and René Descartes to the twentieth-century French philosopher Jean-Paul Sartre, who saw *death* as a reflection of our meaningless existence, struggled to understand the nature of death and how to cope with it. Friedrich Nietzsche argues that humans must face the truth that existence is meaningless. Philosophy, in his case, is bound to surrender to despair.

Our memory is still fresh with the devastated reality, marked by anxiety, grief, and the terrifying specter of death, of the recent COVID-19 pandemic. In an illuminating article in the *New York Times* on how to cope with the specter of death during the pandemic, Simon Critchley, a professor of philosophy, shared his philosophic argument to cope with death positively by reexamining Michel de Montaigne's essay on the subject.[3] His main argument is summed up in his article's title, "To Philosophize Is to Learn How to Die." We will bring up some of his and Montaigne's points later as an attempt to deal with the fear of death, when discussing the nature of death.

Major world religions, including Christianity, teach about death and the afterlife based on the kind of life lived on earth. Christianity offers a unique perspective on the cause of death: it is the consequence of sin, viewed as a rebellion against God and his commandments. Whatever issue this may raise for those who hold a scientific worldview, the Bible repeatedly teaches that death is the consequence of sin. This explains that death is not natural, and it is the just penalty. That is why it raises

---

1. Ferguson, *Christian Life*, 169.
2. Bavinck, *Sin and Salvation*, 607.
3. Critchley, "To Philosophize."

fear among those without hope of forgiveness of sin in Christ. Christianity also offers salvation as a way to heaven through the atoning work of Christ, while other religions emphasize your own merits in your life on earth in determining the destination of the afterlife.

While the precise nature of death has evoked considerable debate within Christianity, Genesis certainly implies that physical death is involved (Gen 2:17, 3:19), which is confirmed by Paul's teachings in the New Testament (Rom 5:12, 14, 17; 1 Cor 15:22). Within Paul's letters, death has been described as the one sure certainty; he also talks about the physical death of the believers as a means of entry into fuller participation of life with Christ (Phil 1:23, 2 Cor 5:6–8). More importantly, the Scripture does not portray death as the end of our existence; There is more to come. The Bible attests to the reality of some afterlife, whether in a disembodied or reembodied state. At some future point, our Lord Jesus will return in majesty and glory with the resurrection of the body and final judgment to take place, which will be finally followed by the arrival of a new Jerusalem, new heaven, and new earth.

Misunderstandings of Death

1. Death is natural because it is part of the life cycle.

This statement is true mainly from a biological viewpoint. All living things are born, grow, reproduce (usually), and then die. So, death is a necessary part of the cycle that allows for new generations and the adaptation of species. While death is a natural biological process, death is never "natural" in the sense of true nature or being "built into our humanity." Death is an intruder because of sin and thus unnatural. In the biblical sense, death is never natural but the last enemy (1 Cor 15:26; cf. 15:54) that will be conquered finally and forever at the return of Christ (Rev 21:4). Christianity sees it as a consequence of sin that disrupts the creation as intended, resulting in a separation from God. Many other religions and philosophies have their own views of death. Some may see it as a transition or a return to a source. Ultimately, how one views death depends on one's beliefs and perspectives.

2. Death is the end of human existence.

This view of death is based on scientific materialism, which suggests that consciousness arises from the physical processes in the brain. When these processes cease, consciousness ceases too, which is the definition of death. From this perspective, no evidence suggests continued existence after death. Not everyone agrees with this view of death based on scientific materialism. Some philosophies and major world religions posit an afterlife or soul that continues. As Herman Bavinck teaches us, Christianity has a unique and positive perspective on death. Since the restoration of life is accomplished through Christ's death and resurrection, death is no longer the end but a passage into eternal life, especially for those in Christ.[4]

3. When we think of death, we think of death in a physical and biological sense.

This is the most common way of understanding death. This means death is seen as the end of all the biological functions that keep us alive. This view is consistent with the conclusion of scientific materialism. While the physical and biological aspects are crucial, death can be viewed more broadly to encompass other dimensions. Being ostracized or forgotten by society can be seen as "social death." More importantly, we can speak of death as a separation from God, as in Christianity. We call this "spiritual death." The Bible also understands death in light of eternity. Those who die impenitently enter into "eternal death." These three dimensions of death (physical/biological, spiritual and eternal) are not separate from one another; they are closely related.

4. According to the scientific worldview, there is no afterlife.

This is the view of philosophical naturalism or materialism. According to this view, nature, matter, or material is all that exists. Carl Sagan, the late Cornell astronomer, promoted this view in his television series *Cosmos* by saying, "The cosmos is all that is, or ever was, or ever will be."[5] However, most great founders of modern science, like Galileo, Newton,

4. Bavinck, *Holy Spirit*, 607.
5. Malone, *Cosmos*.

Robert Boyle, Michael Faraday, James Clerk Maxwell, and Max Planck, believed in God. Naturalism is a philosophic belief that may or may not be associated with science. Naturalism is a worldview that penetrates the minds of the modern world to be ingrained and considered normal. Naturalism in modern secular minds has displaced the traditional Christian worldview with its confidence in God and sacramental and holistic view of the universe.

5. When Christians die, they go to heaven.

This widely held view is too general a statement to be meaningful. So, clarification of the terms used in the statement is required. First, who is Christian? Those who are church members or attend the church are not necessarily Christians. Those who merely accept Christian doctrines are not necessarily Christians either, in the true sense. Though defining Christians precisely is not an easy task, we can rely on Charles Hodge, who defines a Christian as "one who recognizes Jesus as the Christ, the Son of the living God, as God manifested in the flesh, loving us and dying for our redemption; and who is so affected by a sense of the love of this incarnate God as to be constrained to make the will of Christ the rule of his obedience, and the glory of Christ the great end for which he lives."[6]

Hodge's definition of Christians could be enhanced by replacing the idea of "recognition" with "heartfelt knowledge" because the latter reflects a commitment deeper than mere recognition. Christians are characterized as those who possess heartfelt knowledge of three key aspects: (1) who Jesus Christ is (the Christ and the incarnate Son of the living God), (2) what he did (loved, died, and resurrected for our redemption), and (3) how to live a Christian life motivated and guided by a sense of Christ's love in obedience to his rule for the glory of Christ (2 Cor 5:14). According to this perspective, it's what Jesus did, not just the example of his life, that defines Christians. The genuine Christianity depicted here encompasses a comprehensive and robust acceptance of the teachings of the entire Bible, understanding the OT as pointing toward the coming Christ and the NT as the story of Christ coming to fulfill our salvation.

With this authentic Christianity in mind, we must now turn to the question of what happens to Christians after we die. Succinctly, their souls go immediately to be with Christ (Luke 23:43; Phil 1:21, 23) while their

---

6. Hodge, *Exposition*, 133.

bodies return to the earth. The death, more specifically physical death, is a temporary dissolution of the bond between a person's soul and body. The body undergoes corruption, and the soul goes to heaven, where Christ has returned after his resurrection and waits for his people. A soul is the incorporeal (nonphysical) essence of a living being, often contrasted with the physical body, seen as the immaterial essence that animates it. The soul makes a living being truly alive, distinct from its physical form. The concept of the soul is most often applied to humans. For a fuller understanding of heaven, see the next chapter, "Heaven and Hell."

6. Death is a gain and blessing for Christians because they are relieved of the struggles, pains, and sufferings of this world.

We often hear a similar message from funeral sermons, motivated by a good intention of comforting grieving families. But we should not lose sight of what death itself is. It is the destroyer of the life that God gave to man in creation. In his short essay on death, the late Timothy Keller describes death honestly and forthrightly.[7] Though his descriptions of what death does and what it is are blunt and grim, they speak the truth: death tears loved ones away from us or us from them; death rips apart the material and immaterial parts of our being and sunders a whole person, who was never meant to be disembodied, even for a moment; death reminds us that our bodies will be corrupted; death is hideous, frightening, cruel, and unusual because it is not the way life was supposed to be in the creation account, and our grief in the face of death acknowledges that; finally, death is our last enemy because it pursues us relentlessly throughout our days.

What are we supposed to do in the face of the death of loved ones? Jesus sets a good example for us to follow in the face of Lazarus's death, as described in chapter 11 of John's Gospel. He went to Bethany to bring him back to life, teach us about resurrection, and comfort the family. When he went to the tomb where Lazarus was laid, he wept. We need to be with grieving families to comfort them in their time of loss, but with the sustaining hope of resurrection, as 1 Thess 4:13 teaches us: "But we do not want you to be uninformed, brothers, about those who are asleep, that you may not grieve as others do who have no hope."

---

7. Keller, *On Death*, 1–3.

The Nature of Death

Death is inevitable to us all, and so we will die at some point. But we tend to think and act, regardless of age, as if we can live indefinitely, and rarely think about it seriously. A moment's serious reflection, however, will convince us that we need to be prepared for the eventual demise of some of our family members and ourselves. To do so requires a good understanding of the true nature of death, what is involved in it, and how to prepare for it. To find answers to some of these questions is not only the best way to prepare for it but also the best way to live on this earth. Gregory R. Jenks summarizes what is involved in preparing for death. He points out that the study of mortality, or thanatology, is oddly a study of life. Many report that facing impending death squarely energizes the present life. The urgency of the short span of remaining life helps us focus on living with the sense of mission, in step with God who sustains life now for the time being, even though the number of days remaining is limited.[8]

Word Study of Death

The Hebrew term for "death" in the OT is *mawet*, which primarily refers to physical death and rarely to situations that feel deadly or lead to death.[9] It is a noun often translated verbally, such as in the phrase "[he] did not deserve to die" (Deut 19:6) and "in the year that King Uzziah died"(Isa 6:1). Death is also personified in several occasions and has been associated with negative feelings, such as bitterness and fear. The place of death is referred to as Sheol. Finally, the Lord takes no pleasure in the death of anyone (Ezek 18:32) and promises to swallow up death forever (Isa 25:8). The Lord can ransom from Sheol and redeem from death (Hos 13:14) and accomplishes this through the suffering servant who willingly submits himself to death on behalf of sinners (Isa 53:12). So, *mawet* can convey a variety of meanings, and this creates difficulties in interpreting some passages.

In the NT, *thanatos* refers to death as the termination of physical life. For Paul, death is a personified power that has entered the world through Adam's sin (Rom 5:12). Since then, death has ruled and reigned on the earth (Rom 5:14, 17) by enslaving mankind (6:16), which leads

---

8. Jenks, *Paul*.

9. The following discussion draws from Longman and Strauss, "Death, Put to Death," *BED* 211–13.

to shame (6:21), alienation from God (Eph 2:12–13), and ultimately to death (Rom 6:23). Death is thus seen in the NT as the necessary and just consequence and punishment for sin. The only way to resolve the problem of sin and the resulting death is to reconcile with God through the death of Jesus (Rom 5:10, Col 1:22). Believers must participate and share in Christ's death so that they also partake in his resurrection (Rom 6:4–6). Christ was raised from death, and it no longer has dominion over him. For Christians, death has also been conquered as they participate in Christ's death and resurrection (Rom 6:9, 2 Tim 1:10). However, since Christians still experience physical death, their victory over death is still a future reality (1 Cor 15:26), which will materialize when Jesus returns (Rev 20:14, 21:4).

In the Gospel, *thanatos* always refers to physical death. Still, in the book of Revelation, it is used to signify the eschatological judgment of unbelievers after their physical death—the second death (2:11). In John's Gospel, those who hear Jesus' words and believe in God receive eternal life and will not face judgment but pass from death to life (John 5:24).

In conclusion, the terms "die" or "death" in the Scripture are used in three different senses. *Physical death* is both a process and an event, denoting the gradual debilitation of physical powers, exposure to danger that could prove fatal, or the actual termination of bodily functions. *Spiritual death* refers to man's natural alienation from God and hostility to God that expresses itself in sin (Matt 8:22, John 5:24–25, Rom 6:23, Jas 5:20, Jude 12). Both physical and spiritual death are portrayed as the consequence and penalty of sin and the common lot of mankind (Rom 5:12; 6:23; 7:13; Eph 2:1, 5; Heb 9:27). The *second death* describes the permanent separation from God that befalls those whose names are not found written in the book of life (Rev 2:11; 20:6, 14–15; 21:8).

What Is Death?

As mentioned earlier, death is a complex and multifaceted subject with practical implications, especially in science, philosophy, and religion. Each of these fields theorizes and defines death from their unique perspective. The scientific view of death is limited to physical death, which occurs when the heart stops beating. We call this death by cardiopulmonary criteria, and it is how death is defined for more than 95 percent of people. A person stops breathing, and their brain shuts down, causing all life processes to cease.

The philosophic perspectives on the nature of death vary greatly across different thinkers and schools. Socrates viewed death as liberating the immortal soul from the physical body and that it should be welcomed, as it allows the soul to engage in purely intellectual pursuits in the afterlife without everyday physical concerns of life. The ancient Greek philosopher Epicurus viewed death as the complete cessation of existence and consciousness. According to this view, what follows death is nonexistence; we should not fear it. The stoics, like Zeno, believed that the universe is governed by reason and natural law, and they advocated accepting one's mortality with equanimity, as death is both natural and inevitable. A good death involves facing it calmly and rationally without fear or excessive grief. The German philosopher Arthur Schopenhauer had a pessimistic view of life as constant suffering and wanting, and he thus saw death as a release from the torment of unfulfilled desires and the "will to live" that drives human suffering. Nietzsche, instead, upholds embracing and affirming life despite its difficulties and advocates dying at the right time.

Earlier, when we discussed the terrifying specter of death during the recent COVID-19 pandemic, I brought up Simon Critchley's *New York Times* essay, "To Philosophize Is to Learn How to Die," to find out what we can learn from a philosophical perspective on death, especially from Michel de Montaigne's essays. Montaigne begins his essay on death by quoting Cicero, saying, "To philosophize is nothing more than to prepare for death."[10] Montaigne says he has developed the habit of thinking about death all the time, not to be frightened by it but to overcome the fear of death. So he writes, "Let us learn to stand our ground and fight it. . . . We cannot know for certain where death awaits us, so let us expect it everywhere."[11] Then, he capped his main points with three key sentences: "Preparing for death is preparing for freedom. Those who have learned to die have unlearned to live in servitude. . . . Knowing how to die frees us from subjection and servitude."[12] So, the main idea put forth here is to accept and affirm anxiety and fear of death positively. Acknowledging and accepting death as natural and inevitable, one can develop a philosophic mind, which may serve as a vehicle of freedom and liberation.

10. Montaigne, "To Philosophize," par. 1.
11. Montaigne, "To Philosophize," par. 12, 13.
12. Montaigne, "To Philosophize," par. 13.

The philosophic approach to death outlined above shares similarities with the beliefs of stoics like Zeno. Critchley, Montaigne, and the Stoics believed that the universe, including the earth, human life, and death, is governed by reason and natural laws. They advocated for developing qualities such as wisdom/knowledge, courage, temperance, and justice to lead a life of moral excellence and fulfillment. According to this philosophy, the best approach to dealing with death is to learn to accept one's mortality with equanimity because death is both natural and inevitable.

However, acknowledging and accepting death as natural and inevitable is one thing, and connecting the knowledge of death as a vehicle for freedom and liberty from the fear of death is another. Montaigne encouraged his readers to constantly contemplate death, stating, "Having nothing more often in mind than death. We must imagine it in everything, at all times."[13] If we are to follow his advice, the challenge is to figure out how we can find a delicate balance between constant reflection on the concept of death to free us from the fear of death, and constantly being preoccupied with death without resulting in mental health problems. A prolonged and intense focus on death can easily lead to thanatophobia, an anxiety disorder characterized by a fear of death. This goes against the intended purpose of philosophical contemplation of death.

Christianity offers a unique perspective on death and the afterlife compared to all other major religions. Its uniqueness lies in, among other aspects, its ways of dealing with death. First, when Christians consider death, they don't see it as a separate or final event in life. The biblical perspective of death requires us to consider it part of the interconnected life-death-afterlife cycle nexus. To begin with, Christians believe that life is a gift from God, as stated in Genesis, where it is declared that God created human beings in his image and blessed them to prosper (Gen 1:27–28). The Bible explains that the Lord God formed man from the dust of the ground and gave him the breath of life, making him a living being (Gen 2:7). When Adam and Eve rebelled against God and his commandments, they lost their relationship with God, the source and giver of life, experiencing spiritual death. This ultimately led to physical death, which is the just penalty of sin. So, the cause of death is sin, and the only way to regain life is through forgiveness of sin, which can be accomplished through Christ's atoning works.

---

13. Montaigne, "To Philosophize," par. 12.

Let's focus now on the second link between death and the afterlife. In the secular modern world, people do not believe in God and the afterlife. To them, death is the absolute end of everything, which leads to a tragic sense of insignificance and nothingness. Unlike other religions, like Hinduism and Buddhism, which believe in reincarnation, Christianity teaches the reality of resurrection and eternal life in either heaven or hell after death. The central belief in Christianity is the resurrection of Jesus Christ, celebrated every Easter. Christians believe that just as Christ was resurrected, they will be resurrected to eternal life after death. This belief in bodily resurrection sets Christianity apart from other religions. Additionally, the concepts of heaven and hell as eternal destinations for the soul are unique to Christianity among major religions.

Secondly, Christians do not fear death because they believe they will be supported by the Lord Jesus Christ in life and death. Jesus Christ, who was born with a physical body, died, and was resurrected, understands the nature of death and has promised to always be with his people in life and death. Building a close and intimate relationship with Jesus throughout life on earth can provide comfort and stability even during death, especially when believers understand that death is a necessary passage into eternal life.

With this general background of Christianity's unique approach, let us examine the true nature of death more thoroughly by relying on published materials on this subject.[14] In a recent book on dying and death, Guy Prentiss Waters defines death in five closely related statements based on creation accounts in Gen 1–3.[15] The five key points are as follows:

1. Death is not part of the original creation.
2. God created man, a living being, body and soul.
3. Death is the penalty of sin.
4. Death is universal in its scope.
5. Death is cosmic in its reaches.

These five statements together form the basis for the biblical concept of death. Death was not part of the original good creation; God created the human being with the two constituent parts, body and soul; death is

---

14. See Beeke and Bogosh, *Dying and Death*; Nichols, *Death and Afterlife*; Waters, *Facing the Last Enemy*.
15. Waters, *Facing the Last Enemy*, 7–11.

the consequence of sin, explaining how death originates and why it exists; and death is universal in its scope and cosmic in its reaches.

Among the five key points, the third statement is the most important, and potentially controversial, for our purpose. Therefore, it requires some explanation. The Lord God commanded Adam and Eve not to eat of the tree of knowledge with a clear warning that "in the day that you eat of it, you shall surely die" (Gen 2:16–17). This is the first time the term "die" appears in the Bible. What kind of "death" does this threaten: physical, spiritual, or some combination? The Hebrew word can be used for any of these ideas, and the only way to find out is by reading to see what happens as the story unfolds. A short answer is both. Adam died when he had lived nine hundred and thirty years, but the sense of guilt from sin made him become a slave to evil. While they do not cease to exist physically, they are in the realm of the dead, experiencing spiritual death.

However, one must realize that the third statement represents an answer to a more fundamental question of whether death in the OT is viewed as a natural consequence of man's mortality or as a punitive consequence, a result of man's disobedience. As described earlier, all living things are born, grow, reproduce, and die. Death is necessary for new generations and the continuation of species. Since Abraham died at "a good old age, an old man and full of years" (Gen 25:8), his death may be viewed as a natural consequence of man's mortality; a similar "good death" is also reported in the words of Eliphaz about the fate of the righteous (Job 5:26). On this issue of death as natural or punitive, modern scholarship seems to be almost equally divided.[16]

So we learn that the OT emphasizes two perspectives on the cause of death: natural and punitive. These perspectives can be viewed through biblical anthropology, which considers humans as biological and spiritual beings. From a biological perspective, death occurs naturally due to the mortality of all living beings. However, from a spiritual perspective, sin causes separation from God, the source of life, ultimately leading to death.

A strong case can be made, however, for the view that death is caused by sin, particularly in light of references in Gen 2:17 ("But of the tree of the knowledge of good and evil you shall not eat, for in the day that you eat of it you shall surely die") and 3:4 ("But the serpent said to the woman, 'You will not surely die.'") These texts clearly show

---

16. Westermann, *Genesis 1–11*, 266–67.

that Adam's sin was both an act of conscious rebellion against God and failure to carry out his divinely ordained responsibility to keep both the garden and Eve. Additionally, the laws on what is clean and unclean in Leviticus and Numbers provide further evidence supporting the idea that death is unnatural. These laws include specific regulations on exposure to a corpse or a grave, which are presented in negative terms, indicating that death is viewed as defiled and polluted.

Death is not, therefore, what we sometimes mistakenly understand—a blessing, a release from all worldly struggles, and a peaceful end. No, the true nature of death is disintegration, the breaking up of the relationship God created. As Ferguson aptly says, "In and of itself, it is an ugly, destructive thing—it is 'the last enemy,'" to be finally overcome and destroyed. "Death severs us from those we love. It breaks the cords that have joined us physically, mentally, spiritually to others." Death is a loss because it "deprives us of the most precious possessions we have on earth. The death of others separates us from them and places them in realms with which we cannot communicate."[17] Turning our attention to our own death, it forces us to leave everything, including our family, to whom we devoted our whole lives. In death, we are taken from our spouses, children, grandchildren, and dear friends.

Death not only takes us from those whom we dearly love. It also separates our inner self from our body. I am body and soul together as one cohesive unit. That is who I am, who I have been living, and how I am known to others. But death separates body from soul and spirit. This separation is contrary to the original design and creation of life. That is why death is unnatural. "Sin came into the world through one man, and death through sin, and so death spread to all men because all sinned" (Rom 5:12). "For the wages of sin is death" (Rom 6:23).

Death is regarded as part of the curse of sin. Death is not a blessing, a release, a peaceful end. The true nature of death is the breaking of a union which God created. In and of itself, it is an ugly, destructive thing—it is "the last enemy." Ferguson warns us by emphasizing that we should not lose sight of what death itself is. He caps it by saying, "It is the destroyer of life, which God gave to man in his infinite love for him. It is, therefore, not only our last enemy but God's enemy also."[18]

---

17. Ferguson, *Christian Life*, 171.
18. Ferguson, *Christian Life*, 172.

Christian Perspectives on Death

In modern secular culture, many individuals do not believe in God, the soul, or the afterlife. Consequently, death is perceived as the end of everything they hold dear, leading to feelings of insignificance and hopelessness. How do they cope with the sense of nothingness? One common approach is to make the most of what this world offers within the confines of earthly existence. This often leads to pursuing happiness, comfort, and material achievements as life's primary goals. However, we know deep down that death ultimately will erase the results of all these pursuits, bringing us back to a sense of insignificance and nothingness, regardless of our efforts.

Christianity offers unique perspectives on the true nature of death and the afterlife as its solution. Christian perspective on death differs from other religions and philosophical approaches in several important ways. First, the Bible reveals death's true nature and cause in its opening chapters. Instead of ignoring or avoiding thinking about it, the Bible exposes its true nature as the consequence of sin. Laying bare the role of sin as the cause of death is not intended to make us feel depressed or shameful, neither to blame nor to taunt us, but to point out the seriousness of our sinfulness in understanding the anxiety and fear of death. The true nature of death is as the destroyer of life, which is a loss, something to grieve and lament. So, it is right to weep in the face of the death of loved ones. Jesus at the tomb of Lazarus, his friend, in John 11 provides a good example to follow. He came and grieved. When Mary, Lazarus's sister, showed him his dead friend, we are told, in the shortest verse in the Bible, "Jesus wept" (John 11:35). So grieving is the right thing in the face of the death of loved ones. But Paul exhorts us so that we "may not grieve as others who have no hope" (1 Thess 4:13). We must grieve with hope because God will bring with Christ those who have died (1 Thess 4:14). So, we genuinely hope to see and meet those who have fallen asleep.

The Bible also teaches us that death is not only the consequence but also a just penalty for sin, an active rebellion against God and his commandment. The Bible exposes this grim reality of death as a just penalty to show us the way out of it. God is just, and due penalty has to be paid, which shows us the seriousness of sin and points to the urgent need for a savior, whom the gospel offers to all sinners. Christ came into the world to live, die, and rise again for sinners. Christians embrace the truths of who Christ is and what he did for our salvation. Since the OT is about the coming Christ, and the NT is the story of Christ who has come to accomplish our salvation, Christians embrace the teachings of the whole Bible.

Secondly, while virtually all major religions believe in an afterlife, there is a major difference between all other religions and Christianity in how to attain it. Other major religions teach that living a virtuous and ethical life is how to attain a favorable afterlife. For instance, Buddhism teaches that one's actions in this life determine the quality of one's rebirth in the cycle of reincarnation. Good deeds and right conduct lead to a better rebirth or potential nirvana (release from the cycle of rebirth). Hinduism also emphasizes the law of karma, where virtuous thoughts and actions lead to accumulating positive karma and a better reincarnation. In Islam, righteous deeds and submission to Allah are believed to lead to entry into paradise in the afterlife. So specific beliefs vary, but the world's major religions link ethical behavior in this life to a positive afterlife experience or rebirth. Your good deeds in this life will determine the course of your afterlife. However, since no one can live a perfect life, expressing some regrets is common, and people cannot be certain about their afterlife when they pass away.

In contrast, Christians rely not on the merits of their work but on what has been already accomplished by their Lord and Savior through his atoning death and resurrection. They also believe that Christ has destroyed "the one who has the power of death . . . and [delivered] all those who through fear of death were subject to lifelong slavery" (Heb 2:14-15). Therefore, death is no longer a powerful force but a defeated foe. In light of the victory over death through the works of redemption by Christ, Saint Paul challenges and taunts death by rephrasing an Isaian text (Isa 25:8) and adding to it when declaring, "Death is swallowed up in victory. O death, where is your victory? O death, where is your sting?" (1 Cor 15:54-55). The triumph of God is not limited to overcoming the fear of death. Rather, it is the coherent theme of Paul's gospel, focusing on the hope in the dawning victory of God and the imminent redemption of the created order.

What is the basis for Christians to believe that the Lord Jesus Christ accomplished the victory over death and that believers receive the benefits from his atoning works? It requires a serious examination of relevant biblical texts. Among others, the three most pertinent and important biblical bases for the implication of Christ's atoning works are Col 2:6-15, Heb 2:14-15, and Gen 3:15. The main outline of how this is accomplished, based on these and other related biblical texts, can be summarized as follows:

1. We were all (spiritually) dead in our sin, and death reigns (Rom 2:9, Col 2:13).

2. For sinners, there was "the record of debt that stood against us with its legal demands" (Col 2:14a).

3. Christ came as a man by sharing in flesh and blood, dying as our representative, and being resurrected as the first fruit (Heb 2:14b).

4. In his atoning death and subsequent resurrection, Christ overcame and destroyed Satan, who has the power of death, and delivered those who, through fear of death, were subject to lifelong slavery (Heb 2:15; Col 2:12). His atoning work thus cancels the record of debt by the legal demands.

5. How does Jesus disarm the powers of Satan? The accusation is Satan's chief weapon (Rev 12:10), and the power of sin is the law (1 Cor 15:56). Satan attempted to use the demands of the law to destroy God's people. In taking the law's curse on himself (Gal 3:13), Christ has wrested this weapon from Satan.[19]

6. By participating in Christ's death and resurrection, Christians gain freedom and liberty from the problems of death, ranging from disquieting thoughts, disturbing emotions, and the fear of death.

7. How do Christians participate in Christ's death and resurrection? To answer this question properly, we need to understand the nature of union with Christ. The union with Christ is obviously an extensive subject. Ferguson succinctly summarizes the nature of union with Christ as a federal union, a carnal or flesh union, a faith union, a spiritual union, and an extensive union.[20] The first two (federal and carnal unions) tell us that we are united to Christ by God's covenant and also by divine incarnation. By faith Christians receive Christ and thus get Christ into their lives (faith union). Through the agency of the Holy Spirit, they are joined with Christ (a spiritual union). Finally, the union is extensive because

---

19. See also Wedgeworth, "Jesus Disarmed the Devil."
20. Ferguson, *Christian Life*, 100–102.

it encompasses the total human experience, including dying and death (extensive union).

Third, when we die, we often say that we leave everything behind, and that is one of the causes of the sense of nothingness with death. But this is factually accurate only from a material perspective. Upon death, we do leave behind our physical possessions, relationships, careers, and others in this life. For Christians, however, the most precious possession in this life is the love of God and the love of Christ Jesus our Lord (John 3:16, Rom 8:35–39). Christians firmly believe that the God in Christ accompanies and sustains them through the vicissitudes of this life and the ordeal of death. God's love will accompany us, Paul says, in all life's challenges, including death: "Who shall separate us from the love of Christ? Shall tribulation, or distress, or persecution, or famine, or nakedness, or danger, or sword? ... No, in all these things, we are more than conquerors through him who loved us. For I am sure that neither death nor life, nor angels nor rulers, nor things present nor things to come, nor powers, nor height nor depth, nor anything else in all creation, will be able to separate us from the love of God in Christ Jesus our Lord" (Rom 8:35–39).

Christians grieve for their loved ones when they pass away, but they do so with the hope of meeting them again. This hope is based on the belief that God will bring back those who have died when Christ returns (1 Thess 4:14). The hope of reuniting with those who have passed away is central, but the Bible's teachings about the afterlife go even further. What are the specific aspects of this hope in Christ when faced with death?

Timothy Keller outlines three important ones: the hope in Christ is personal, material, and beatific.[21] The Christian hope is for a personal future of love relationships, as emphasized in Jonathan Edward's famous sermon "Heaven Is a World of Love." The Christian hope is also a material hope, built and based on the promise of the bodily resurrection with our Lord's second coming, to culminate in the new heaven and earth (Rev 21:1–4). Along with personal hope and material hope, the third feature of our hope is beatific, meaning that we will see God when we will be with the Lord (1 Thess 4:17, 1 John 3:2).[22] First John 3:2 says, "When he appears we shall be like him, because we shall see him as he is." This hope is to be realized in the future. Concerning seeing God's

---

21. This discussion relies heavily on Keller, *On Death*, 43–72.

22. For the beatific hope, see Ferguson, "What Is the Beatific Vision"; Sproul, "Beatific Vision."

glory (John 1:14), while we are in this life on earth, "it is a 'faith-sight' that we can have now. We cannot see God's glory yet with our physical eyes, but through faith, the Word and the Spirit can give us a powerful sense of his presence and reality in our lives and hearts."[23]

Conclusions

We have examined several important aspects of death and the afterlife by focusing on the true nature of death and various approaches to death, especially in science, philosophy, and other major religions. From this examination, we learned several important things about death. First, death is a profound mystery that has puzzled humanity throughout history. We also recognize that death is a complex and multifaceted subject with practical implications, particularly in science, philosophy, ethics, and religion. The scientific view of death is limited to physical death, which occurs when the heart stops beating. Philosophical perspectives on the nature of death vary greatly among different thinkers and schools. What the modern philosophical mind can offer in the face of death is a twofold approach: first, acquiring wisdom through recognizing and accepting that death is natural and inevitable, and second, striving to free ourselves from the fear of death by confronting it, neutralizing it, and attaining the freedom to enjoy life truly. This wisdom is already included in ancient Israel's wisdom literature, as recorded in Ps 90:12, which says, "So teach us to number our days that we may get a heart of wisdom." This teaches us that our attempt to repress thinking deeply about death is not wise, but the wise thing to do is to learn to make the most of one's days in this life since our days are few. All major world religions other than Christianity teach that living a virtuous and ethical life is how to attain a favorable afterlife.

Christianity offers a unique approach to death in several important respects. First, the Bible reveals death's true nature and cause in its opening chapters. The Bible exposes its true nature as the consequence of sin. Laying bare the role of sin as the cause of death is neither to blame nor to taunt us but to point out the seriousness of our sinfulness and the need for the Savior. He will save us from sin, the root cause of death, which removes the specter of anxiety and fear of death.

23. Keller, *On Death*, 59.

Unlike in other religions, the Bible teaches that we cannot earn salvation through our own works. Instead, the Bible teaches us to believe that we are saved by accepting, through faith, what has already been accomplished through Christ's atoning works. Christians believe that we were spiritually dead in our sins and that Christ, through his atoning work of death and resurrection, took on our sins and destroyed the power of Satan, freeing us from the fear of death. By being united with Christ through faith and the Holy Spirit, we are sustained at the time of death by the love of God and have hope for the afterlife. This faith gives us a powerful sense of the presence and reality of Jesus Christ both while living on this earth and when we depart from it, with hope and expectation of heaven.

The Christian faith provides us with two important sources of help for facing death. The first is the love of God and Christ, which supports us through the ups and downs of life and in facing death. Jesus himself died and overcame it, and he still lives. He promised to be always with his followers, even in death. The apostle Paul declared that nothing in this world or the afterlife can separate us from the love of God in Christ Jesus our Lord (Rom 8:35–39). The second is the hope and assurance of an afterlife awaiting us. Through faith, the word, and the Spirit, Christians already experience a strong sense of the presence and reality of Jesus Christ in their lives, helping them to complete their journey on earth. This is truly a blessed life with hope for the return of our Lord.

Charles Spurgeon delivered seventeen sermons on death before he died at age fifty-seven on January 3, 1892, in Menton, France. He left many powerful and illuminating thoughts on the subject. Five of them are listed below for our consideration.

1. "To be prepared to die is to be prepared to live."
2. "It is the very joy of this earthly life to think that it will come to an end."
3. "The best moment of a Christian's life is his last one, because it is the one that is nearest heaven."
4. "It is not a loss to die, it is a gain, a lasting, a perpetual . . . gain."
5. "He who learns to die daily while he lives, will find it no difficulty to breathe out his soul for the last time."[24]

24. The quotes, in order, are from Spurgeon, "Our Last Journey," 6; "Epistle," 9; "Dumb Become Singers," 9; "Precious Deaths," 4; and "Saintly Death-Beds," 2.

CHAPTER 9

Heaven and Hell

DEATH IS AN INEVITABLE part of life, and people have been curious about what happens after we die for ages. In the book of Job, Job asked whether a man could live again after dying, which raises the question of the afterlife. Many religions believe in heaven and hell, including Christianity, Islam, and Judaism. In these religions, heaven is viewed as the afterlife where good deeds are rewarded, and hell is where evil deeds are punished for eternity. Some philosophers grapple with the concept of an afterlife based on ideas of justice, the human soul, or the nature of good and evil. These arguments can be complex and remain controversial.

Those who deny or question the reality of heaven and hell abound. Some in this group argue that heaven and hell are merely figurative concepts that symbolize our future fate. Others say these concepts are products of human imagination, cultural conditioning, or wishful thinking rather than objective realities. Finally, those who follow a secular scientific worldview deny the existence of heaven and hell, citing empirical grounds as their evidence. In response to this skeptical view, J. I. Packer offers a piece of cogent advice: "While we are in our present bodies, the realities of heaven are invisible and ordinarily imperceptible to us, and we only know them by faith (2 Cor 4:18, 5:7)."[1] As long as one believes that reality is not limited to the physical realm, grasping the reality of heaven and hell by faith is possible and encouraged and should not be quickly rejected.

1. Packer, *Concise Theology*, 265.

The concept of hell as a dreadful place is a difficult one to come to terms with, not only for those with modern sensitivities but also for those who struggle to reconcile it with the gospel of Christianity. Some well-known scholars, like Bertrand Russel (British intellectual) and John Hick (British philosopher of religion), have expressed strong opinions against the concept of hell. Even when R. C. Sproul, the highly respected theologian, was asked which doctrine he struggles with most, he replied, "Hell."[2] At a more popular level, John Lennon's well-known piano ballad "Imagine" presents a world without heaven or hell. The language in his song is simple and direct, making it easy to understand. This explains why his song has a more powerful influence in denying the existence of heaven and hell than many logical arguments against it.

Scripture clearly distinguishes between the destiny of the righteous and the unrighteous after death. Heaven is referred to as God's abode in the Bible (Ps 33:13–14, Matt 6:9) where his throne is (Ps 2:4), and a place where the glorified Christ has returned. Heaven is also a place for rest where Christ's people will be with their Savior. Death separates the body and soul, and the souls of believers in heaven are received to be with Christ, and they grow in their knowledge and love of God. At a future point, at the time of Christ's return, it will take the form of a newly constructed cosmos. While the Bible contains hundreds of references to "heaven," "heavens," and "hell," not much information is available about the locations and exact conditions of these places.

In the early period of its history, Christian theology limited itself to what was simply a given in the Scripture. The apostolic fathers believed that at death, the righteous immediately experience the blessedness of heaven; and the unrighteous, the punishment of hell. Since then, however, detailed theories of the afterlife have developed, including the immediate bliss for believers and punishment for unbelievers and the notion of purification by fire and purgatory. The Reformation repudiated the idea of purgatory and again elaborated entry into the intermediate state into immediate bliss or judgment. Other ideas such as soul sleep, annihilation, reincarnation, and a variety of universalisms also sprang up. Unfortunately, these afterlife theories continue to influence people's view of what lies after death. However, the Bible does not tell us much about the intermediate state; perhaps that is good, lest we misconstrue what it will be like.

---

2. Schmucker, "Uncomfortable Subject."

The Scripture describes heaven and hell as places and destinations. So, our natural tendency is to focus on their location and condition. Heaven is "up there" somewhere in its beauty and glory, while we avoid even thinking of hell in misery and torment. But Packer wisely points out, "To think of heaven as a place is more right than wrong, though the word could mislead."[3] It is important to realize that when we think of heaven and hell, we should focus first on God and his attributes, and on Jesus Christ and what he has done for us. When we think of heaven, we should focus on the goodness and love of God and Christ's death and resurrection. When we think of hell, we should focus on the severity of God's judgment against sin and on the seriousness of our own sinfulness. To fully comprehend heaven and hell, we first need to deeply understand God's attributes, particularly his holiness, righteousness, love, goodness, and severity in judgment.[4] Jonathan Edwards understood this principle well. You will know the truth about this argument if you read two of Edwards's best-known sermons on heaven and hell.[5]

What do people, in general, believe about heaven and hell? A recent Pew Research Center survey reports that nearly three-quarters of US adults (73 percent) say they believe in heaven, while six in ten (62 percent) believe in hell.[6] It is not surprising that these figures are higher for Christians. However, there is a paradox here. Despite the high percentage of people who claim to believe in heaven and hell, few seem to have a genuine interest in the topic, and their interest in heaven and hell remains a curiosity and does not seem to impact their lives.

How can we explain this apparent contradiction? People tend to neglect the concept of heaven and hell mainly because they are too busy with their daily routines to think about the afterlife, especially in the secular modern world. Additionally, people in the Western world tend to be comfortable, healthy, and financially secure, which makes them less concerned about the afterlife. Furthermore, people tend not to relate the concept of death to their own existence, but it seems to be someone else's problem. Even Christians tend to avoid discussing the idea of heaven and hell despite believing in it. It is not regularly taught and rarely preached from the pulpit, with little emphasis on its implications for Christian life. Such a lack of interest in the subject is well illustrated by the fact that a well-known

3. Packer, *Concise Theology*, 264.
4. Packer, *Knowing God*.
5. Edwards, *Heaven*; Edwards, "Sinners."
6. Pew Research Center, "Views on the Afterlife."

systematic theology book by Louis Berkhof, a highly respected Reformed theologian, devotes only one page out of 784 to heaven.

The OT doesn't have a lot to say about heaven and hell, but what it does say is significant. When talking about death, phrases like "gathered to one's people" (Gen 25:8) or "resting with one's ancestors" (Gen 49:33) suggest a place for the dead. This place is often called Sheol and is considered everyone's common destiny. However, Sheol is mainly associated with the ungodly and those under divine judgment. By the first century, two schools of thought had emerged on the resurrection of the dead. The Sadducees rejected the idea, while the Pharisees and most Jewish people believed it.

Turning our attention to the NT, we note that Jesus taught the reality of heaven and hell with the goal that his followers might rescue others from hell's road, pointing them to the way that leads to heaven, as in Matt 7:13-14: "Enter by the narrow gate. For the gate is wide and the way is easy that leads to destruction, and those who enter by it are many. For the gate is narrow and the way is hard that leads to life, and those who find it are few." In a story about the rich man and Lazarus in Luke 16, Jesus uses the term hades (the Greek equivalent of Sheol) instead of using gehenna or "the lake of fire" (Rev 20:14).

Reviewing Paul's letters, we find that in speaking of his decision between remaining alive or dying (Phil 1:20-24, 2 Cor 5:6-9), Paul sharply distinguishes between being "in the body" and "away from the body." The latter expression seems to envisage noncorporeal ("naked," 2 Cor 5:3-4) existence, pointing to an intermediate state rather than an eschatological "heavenly dwelling." He also uses another metaphor of sleeping, not as a euphemism for death but as an expression of the believer's ontological existence after life. There are also several expressions of the ongoing existence or heavenly location of the souls waiting for resurrection in both Hebrews and Revelation (Heb 11:35; 12:23; Rev 6:9-11; 20:4-5; 20:11-15), all of which point to the "intermediate state." Given the mystery of death and the afterlife, it is unsurprising that ongoing debates exist. However, a brief review of these biblical references clearly supports the reality of heaven and hell, and we can confidently say that the reality of heaven and hell is an integral part of Christian teaching.

The common saying that Christians may be "too heavenly-minded to be any earthly good" implies that those prioritizing spiritual matters neglect their earthly responsibilities. However, Richard Baxter, Jonathan Edwards, and John Owen disagree. They believe focusing on heavenly things is essential to any good on earth. Baxter's book on heavenly rest (originally written and published in 1650, then updated and abridged by Tim Cooper) includes a quote that supports this idea:

> For Baxter, regularly focusing our thoughts on heaven is no small thing. It changes the color and complexion of our whole walk of faith. If we pursue it diligently, we will gain; if we neglect this duty, we will lose. A heavenly life is one that makes us joyful, secure, lively, patient, and profitable. We will honor God, and we will demonstrate that we really are citizens of another kingdom making our way home.[7]

As to the relevance of heaven, Jonathan Edwards emphasizes that heaven is not just a future destination but also impacts our lives on earth. In his book on Edwards's teachings about heaven, Stephen Nichols explores how we can apply his insights to our modern-day Christian life challenges.[8] Edwards urges us to live our earthly lives in light of heaven and strive to bring the beauty and realities of heaven to earth, even if it's just in a small way.

According to Matt 6:9-10, the Lord's Prayer is a request to God that his kingdom be established on earth just as it is in heaven. This prayer recognizes that heaven is a perfect model for how everything on earth should be. Therefore, our thoughts about heaven should influence our lives here on earth. It's essential to understand that heaven isn't just a future destination; it has everything to do with our lives on earth.

In what follows, we focus on several related questions about heaven and hell. First, what are the common misunderstandings of heaven and hell? Correction and refutation for each misunderstanding will prepare our minds to learn the biblical truth about them. Second, we present what the Bible teaches us about heaven and then about hell. Then, we will summarize the main points in the two essays on heaven and hell by J. I. Packer, an eminent and highly respected theologian, from his well-known book *Concise Theology*, which will be used as the launching point for our further examination of heaven and hell.

---

7. Baxter, *Saint's Everlasting Rest*, 95.
8. See Nichols, *Heaven on Earth*.

Misunderstandings of Heaven

1. Heaven is a place "up there" somewhere around the clouds, where harps are being played and angels march humanity through the pearly gates to live blissfully.

This famous image oversimplifies a complex and multifaceted concept of heaven. The imagery likely comes from a mix of sources. Clouds might reflect the idea of heaven above the sky, harps from the biblical mention of instruments praising God (Ps 150:3), and pearly gates symbolic of a grand entrance. These metaphors are intended to describe something beyond human experience. Perfect peace, joy, and connection with the divine might be felt as a sense of serenity, not in playing an actual harp. This modernist image of heaven is a cultural touchstone. Still, it's important to remember the broader concept of what heaven represents: a state of ultimate peace, joy, and rest in the presence of God beyond earthly limitations.

2. Heaven is not a place but a metaphorical expression and symbolic representation of the future destination after death.

But heaven is an actual place, to and from which Christ (John 1:32; 6:33, 42; Acts 1:2), angels (Matt 28:2, Rev 10:1) and in rare instances people, even before their death, have traveled (2 Kgs 2:11, 2 Cor 12:2, Rev 11:12). On this very subject, J. I. Packer, in his book *Concise Theology*, writes, "To think of heaven as a place is more right than wrong, though the word could mislead. Heaven appears in Scripture as a spatial reality that touches and interpenetrates all created space."[9] The latter statement is highly condensed and requires explanation, which we will provide later when we evaluate Packer's writings on heaven.

3. All human beings will be ultimately saved.

This statement is called *universalism* and is based on several Pauline texts, emphasizing the universal scope of Christ's saving work. Commonly, universalism refers specifically to the salvation of all human beings. People often say, "There are many ways up the mountain to God;

---

9. Packer, *Concise Theology*, 264.

we take different paths." However, carefully evaluating Paul's writings does not support the notion that all will be saved. In other words, the universal scope of Christ's saving work is not the same thing as universalism. The exclusivity of Christ in the matter of salvation is best illustrated in Peter's declaration to the Jewish rulers: "There is salvation in no one else, for there is no other name under heaven given among men by which we must be saved" (Acts 4:12).

4. All believers who die are assured of their eternal salvation, but after death they undergo purification before entering heaven's joy.

Catholic Church gives the name *purgatory* to this final purification of the elect. C. S. Lewis seems to believe in purgatory. A common assumption of both the Catholic Church and C. S. Lewis in their support for purgatory is the assumption that the cleansing through an extended period of time is necessary, which is not biblical. Some use 1 Cor 3:13–15 as a proof text for the notion of cleansing, but it does not even address cleansing of our own impurities through an extended period of time. Some verses like Phil 1:23 and 2 Cor 5:8 suggest an immediate and joyful fellowship with Christ after death. As to the way of change at the time of resurrection, Paul pictures a moment of change in 1 Cor 15:51–52: "We shall all be changed, in a moment, in the twinkling of an eye, at the last trumpet."

Misunderstandings of Hell

1. Bertrand Russell, the renowned British philosopher, said in his well-known essay "Why I Am Not a Christian," "I must say that I think all this doctrine, that hell-fire is a punishment for sin, is a doctrine of cruelty. It is doctrine that put cruelty into the world and gave the world generations of cruel torture."[10] *He also stated in the same essay that belief in hell reflected a serious moral defect in Christ's character, as he could not reconcile such teachings with compassion and justice.*

The biblical teaching of hell as a place of torment in vivid images is hard even for Christians, especially in the secular modern culture. However, it is important to realize that the revelation of hell in the Bible assumes a clear understanding of divine holiness and man's sinfulness. Those who protest

10. Russell, "Not a Christian," 17–18.

the biblical teachings of hell as being excessive demonstrate their delusion of man's sinfulness against God's infinite qualities (especially, holiness and goodness) and his role as the ultimate ruler over creation.

2. The concept of hell is a grim fantasy and a perversion of the Christian gospel.

This is a view expounded by John Hick, a well-known philosopher, and it consists of a twofold misunderstanding. First, hell is a place and destination, not a metaphorical or symbolic future destination after death. The NT teaching of hell is meant to teach us that hell as a dreadful place is meant "to appall us and strike us dumb with horror," assuring us to be forewarned.[11] Hell is a worse place than described in the Bible. Secondly, the Christian gospel emphasizes the love of God, who sent us Christ to be saved from the wrath of God. A long-standing position in the broader Christian circle sets the justice and love of God over against each other. Christianity has always rejected this Marcionite juxtaposition of opposites. We must recognize that the two seemingly opposite attributes of God—namely, justice and love—are not in conflict and are truly proper attributes of God simultaneously. If sin does not deserve punishment, there is no grace either.

3. The concept of hell is inconsistent with the biblical teaching of God's love.

This is a view presented by Clark Pinnock, another well-known theologian. Pinnock questions the idea that God, who gave his Son to die for sinners out of love, would create a place of eternal suffering for those who reject him.[12] While Pinnock emphasizes the love of God, he overlooks the Bible's equally important teaching that God is a God of judgment. Those who are consigned to hell will experience God's anger as a consuming fire (Heb 12:29), his righteous condemnation for defying him and rejecting the gospel by clinging to sins he hates.

---

11. Packer, *Concise Theology*, 262.
12. Rethinking Hell, "Clark Pinnock."

4. Those in hell will be destroyed after they have paid the penalty for their sins.

This view is commonly known as *annihilationism*. Its proponents offer several arguments based on biblical images of hell and other considerations. For instance, hell is described as "the lake of fire" (Rev 19:20; 20:10, 14, 15; 21:8). Fire consumes what is thrown into it, so it will burn up the wicked so that they no longer exist. A counterargument is also provided in Jesus' story of the rich man and Lazarus, where hell is described as a "place of torment" (Luke 16:28) involving "anguish in this flame" (v. 24). Even though the imagery of hell is intolerably tragic to the modern sensibility, we have no right to make it more palatable by toning down the negative imagery of hell.

5. The concept of hell is of a negative relationship to God.

This is partly true because hell may be viewed as the absence of God. However, the concept of hell is better understood as experiencing positively God's wrath and righteous condemnation for rejecting him and his Son, as discussed above. So, it is more accurate to say that hell is not so much the absence of God's presence, but it is experiencing God's anger.

Word Study of Heaven

Heaven signifies the visible realm of the sun, moon, and stars and the invisible realm of God's dwelling to which Christ has ascended.[13] In the second sense, heaven is also an expression of the believer's hope for an enduring homeland and inheritance in the presence of God. The OT word *shamayim* is typically translated as heaven, heavens, or sky. Heaven often refers to the space immediately above the earth or outer space. Most often, heaven is the abode of God. The NT word, *ouranos*, means sky, air, atmosphere, heaven, the dwelling place of God, and the dwelling place of the sun, moon, and stars. The primary meaning it conveys in the NT pertains to some location above the ground, above the sky, or transcending the entire physical universe. Frequently, *ouranos* refers to the place of eternal reward for the faithful. Most commonly, *ouranos* refers to the

---

13. The following discussion draws from Longman and Strauss, "Heaven(s)," *BED* 395–97.

domain where God dwells and from which he governs his creation and executes his judgments. The phrase "the kingdom of heaven" refers to the rule and reign of God. Heaven, in this sense, refers to the domain of God (Matt 3:16–17; 5:16; 6:9, 20; 7:11; 10:32–33).

What Does the Bible Say About Heaven?

Heaven in the Old Testament

Heaven is one of the creations of God (Gen 1:1, Ps 33:6, Amos 9:6). The phrase "heavens and earth" in Gen 1:1 refers to celestial and terrestrial realms of the physical universe that are initially unformed and unfilled. Given God's dominion over it, it is understood to be the source from which he sends the various physical phenomena which affect the earth. Heaven is also viewed as the habitation of God (1 Kgs 8:30, Ps 14:2, Is 63:15). God's throne is in heaven, and he is referred to as the "God of heaven" (Gen 19:24, 1 Kgs 8:32). Alongside these views of heaven, it is also the source of many blessings (Gen 4:25, Deut 33:13, 1 Kgs 8:35).

Heaven in the New Testament

Jesus, in the Gospels, speaks of heaven in several ways. As *shamayim* is used in the OT, he uses *ouranos* here to refer to the sky or the air, as well as the abode of the clouds. More significantly, heaven is the abode of God, from which the Spirit and the Son are sent; it is also the place to which Jesus ascended. "Heaven" is also used by Jesus as a roundabout way of referring to God (Mark 11:30, Matt 21:25, Luke 20:4). Finally, Jesus refers to heaven as the place of future bliss for the righteous (Matt 13:43). Though no explicit discussion is provided in the Gospels regarding when heaven begins, most sayings point to the "end of the age" (Matt 13:30, 40–43; Mark 10:30) or the return of the Son of Man (Matt 24:46–47; 25:10, 31–34).

The author of Hebrews uses the term "heaven" to refer to two different realities. One refers to the changing and temporary creation, which will "wear out like a garment" (Heb 1:10–12), in contrast to the unchanging, eternal, and abiding realm beyond the material and visible creation, where Jesus serves as high priest in the greater and perfect tabernacle "not made with hands, that is, not of this creation" (Heb 9:11). This is described as "a better possession and an abiding one" (Heb 10:34), "a better [heavenly] country" (Heb 11:16). Through Jesus Christ, believers may have access to the throne of God, that is, God's presence (Heb 10:19–22). The concept of heaven in the latter sense and its access must have been comforting and encouraging to the recipients of this epistle amid their trials and persecutions in the first century.

Acts refers to heaven as the place that has received Jesus "until the time for restoring all the things" (Acts 3:21), from which Jesus continues to direct his churches (Acts 9:10–16, 16:7–8). The notion that heaven serves as the center of supernatural influences, not only for churches but also all believers on earth, is an important idea, which will be examined later.

In the book of Revelation, John shares the belief that the heavens are open to visionaries and that the events in the heavenly realm hold ultimate authority over the earthly realm. John's vision of heaven, as described in Rev 4, gives us a glimpse into the heavenly realm. He saw a door standing open in heaven and witnessed a vision of God on his throne receiving continuous worship and the Lamb receiving a sealed scroll from him. In a broader sense, this scroll contains God's plan for history. Revelation shows that it is from heaven that judgments and agents of judgment are released upon the earth. Revelation's insight into the heavenly realm encourages believers to resist Roman imperial ideology and the pressure to conform to the Greco-Roman way of life. In the current age, heaven and earth are separate realms. Revelation anticipates the merging of these realms when the new heavens and new earth arrive, allowing God to dwell with humanity finally.

Paul used the term "heaven" or "heavenly place," a literal variant of heaven (*ouranos* in Greek), both in the singular and in the plural, to communicate various views of "heaven." They include:

1. The description of the universe as heaven and earth (1 Cor 8:5; Eph 1:10; 3:15; Col 1:16)

2. The abode of angels (Gal 1:8)

3. The dwelling place of Christ from which he came down (Eph 4:9, Rom 10:6), and to which he returned (Eph 4:10), and from which he will come again (Phil 3:20–21; 1 Thess 1:10; 4:16; 2 Thess 1:7)

4. The center of all supernatural influence that exerts its influence upon the believers on earth (Eph 1:3, 20; 2:6; 3:10; 6:12)[14]

5. The eternal home of the believer (2 Cor 5:1, 2; Phil 3:20; cf. Gal 4:26), where the citizenship of believers is being kept and the hope of believers is laid up (Col 1:5)

This brief survey shows that Paul's view of heaven is not just a mere future reality; it is, as J. I. Packer puts it, "a spatial reality that touches and interpenetrates all created spaces."[15] J. F. Maile expresses the same idea, in his entry on "Heaven," as "a spiritual sphere coexisting with the material world of space and time; it is where the exalted Christ now is, seated at God's right hand; it is also where the believer is united with Christ, is in Christ."[16]

J. I. Packer's View of Heaven

So far, we have briefly examined what the Scripture teaches us about heaven. This review shows that heaven is a complex and multifaceted topic, like many other key biblical terms we have chosen to examine. While there are a few concise articles on heaven,[17] the most well-balanced and lucid, and therefore the most helpful, writings about heaven and life in heaven for our purpose, is in J. I. Packer's popular book *Concise Theology*. He offers separate entries on heaven and hell, making it a handy and accurate resource for those interested in grasping a basic understanding of the topics.[18]

Packer's essay on heaven has several desirable and important features. First, heaven is described succinctly at the outset, which provides a clear picture of heaven drawn from various biblical sources, mostly cited above. Second, heaven is viewed as a place, a spatial reality that influences what is on earth. We will discuss this feature in more detail later. Third, his essay clearly distinguishes between heaven and life in heaven. Most other writings combine them together and create confusion.

14. See Vos, "Kingdom of God," 306.
15. Packer, *Concise Theology*, 264.
16. Maile, "Heaven, Heavenlies, Paradise," 382.
17. Lunde, "Heaven and Hell"; Acorn, "What Does the Bible Say"; "What Does the Bible Teach About Heaven and Hell?" in Waters, *Facing the Last Enemy*, 123–32. Nichols, *Heaven on Earth*.
18. Packer, *Concise Theology*, 264–67.

Our plan is to present a detailed summary of his entry under "heaven" in five paragraphs, which will be used as a starting point for further examination of the subject. The following is a brief summary with some minor additions.

1. Heaven is the biblical term for God's abode (home), where his throne is. Heaven is also the place of his presence to which the glorified Christ has returned, where the church militant and triumphant now unite for worship. In the future, heaven *will be* the place where Christ's people *will be* with their Savior forever, and it is pictured as a place of rest, a city, and a country. When Christ returns for the final judgment in the future, heaven *will* take the form of a new heaven and earth. Other obvious features of heaven, not included in Packer's essay but which are prominent, are that it is a place of everlasting rest and joy. At the same time, sin and misery are permanently gone, as explained in Baxter's well-known classic on heavenly rest.[19]

2. Heaven appears in Scripture "as a spatial reality that touches and interpenetrates all created space."[20] How heaven as a spatial reality affects the created space and its inhabitants is a crucially important subject, especially for Christian life, and we will further examine this subject later.

3. The realities of heaven are invisible and ordinarily imperceptible to us as long as we are in our present bodies. What we have now is our keen awareness of the realities of heaven and hell, our biblical teachings on them, and our close but less-than-perfect knowledge and relationship with the Father, the Son, and the Holy Spirit in heaven. These are a matter of solid spiritual fact.

4. Scripture teaches us to form our notion of the life of heaven in three ways: (1) by extrapolating from our less-than-perfect current relationship "with God the Father, the Son, and The Holy Spirit, with other Christians, and with created things to the thought of a perfect relationship, free from all limitation, frustration, and failure,"[21] (2) by eliminating from our idea of a life lived here on earth for God all limitation, frustration, and failures, and (3) by

---

19. Baxter, *Saint's Everlasting Rest*.
20. Packer, *Concise Theology*, 264.
21. Packer, *Concise Theology*, 265.

enriching our imaginings of that perfect and happy future instead by the visions of heavenly blessings.

5. Scripture also teaches us that the constant joy of heaven's life for the redeemed, while living on the earth, arises from four sources: (1) their vision of God in the face of Jesus Christ (Rev 22:4), (2) their ongoing experience of Christ's love through the ministry of the Holy Spirit (Rev 7:17), (3) their fellowship with other church members, and (4) continuing growth, maturity, learning, and strengthening of our abilities to witness and serve others. The redeemed desire all these things, yet the goals are not met here on earth. But in heaven, there will be no unfulfilled desires. In conclusion, the glory of heavenly life is composed of seeing God in and through Christ and being loved by the Father and the Son, of rest (Rev 14:13) and work (Rev 7:15), of praise and worship (Rev 7:9–10, 19:1–5), and of fellowship with the Lamb and saints (Rev 19:6–9). And the best part is that the heavenly glory never ends; it continues forever![22]

Evaluation of Packer's View of Heaven

Although Packer's short writings on heaven and life provide a clear and well-balanced explanation of heaven, a careful reading would reveal that his writings on the subject leave out some important details in grasping the concept of heaven. Specifically, he describes what heaven is and what heaven will be without clearly distinguishing between the two major phases of heaven. Traditionally, the biblical concept of an afterlife has been understood in terms of two major phases: a disembodied intermediate state between the believer's physical death and bodily resurrection, and a consequent reembodied, or eternal state associated with an eschatological resurrection and final judgment. Since Packer's writings on heaven and hell are part of concise theological essays on the subject, they must be brief, and thus it is understandable to leave out some important discussions on the two major phases of heaven.

More concretely, Packer's descriptions of heaven, presented in summary form, contain several well-known features in the Bible. But then he discusses what heaven will be like after the final consummation in the same paragraph. One should pay particular attention to the tense Packer uses. For instance, heaven is the place where *one day*, Christ's people *will*

---

22. For more on life in heaven, see Nichols, *Heaven on Earth*.

be there with their Savior *forever* (John 17:5, 24; 1 Thess 4:16–17). It is also pictured as a place of rest (John 14:2), a city (Heb 11:10), and a country (Heb 11:16). Packer finally writes, "*At some future point*, at the time of Christ's return for judgment, it *will* take the form of a reconstructed cosmos."[23] Astute readers will notice that these descriptions of heaven in the future tense will be realized after the parousia.

It's clear that Packer's depiction of heaven doesn't differentiate between the two significant phases of heaven—the intermediate state and the eternal or final state. The intermediate state is a somewhat technical term to describe the state of a believer between his or her death and the consummation of the created order at the parousia of Christ. At this time, a new bodily existence is begun. To understand the discussion of death and the afterlife in theology, one must have a basic understanding of biblical eschatology, particularly Pauline eschatology, which most of us lack. Packer avoids discussing the two major phases of heaven and only presents some crucial conclusions. However, the issue with this approach is that it becomes quite difficult for individuals without the necessary background to understand and grasp the concept being taught.

In the second paragraph of his essay on heaven (summarized in the second point above), Packer discusses the meaning and significance of viewing heaven as a place. As our brief word study points out, the primary meaning and significance of the word "heaven" relates to the location as a spatial reality. Packer says, "To think of heaven as a place is more right than wrong, though the word could mislead."[24] He probably meant to convey that if we understand "space" as we know it in the conventional sense of a time and space continuum, that would be misleading.

Packer writes then that "heaven is a spatial reality that touches and interpenetrates all created space."[25] This highly condensed theological statement requires serious effort to understand its meaning and significance. After providing the biblical basis for his statement, Packer also emphasizes that while we are in our present bodies, the realities of heaven are invisible and ordinarily imperceptible to us, and we know them only by faith (2 Cor 4:18, 5:7). Upon carefully reading these two statements, we would want to know why and how heaven serves as the center of all supernatural influence on those believers who believe in the reality of heaven by faith. The significance and implications of the

---

23. Packer, *Concise Theology*, 264. Emphasis mine.
24. Packer, *Concise Theology*, 264.
25. Packer, *Concise Theology*, 264.

truth in the two statements are very important issues in the Christian life. To understand and appreciate this truth, however, requires some essential background in Paul's eschatology, because death and the afterlife belong to the field of eschatology.

Vos's View of Heaven[26]

To find answers to this important question, we now turn to Geerhardus Vos's early writings on the kingdom of God. Vos defines heaven in four different but related ways.[27] Firstly, "heaven is the center of all supernatural influence brought to bear upon the lower world. To say that work is done by God leaves the mode of its accomplishment undetermined. To say that it is done from heaven is the strongest possible affirmation of its strictly supernatural origin." Secondly, "heaven means God in a special mode of activity (cf. Dan, 2:44; 7:13; Matt 16:17; 18:35; Rom 1:10; 1 Cor 15:47; 2 Cor 5:1, 2)." Thirdly, "heaven is also, as the mode of God, in relation to earth, the ideal pattern to which all things here below ought to conform. In this sense, to say that a thing is 'of heaven' means not only that it is 'of God' in general but in that specific sense in which the heavenly realities agree with God's nature (cf. Matt 6:10)." Fourth and finally, "heaven is in the consciousness of Jesus the goal toward which every aspiration of the disciple in the kingdom of God ought to tend (cf. Matt 6:19–21)."

To better understand how the reality of heaven, as described in the four different ways above, affects believers' lives on earth, we need to understand essential features of Pauline eschatology, focusing on understanding how Christ's presence in heaven influences his people on earth.

Pauline teaching contains five important broad structural lines. They consist of the idea of the resurrection, the thought of salvation, the doctrine of judgment and that of justification, and the conception of the Spirit. Ridderbos summarized the whole content of Paul's preaching "as the proclamation and explication of the eschatological time of salvation inaugurated with Christ's advent, death, and resurrection," and continues to argue that "it is from this principal point of view and under this denominator that all

---

26. This and the following subsections explain why and how heaven is the center of all supernatural influence on believers who live on earth. Those interested simply in the basic understanding of heaven and hell may skip them.

27. Following quotes are drawn from Vos, "Kingdom of God," 306.

the separate themes of Paul's preaching can be understood and penetrated in their unity and relation to each other."[28]

For our purpose, a succinct summary of the content and structure of Pauline eschatology will suffice. Toward that goal, we now turn to an entry titled "Eschatology" in the *DPL* by L. J. Kreitzer. As is well-known, Pauline eschatology is a broad and complex subject. Kreitzer briefly and clearly presents seven central tenets of Pauline eschatology.[29] They are (1) the messiahship of Jesus of Nazareth, (2) the presence of the eschatological age, (3) the resurrection of Jesus Christ from the dead, (4) the awaited day of the Lord and final judgment, (5) the gentile mission and the fate of the Jewish nation, (6) the eschatological gift of the Spirit, and (7) the transformation of the cosmos. To understand Vos's four different views of heaven and how heaven affects what is on earth, we need to briefly explain the second feature—namely, the presence of the eschatological age.

The Presence of the Eschatological Age

The arrival and the presence of the eschatological age in Paul's teaching reflects the influence of both the OT and the Jewish eschatological dualism of two ages (or eons), and it is the arrival of the eschatological time of salvation inaugurated with Christ's advent, death, and resurrection. Numerous eschatological phrases support this contention. For instance, a phrase like "in the fullness of time" in Gal 4:4 and Eph 1:10 announces the arrival of this eschatological age, expressed as "the age to come," as the new age in contrast to "the present age," which is seen as the old age. Therefore, this antithesis between the ages should be viewed against the backdrop of a temporal dualism. The declaration of the commencement of a great time of salvation in 2 Cor 6:2, "Behold, now is the favorable time; behold, now is the day of salvation," also announces that God's decisive, long-awaited, and expected coming has finally dawned.[30] Ridderbos expresses it as "the hour of hours, the day of salvation in the fulfilling, eschatological sense of the word."[31]

---

28. Ridderbos, *Paul*, 44.

29. Kreitzer, "Eschatology," 256–68.

30. Bromiley, "*Vuv*," *TDNTA* 1122, provides an excellent summary of the full significance of the NT view of the "now."

31. Ridderbos, *Paul*, 45.

Believers still live in the present time on earth. How does the presence of the eschatological age then relate to the present realities of believer's lives? Or how does the reigning Lord in heaven—which is, for all practical purposes, eschatological reality—vitally interact with believers who live here in the world below? To find an answer to this important question, which Vos refers to as a "fundamental problem,"[32] we now turn to his famous diagram of the original scheme and the modified scheme in the eschatological process with the resurrection of Christ (see below).[33]

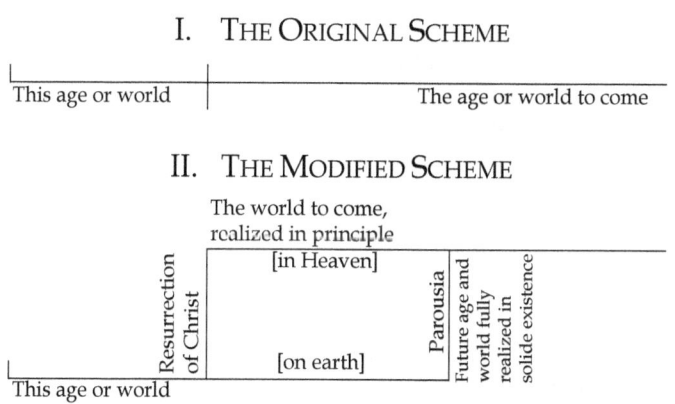

According to the original scheme in the OT and intertestamental Judaism, the age or world to come is in the distant future. For Paul, the chief actor in the divine drama of redemption—Jesus the Messiah—had come upon the stage and had been made present. With the resurrection of Jesus Christ and the outpouring of the Holy Spirit, which are dramatic events only possible in the age to come, while "this age" continues, the emergence of a new age ("the age to come") has come upon the scene, thus now with resulting coexistence of the two worlds or states. As to what is really happening here, Vos says, "As soon as the direction of the actual spiritual life contact becomes involved, the horizontal movement of thought on the time-plane must give way immediately to a vertical projection of the eschatological interest into the supernal region, because there, even more than in the historical development below, the center of all religious values and forces has come to lie." He continues, "The other, the higher world is in existence there, and there is no escape for

---

32. Vos, "Structure," 46.
33. Vos, "Structure," 1–41.

the Christian from its supreme dominion over his life. Thus, the other world, hitherto future, has become present."[34]

Vos's conception of the two schemes in the eschatological process is based on several Pauline texts. One is 2 Cor 5:17: "Therefore, if anyone is in Christ, he is a new creation. The old has passed away; behold, the new has come." Another verse, 1 Cor 10:11, affirms that the end of the age "has come" using the deliberate perfect tense verb *katenteken*. Finally, in 1 Cor 7:31, he asserts that the "form of this world is passing away," that the one who is in Christ participates in—belongs to—this new world of God and is a "new creation," and that the same truth that applies to all believers in the aggregate was kept "hidden" or "kept secret" until now.[35] All these affirm that the eschatological future somehow impinges upon the present, but at the same that the assurance of the arrival of the eschatological future should not lead the Corinthians, or us, into an overly realized eschatology. In other words, we should avoid the danger of "eschatologism," where eschatology is overly emphasized. Instead, we should not overlook that, for Paul, the consummation of the final eschatological age still lies in the future. The ultimate transformation of the world order, the final redemption of the believer with a resurrection body, and the final judgment have yet to arrive. The Gospel is a mystery in that what has been kept secret for ages is now revealed by the advent of Christ (Gal 4:4). But the full and final redemption is yet to be realized in the future. Therefore, the tension between the present and future is to be maintained. What has been said in the first two major features points to the convergence of the general eschatological character of Paul's teaching with the advent and revelation of Jesus Christ. As Ridderbos succinctly said, "Paul's 'eschatology' is 'Christ-eschatology,' and the Pauline approach to history is faith in Christ." This observation suggests that "the fundamental structure of Paul's teaching has to be approached from his Christology."[36] Many already quoted eschatological passages represent the close relationship between Paul's eschatology and Christology.

The interface between Paul's eschatology and his Christology is extensive. Given that, the christological and eschatological ground motif of Paul's teaching clearly shows that these two are closely related, and the interdependence between them is the critical element for

34. Vos, "Structure," 38.

35. For the revelation of the mystery, see Rom 16:25, 26; Col 1:26; Eph 1:9, 10; 3:4–5; 1 Cor 2:7; 2 Tim 1:9.

36. Ridderbos, *Paul*, 49.

understanding both. On the redemptive aspect of Paul's Christology, Ridderbos adds two additional comments. First, Paul's preaching of Christ has, in principle, a "redemptive-historical, eschatological content." In his words, "Paul's Christology is a Christology of redemptive facts."[37] This historical-eschatological character of Paul's Christology is presented in an organic relationship with the prophetic revelation of the OT. Ridderbos affirms that "this all-embracing character of Paul's eschatology and Christology" reveals all of Paul's preaching presuppositions.[38] Another perspective on Pauline Christology is provided by Beale in his recently published book, *A New Testament Biblical Theology*. In it, Beale treats the OT as a story without a conclusion and affirms that "the main elements of the OT plotline become the basis for the formulation of NT storyline."[39] The NT writers see the OT as a promise, which is fulfilled now in the person of Jesus Christ. Still, it is not yet completely fulfilled until Jesus returns in glory.

Hell

A succinct summary of J. I. Packer's entry under "Hell" in his book *Concise Theology* follows.[40]

1. Secular modern culture in the West makes it hard for Christians to take the reality of hell seriously. The revelation of hell in Scripture assumes/presupposes both deep insights into the holiness of God and into human and demonic sinfulness that most of us do not have. However, the doctrine of hell in the NT is essential to Christianity, and thus, we are called to try to understand it as Jesus and his disciples did.

2. The NT views hell (gehenna, as Jesus calls it, the place of incineration) as the final abode of those consigned to eternal punishment at the last judgment. It is described as a place of fire and darkness, with weeping and grinding of teeth, destruction, and torment—in other words, of total distress and misery. These descriptions are symbolic rather than literal. However, they teach us that the reality

---

37. Ridderbos, *Paul*, 49.
38. Ridderbos, *Paul*, 50.
39. Beale, *New Testament Biblical Theology*, 6.
40. Packer, *Concise Theology*, 261–63.

and situations of hell are far more dreadful than symbolic descriptions. The NT teaches about hell as a place of terror to prevent us from ending up going there.

3. Hell is often described as the absence of God's presence, but it's more accurately perceived as experiencing his wrath and displeasure. This dreadful experience is described in the Bible as a consuming fire, his righteous condemnation for defying him and clinging to the sins he hates. Hell is formed by systematically negating every element of experiencing God's goodness. Hell is the opposite of heaven, with heaven and hell forming a dichotomy in Scripture. We need to examine both words together to appreciate the link and bring distinction and contrast between them. To conclude, the reality of hell will be more terrible than the concept; no one can imagine how bad hell will be.

4. Scripture envisages that it never ends and continues forever and ever. Speculations of a "second chance" after death or a personal annihilation of the ungodly at some stage have no biblical merit.

5. Scripture also sees hell as self-chosen. So, those in hell will realize that they sentenced themselves to it by their own will and decision. Though what can be known about God is plain through general and special revelations to them, they chose to defy him as their Lord and rejected Jesus rather than coming to him. Therefore, they deserve it. In a sense, God appears to respect their decision.

6. The purpose of the biblical teaching about hell is to point out the critical importance of the choice and decision to be with God forever, worshiping him, or without God forever, worshiping ourselves. Some may find warnings of hell irreconcilable with the love and mercy of God, but it is his love and mercy to mankind that God has shown which makes Scripture so explicit about the dreadful conditions of hell.

Teachings We Have Learned About Heaven and Hell

So far, we have focused on examining three main topics: (1) what heaven and hell are, (2) the meaning and significance of viewing heaven as a spatial reality, and (3) why and how heaven is the center of all supernatural power that influences our world for those who live on earth, waiting for the return of our Lord Jesus Christ. Let us now turn our attention to the lessons we learned and their implications for Christian life. There are several important lessons to learn.

First, biblical teachings on heaven and hell teach us the true identity of believers, i.e., who we are. We are citizens of heaven, and while we live on earth, we belong to a different nation with its king and its laws, goals and priorities, and lifestyle. Philippians 3:20–21 teaches us that our citizenship is in heaven, and we are waiting for the Lord Jesus Christ in heaven to return, who will transform our lowly body to be like his glorious resurrection body. Colossians 3:1–2 teaches us to seek the heavenly things where Christ is and set our minds on heavenly things, not earthly things.

While it is recognized that dying, death, and the afterlife in heaven and hell properly belong to eschatology (the doctrine of the last things), we need to think of them as an integral part of the whole biblical narrative. Furthermore, death is the opposite of life, forming a part of a two-word concept, a dichotomy, in Scripture. Examining death fully requires examining life's meaning and significance to appreciate the link and bring distinction and contrast between them. If we study only one word without the other, we will do a great disservice to a rich and full understanding of the word under consideration. Philippians 3:20–21, as referred to above, illustrates this point well. Both believers on the earth and those with the Lord in the "intermediate state" in heaven are waiting for our Lord's return, who will restore us to everlasting heavenly life. As a matter of fact, the new creation is the storyline of the whole Scripture.

Second, the Bible teaches us that while we are in our present bodies, the realities of heaven are invisible and ordinarily imperceptible to us, and we know them only by faith (2 Cor 4:18). This truth points to the critical role of faith in perceiving and embracing the reality of heaven and hell. In our modern secular culture, which is bent on scientific thinking, what is real and true is limited to the physical and material things that can be observed and measured. Since heaven and hell are unseen and transcendent and cannot be objectively verifiable, many reject the realities of heaven and hell. Broadly speaking, this is the question of the methods of knowledge, specifically the role of faith versus sight in perceiving and embracing the realities of heaven and hell. Empiricists argue that knowledge comes primarily through sensory experience. Conversely, rationalists believe that reason and intuition can lead us to truths beyond sensory perception. They acknowledge the limitations of the senses but emphasize the role of reason and faith.

Our faith allows us to grasp the unseen realities of heaven, even though they remain imperceptible to our physical senses. Faith bridges the gap between the visible and the invisible. It enables us to believe in God's promises, including the hope of resurrection, eternal life, and the existence of heaven and hell (2 Cor 4:17–18). Hebrews 11:3 says, "By faith we understand that the universe was created by the word of God, so that what is seen was not made out of things that are visible." As discussed earlier in the chapter on faith, a condensed definition of faith is a heart-knowledge of God, far more than a merely intellectual assent to certain doctrines or dogmas; it is a deep-seated conviction that God is real and has a personal and intimate relationship with each individual believer. As a deep and intimate knowledge of God the Father, the Son, and the Holy Spirit in heaven is real, so are the realities of heaven and hell. They are a "matter of solid spiritual fact," as Packer describes it in his essay on heaven.[41]

The eleventh chapter of the book of Hebrews is filled with examples of faith heroes from the OT who could see beyond the physical world. While it was important for the apostles to witness what they heard, saw, and touched regarding Christ (as stated in 1 John 1:1), faith allows us to look beyond the senses and perceive the unseen. Since the things we see and experience in this world are temporary and fleeting, faith helps us diminish the value we place on the physical world, its goals, and its desires, instead focusing on the world to come. This idea is emphasized by Paul in 2 Cor 4:17–18, stating that the troubles and trials we experience in this life are only momentary and are preparing us for an eternal glory that far exceeds anything we can imagine. Therefore, we should not focus on the things that we can see, which are temporary, but rather on the things that we cannot see, which are eternal.

Third, although Jonathan Edwards is often remembered for his famous sermon on hell, "Sinners in the Hands of an Angry God," he also wrote extensively about heaven. One of the most important lessons we can learn from his writings is captured in the title of his sermon, "The True Christian's Life Is a Journey Towards Heaven," which he delivered in September of 1732. Edwards's vision of heaven reminds us of our responsibility to live on earth with a heavenly perspective, striving to

---

41. Packer, *Concise Theology*, 265.

bring the beauty and reality of heaven to earth in our own small way.[42] According to his vision of heaven, life is a pilgrimage, a journey. We should remember this insight daily. On a journey, though one is provided comfortable accommodation at an inn, he entertains no thought of settling there. As a man on a journey does, he enjoys and appreciates comforts and good things in life, but his sight and heart are also on the journey's end, heaven, as his inheritance in eternity. He also pays close attention to a piece of good travel advice on the merit of traveling light. When we learn to hold life's blessings not too tightly, it will be easier to let them go when it's time to leave this earthly journey.

Fourth, regularly focusing on heaven can enhance the quality of life for believers during their journey on earth. As quoted earlier, Tim Cooper, in an updated and abridged book by Richard Baxter, expressed this notion well:

> For Baxter, regularly focusing our thoughts on heaven is no small thing. It changes the color and complexion of our whole walk of faith. If we pursue it diligently, we will gain; if we neglect this duty, we will lose. A heavenly life is one that makes us joyful, secure, lively, patient, and profitable. We will honor God, and we will demonstrate that we really are citizens of another kingdom making our way home.[43]

Fifth, as we learn about heaven and hell, we become ever more convinced about the need for the assurance of salvation in Jesus Christ. As we face the grim reality of death, we can move on with much anticipation, not for the process of dying but for what lies ahead—heaven, as described in the Scripture.

Sixth, we also learn that heaven is not only the destination for Christ's people to go after death but also the reality we can experience while we live on this earth. This is in union with Christ, and Vos teaches us that heaven is the center of supernatural influences on believers who live on earth.

Seventh and finally, John's vision of heaven in Rev 4:1–6 and the throne room show us who is in control. This vision reassures believers that no matter what happens on earth, God our Lord reigns in heaven and fully controls everything seen and unseen.

---

42. Edwards, "True Christian's Life."
43. Baxter, *Saint's Everlasting Rest*, 95.

CHAPTER 10

Eternal Life

> This knowledge (of God) is a matter of head and heart both. It does not make us more "learned," at least not in the first place, but it makes us wiser, better, happier. It makes us *blessed* and gives us *eternal life*, hereafter indeed, but here and now also.
>
> BAVINCK, *WONDERFUL WORKS*

THE CONCEPT OF ETERNAL life can evoke different images and thoughts, depending on an individual's perspective. For many, eternal life is seen as the everlasting existence of consciousness or the soul's existence after death. Others believe that eternal life is equated with a blissful and everlasting life in heaven and communion with God. At the same time, for some doubters, it may be perceived as a wishful imagination of the mind and a distraction from the beauty of life on earth. The Apostles' Creed bears witness to the reality of eternal life: I believe in the resurrection of the body and life everlasting. In this view, eternal life commences with the bodily resurrection with the second coming of Jesus and the resurrection of the dead. Whichever view one subscribes to, most would agree that beliefs about eternal life influence daily life and decision-making on the earth. We can also agree that these varied perceptions often stem from a lack of understanding of the teachings of the Bible.

The Bible teaches that eternal life, the true and perfect life intended by God at creation, is experienced through knowing and walking with God. This biblical view of life is based on the belief that life is a gift from God. It means that life is not something we inherently possess on our own, but rather it is given to us initially at creation and then again through redemption. God gives life and makes it possible for it to be eternal. Recognizing that time is passing and that everything we cherish in this life will eventually be taken away from us can diminish the joy of life. Given this grim reality of the finitude of life, the promise and assurance of eternal life can give us peace as we face death, and they can change how we value the joys of this earthly life.

However, eternal life, in the true sense, is far more than an everlasting life in the future. It includes that but surpasses it in several ways. First, it is also a present reality relevant to a vibrant, fruitful, and fulfilling life on this earth. Second, it is new, not in the sense of time but in the sense of nature and kind, with the meaning of "better." This new kind of life was promised in Isa 25:8: "He will swallow up death forever; and the Lord God will wipe away tears from all faces, and the reproach of his people he will take away from all the earth, for the Lord has spoken." But it was finally fulfilled for the first time with the coming of Jesus Christ. Third, Christ came down from heaven to give this life to the world (John 6:33). This life does not come from awakening any innate power in humanity; it is the giving of a new life, mediated through Christ's words and himself. The Bible teaches us that one can only find a genuine and authentic life in Jesus Christ, the Creator of all life. Jesus later says, "I am the way, and the truth, and the life" (John 14:6). As we shall see, "life" in Christ and "eternal life" are essentially synonymous. Correctly understanding the concept of eternal life in the Bible can reshape how we continue to live our lives vibrantly with purpose as we wait in hope for the coming of our Lord Jesus Christ.

An excellent place to start learning about the meaning and nature of eternal life in the Bible is John's Gospel because "life" is a prominent theme in it. We may consider two well-known texts: First, the apostle John states clearly that the purpose of writing John's Gospel is that we may believe that Jesus is the Christ, the Son of God, and that by believing, we may have life in his name (John 20:31). Secondly, we must examine John 3, out of which verse 16 is the most famous summary of the gospel in the entire Bible. It reads, "For God so loved the world, that he gave his only Son, that whoever believes in him should not perish but have eternal life." When we consider these two texts together, we learn a few essential truths about life or eternal life. We first realize that the terms "life" and "eternal life" are used for the same meaning and purpose, so they are interchangeable. We then learn that man must be born again (from above) to inherit eternal life. Third, the way to obtain eternal life is through belief in Jesus. So, knowing the true identity and work of Jesus, which is the subject of Christology, is vital in the pursuit of eternal life. Fourth and finally, the way for man to be born again is through the Spirit (3:6–8), which points to the vital relationship between life and the Holy Spirit.

However, the apostle Paul presents a thorough doctrine of new life in christological and pneumatological frameworks. In light of the pervasive use of "life" or "eternal life" in various contexts in the NT, we realize the importance of linguistic data and the historical origin of the concept of life or eternal life in the Jewish background for a fuller understanding of the term. Before we delve into these tasks, consider a few common misunderstandings surrounding eternal life.

Misunderstandings of Eternal Life

1. Eternal life begins after death.

Many people mistakenly believe that eternal life starts only after physical death. However, the Bible teaches that eternal life is also a present possession for believers, not necessarily something that begins after death. Jesus said in John 5:24 that believers "have eternal life," in the present tense, and will never face condemnation.

2. Eternal life is living forever.

Eternal life is often equated with living forever, whether in heaven or hell. But the Bible defines eternal life as far more than endless existence—it is knowing God in an intimate, personal relationship (John 17:3) and walking with God. The quality of life matters here, not just the duration.

3. Eternal life can be earned.

Some wrongly believe eternal life is a reward earned by good works or moral living. However, the Bible clearly states that eternal life is the gift of God, received by grace through faith in Jesus Christ, not by works (Rom 6:23, Eph 2:8–9).

4. Eternal life cannot be lost.

While eternal life is "eternal" and can never be lost once received (John 1:28–29), some mistakenly think a believer's lifestyle is irrelevant. Scripture warns against falling away from the faith (Heb 6:4–6) and teaches that perseverance in faith leads to eternal life (Matt 24:13).

5. We do not know whether we have eternal life until we get there after death.

Belief can be shaky at times. John reassures his original hearers and us that eternal life is a sure thing. This is the first of the seven *know*s in his final summaries of assurances (1 John 5:13–20). First John 5:13 begins, "I write these things to you who believe in the name of the Son of God, that you may know that you have eternal life."

Word Studies

Four Hebrew words for life deal with different aspects of life.[1] They are *basar* (often translated as "flesh"), *chayah* (often translated as "life"), *nefesh* (often translated as "soul"), and *ruach* (often translated as "breath" or "spirit"). The Hebrew vocabulary for life centers on the OT word *chayah*, and its word group. It refers to a person's temporal existence (Gen 5:3) at a minimum, but more often it refers to a type of life. In the OT, the concept of living "a good life" is often associated with keeping God's laws and commandments and living according to his will. *Chayah* describes not merely our ability to move and breathe and think but the character or outcome of what we do with our existence. In Hebrew culture, there was less emphasis on the origins of life or the physical

---

1. The following discussion is based on Longman and Strauss, "Life," *BED* 481–82 and Bromiley, "*Zao* (To Live), *Zoe* (Life), *Bioo* (To Live)," *TDNTA* 290–96.

aspects of existence and more on the complete experience of living. The fundamental belief about life in the OT is that all living beings originate from God and are sustained by him. Therefore, life is considered a gift, and we do not inherently possess it independently.

The typical expression of God as the living God is meant to teach an essential truth about the vital and intimate relationship between God and all living beings and his activity on their behalf. This basic idea of life from God is evidenced by Gen 2:7, where the noun appears in the phrase "[God] breathed into his nostrils the breath of life; the adjective follows in the second clause, "and the man became a *living* creature,"[2] the same phrase used for the animals. This shows that all physical life is similar because it comes from God, and life is the same at the most basic level. The biblical view of life thus opposes the notion that life is simply a by-product of nature and that life is native to all creatureliness. According to that naturalistic view, God is incidental, and nature will care for itself without God.

One closely related Hebrew term for life is *nefesh*, often translated as "soul," that which animates the body. Another related term used to describe this animating dimension of life is *ruach*, usually translated as "spirit."

The *Baker Expository Dictionary* also emphasizes that life for mankind is holistic, leads to experience, is active, and expresses general vitality. So, the word opposite of life is death.

The NT has three Greek words for life: *bios*, *psyche*, and *zoe*. *Bios* almost always refers to an aspect of human life in the present world. *Psyche* denotes self-conscious physical existence and closely corresponds to the Hebrew word *nefesh* (Acts 20). Third and finally, *zoe* means life, existence, or spiritual life. This noun has four essential characteristics: (1) it generally refers to spiritual life, which is eternal (John 3:16, Rom 6:23); (2) it is obtained through faith (John 5:24, 1 Tim 1:16); (3) it is derived from being in Christ, its source (John 1:4; 5:39–40; 6:35; 17:2–3; 1 John 5:11, 20); and (4) it is fundamentally more important than physical life and all that the latter offers (Matt 18:8–9; 19:29; Luke 12:15; John 6:27; 1 Tim 6:19).

---

2. Emphasis mine.

Eternal Life in the Bible[3]

The Jewish Background

The term "everlasting life," which occurs in the LXX only at Daniel 12:2, where it translates the Hebrew term *hayye olam*, ("the life of the age"). It describes the life of the future age after the resurrection of the dead. Remembering that the book of Daniel was written in the sixth century BC during the time of exile under the Medo-Persian rule, we know that exiled Jews were at the most challenging time in their history. This verse expresses an ardent hope for the faithful to be raised to glory, honor, and everlasting life in the final kingdom in the coming age. The everlasting or eternal life is the life of the future age after the resurrection of the dead. However, the basic meaning of life in the OT is a complete well-being in earthly existence. Since life is God's gift, enjoying life is to enjoy the fullness of God's blessings and gifts. This includes long life, family blessings, prosperity, security, and especially fellowship with God.

Eventually, this sense of divine presence and assurance of God's blessings led to the conviction that even death could not destroy the close relationship between God and his people and that God would somehow enable his people to transcend death (Pss 16:9-11, 49:15, 73:24). The age to come is in the distant future, and the conviction might be dimly seen at first, but in time it developed into a solid hope of the resurrection of the body and life in the age to come (Isa 26:9, Dan 12:1-2).

In intertestamental Judaism, the belief that death is not the end of human existence gave rise to the concept of Sheol as an intermediate state where the dead await resurrection. Two contrasting terms emerged in the Jewish language during this period: "this age" and "the age to come." The rabbis often referred to "the life of the age to come," suggesting that the age to come would bring the blessing of immortality.[4] Considering these developments in the Jewish background, "eternal life" in Judaism, as expressed in Dan 12:2, is primarily the life of the age to come, the life of the resurrection.

---

3. Several good sources of information on this topic are Ladd, *Theology*, 290-305; Burge, "Life," 655-61; and Johnson, "Life."

4. Ladd, *Theology*, 291.

Eternal Life in the Synoptics

A quick review of *Strong's Concordance* reveals that "eternal life" appears six times, but the context of the phrase "eternal life" is the final judgment in the age to come, as in Judaism.[5] The best-known example is the rich young man's question, "What must I do to inherit eternal life?" and our Lord's answer (Mark 1:17–31, Matt 19:16–30, Luke 18:18–30). The young man was thinking of the life of the resurrection, and Jesus answered him in the same context. Eternal life, or simply life, is the life of the kingdom of God, which will be inherited in the age to come (Mark 10:23, 30; Matt 25:46). Other texts regarding eternal life appear in Matt 25:31–46, which tells us of the final judgment with the Son of Man, who will separate the righteous (who will go into eternal life) from the wicked (who will go into the eternal punishment).

Eternal Life in John's Gospel

Life in John's Gospel retains its eschatological character. It is the eternal life in the age to come, as in the Old Testament and the Synoptic Gospels. John's Gospel features forty-four references to life or eternal life, and 1 John has fifteen references. These references describe and depict various aspects of life.[6] Given the pervasiveness and the diversity of the use of life or eternal life throughout John's Gospel, our approach to viewing eternal life in John's Gospel is to present a succinct summary by focusing on its three unique features under four separate headings: (1) eternal life as present and future reality, (2) the relationship between life and Jesus Christ, (3) the knowledge of God and Jesus Christ as eternal life, and (4) the relationship between life and the Holy Spirit.

LIFE AS PRESENT AND FUTURE

While eternal life is eschatological in John's Gospel, the central focus is emphasizing the present experience of this future life in the coming age. The present experience of this eschatological life is declared in his saying, "Truly, truly, I say to you, an hour is coming, and is now here,

---

5. Strong, s.v. "Life," 237.
6. Strong, s.v. "Life," 237.

when the dead will hear the voice of the Son of God, and those who hear will live" (John 5:25).

Jesus came down from heaven to give life to the world (6:33) to satisfy the world's spiritual hunger and thirst (6:35). He has come down from heaven to do the will of God, and the Father's will is that "everyone who looks on the Son and believes in him should have eternal life, and I will raise him up on the last day" (6:38-40).

In John 6:40 and 6:54, it is promised that believers will experience bodily resurrection on the last day. Even if those who believe in Jesus physically die, they will receive a new resurrection body at the time of Jesus' second coming. By having faith in Jesus, they have received life and will live again in the resurrection body, never to die (11:25-26).

Life and Jesus Christ

One should note that John's Gospel begins the creation narrative with the phrase, "In the beginning," to introduce who Jesus is. "In the beginning, God created the heavens and the earth" (Gen 1:1). John presents Jesus as the eternal, preexistent, now incarnate Word (1:1, 14) and as the unique and only Son of the Father who is himself God (1:1, 18). Verse 3 says, "All things were made through him, and without him was not any thing made that was made." This verse says that God the Father carried out his creative works through the activities of the Son (1 Cor 8:6, Col 1:16, Heb 1:2). John uses the word "life" twice in verse 4: "In him was life, and the life was the light of men."

John informs us that Jesus came to this world so that we would have life and have it abundantly (10:10). He further informs us that he is the resurrection and life (11:25), the real life, and that life is both present and permanent. Considering these verses together, we learn that not only is life in him, but he himself is life (11:25). Finally, he comforted his beloved disciples in his farewell remark, "Let not your hearts be troubled. Believe in God; believe also in me" (14:1). What would be the substance of the belief in God and Jesus? Among others, the belief includes a conviction in God's decisive intervention in human history and life by sending his only Son so that they would not perish but have eternal life (3:16). There are two groups of people in terms of their response to the Gospel message: those who believe and follow, and those who will not. Those who believe will be born into this new life; the unbelief of the others may be considered part of judgment.

He comforted his followers by saying he would prepare a place for them. When he comes again, he will take them to where he is for them to be with him (14:2–6). When Thomas asked about the way to where he was going, Jesus said, "I am the way, the truth, and the life" (14:6). This is an unambiguous statement about who Jesus truly is, especially when considering the three definitive articles in the claim.

Life as Knowledge of God and Jesus Christ

After some critical teachings in the farewell discourses, Jesus lifted his eyes to heaven at the beginning of chapter 17 and said, "Father, the hour has come; glorify your Son that the Son may glorify you, since you have given him authority over all flesh, to give eternal life to all whom you have given him" (John 17:1–2). In verse 2, we see the tension in that the Son came as God's regent for all people to have eternal life, but only those given to him will have eternal life. Verse 3 defines eternal life: "And this is eternal life, that they know you, the only true God, and Jesus Christ whom you have sent." To put it concisely, eternal life is knowing or the knowledge of the true God through Jesus Christ. There are two essential things to be noted in this vitally important verse in understanding the nature of eternal life. First, knowing Jesus' true identity is vital in pursuing eternal life. The question of who Jesus is reaches the boiling point toward the end of chapter 8 ("Before Abraham was, I am," John 8:58). The more fundamental question than the identity of Jesus is, Who is God? John 3:16 provides the answer: he is described as the one who so loved the world and gave his only Son, not to condemn but to save them through him. Second, this (John 17:3) is the first time Jesus refers to himself as Jesus Christ (cf. 1:17).

This verse also leads us to the question of the nature of knowledge in the Bible, particularly in John's Gospel. This question deals with an important biblical and Hebraic epistemology question, using the Greek word *ginosko* and the Hebrew word *yada*. The Greek word is usually used to signify intelligent comprehension ("to perceive," "to understand," and "to know"), initially with an emphasis on the act.[7]

---

7. Bromiley, "*Ginosko*," *TDNTA* 119–23.

The concept of knowledge used and understood in the OT is based on the Hebraic concept and differs significantly from knowledge in Greek philosophy.[8] The Bible emphasizes knowledge's existential and covenantal nature, highlighting its connection to ultimate reality. Its existential aspect means "to know by experience," which includes "knowing" such things as afflictions, loss, disaster and grief, and in the sense of a husband knowing his wife with a sexual connotation. It implies that "to know" does not simply mean to have theoretical knowledge of an object and its nature. Rather, it refers to a personal, intimate relationship between the knower and the object known, a close experiential relationship evidenced by care, concern, love, and loyalty.

The covenantal aspect of knowledge means that its purpose is to promote obedience to the covenant between God and his people. Covenantal epistemology emphasizes knowledge as a means to carry out responsible action. This approach links knowledge with the right behavior, connecting epistemology with ethics and belief with behavior. Knowledge as a mere idea and conception without these deep and intimate connections and links often leads to hypocrisy, guilt, and personal disintegration.

Knowledge in John's Gospel is expressed in Greek, but its underlying concept is Hebraic. Knowledge in John's Gospel is the intimate and experiential relationship. One may begin with an intimate, mutually loving relationship between the Father and the Son; moving on, Jesus knows his disciples, and they know him; in knowing him, they also know God. Jesus said, "I know my own, and my own know me, just as the Father knows me and I know the Father; and I lay down my life for the sheep" (John 10:14–15). One important benefit of learning the true and intended meaning of knowing and knowledge in John's Gospel is to start to recognize the abundant use of the word "know" with its deep and intimate relationships among God, Jesus, and his people.

This knowledge of God is further associated with the visions of God. "If you had known me, you would have known my Father also. From now on you do know him and have seen him" (John 14:7). This verse reinforces what John 1:18 says: "No one has ever seen God; the only God, who is at the Father's side, he has made him known." Now, since Christ has come into the world, the one who has seen him has seen the Father (14:9). So, the vision of God, the blessings of the age to come, is realized by the coming of Jesus to the world. Continuing in the narrative, Philip's

---

8. Bromiley, "*Ginosko*," *TDNTA* 120.

request to show them the Father prompts Jesus' declaration, "Believe me that I am in the Father and the Father is in me" (14:11). The main point of all these teachings means that the knowledge of God in John's Gospel is mediated through Jesus the Son, the Word who became flesh. Knowledge of God is also mediated by faith through the Holy Spirit. Being born again is possible through the Spirit (John 3:3–5, 8).

LIFE AND THE HOLY SPIRIT

John 17:3 defines eternal life as knowing God through Jesus Christ, with the underlying meaning of knowledge as an intimate and experiential relationship. What does it involve for believers to have such a close relationship with God through Jesus Christ? In what concrete way do believers enjoy such close and intimate relationships? It takes the Holy Spirit. Two distinctive themes of John's Gospel are eternal life and the coming of the Spirit. Thus far, we have been examining the first main theme, eternal life; the spirit's coming, as the second main theme, is explained in the passage of John 14:15–29.

This passage consists of a condition and a promise repeated three times differently. The condition specified is for believers to love Jesus and keep the commandments (vv. 15, 21, 23). The promise offered is threefold. First, Jesus will ask the Father, and he will give them another Helper (v. 16), the Holy Spirit, and the Spirit of truth (v. 17), to be with them forever (v. 16). When Judas (not Iscariot) asked why Jesus manifested himself to his disciples but not the world (v. 22), Jesus' answer, recorded in verse 23, is revealing: "If anyone loves me, he will keep my word, and my Father will love him, and we will come to him and make our home with him." This is the second promise signifying such a close and intimate fellowship. Third, the Helper, the Holy Spirit, whom the Father will send in Jesus' name, will teach believers all things and bring all that Jesus taught them to their remembrance. Jesus said that he was going away *and* would come to them (v. 28), and this promise was fulfilled by the coming of the Holy Spirit on the day of Pentecost in Acts 2.

The parallelism between the three conditions and promises in one discourse is perhaps intended to teach us the same truth by repetition, emphasizing that it is through the Spirit that Father and Son come to have fellowship with believers. The images of being in each other among

Father, Son, and believers in verse 20 and of coming and making home in verse 23 are apt pictures of close and intimate fellowship.

When we consider John 17:3, which discusses the nature of eternal life as the fellowship of believers, along with John 14:15–29, which examines the mediatorial role of the Spirit, it becomes clear that "eternal life" refers to the fellowship of believers with the Father and the Son, experienced through the coming of the Spirit. From this, we can conclude that in John's Gospel, eternal life is the Father and the Son making their home with the believer through the Spirit. The believer, baptized into Christ, is baptized into his death and resurrection through the Spirit. Therefore, receiving the Holy Spirit and receiving eternal life should not be viewed as separate blessings but rather as the same blessing in a real sense.

Receiving the Holy Spirit by being born again requires Christians to be united with Christ, which encompasses all the blessings of Christian life. In the Gospel of John, however, eternal life has both present and future aspects. John emphasizes that believers experience eternal life now by having fellowship with the Father and the Son, but it will be fully experienced in the future (4:14, 5:29) when believers will be in the presence of God and the Son. Even though believers experience the presence of God and the Son through the Spirit, they are not physically with us, especially since the Son has gone to prepare a place in heaven for his people. It will only be when he returns for his followers that they will be with him and see his glory (14:2, 3; 17:5, 24). We know that eternal life in heaven will be far more beautiful and glorious than our current experience of intimate fellowship with Christ.[9]

Life in Paul's Letter: New Life[10]

Paul speaks of eternal life in several places, and he usually designates a future life in the coming age (Rom 2:7; 6:22; Gal 6:8; 1 Tim 1:16; Titus 1:2; 3:7). But since the new eon (Greek: *aion*) in Christ is the eon of life (Rom 5:18; 6:4; 8:2; Col 3:4), we can argue that Paul's view of eternal life is also in the present reality, even though he does not emphasize it, as John does. The concept of "eon" is often used to describe distinct ages or orders of existence. The "new eon" then designates a shift from

---

9. For a good book to read to catch the vision of heaven, see Baxter, *Saint's Everlasting Rest*.

10. This section heavily relies on Ladd's essay "The New Life in Christ" in Ladd, *Theology*, 521–37; and Ridderbos, *Paul*, 205–52.

death to life, as believers are no longer under the dominion of sin and death (Rom 8:1-2; Titus 2:11-13). So we can say that Paul's eschatology is entirely characterized by God's realized and still-to-be-realized redemptive work in Christ.

Besides viewing life as the present reality, Paul and John share similar perspectives on life in several other ways. Firstly, both teach that true life is found only in Christ, who brings new life through redemption (John 5:26; 6:68; Eph 1:7). Secondly, they divide humanity into two groups: those who are physically alive but spiritually dead, and those who have been brought to life through belief in Christ (John 3:16-21, Eph 2:1-3). Thirdly, they emphasize the importance of the Holy Spirit for believers to experience close and intimate fellowship with the Father and his Son.

Yet, their perspectives on life and eternal life are still distinctly different, especially with the different emphasis, idioms, and imagery used to describe various aspects of life. John's concept of eternal life focuses on the nature of eternal life as knowing God and his Son intimately, thus emphasizing the necessity of a close and intimate fellowship. This knowledge in John's Gospel is also linked to the vision of God. Although no one has seen God, the Son, who has come into the world, has not only made him known (John 1:18) but also made it possible for those who have seen him to have also seen the Father (John 12:45). This underscores the Son's mediating role in understanding God: believers know God through knowing his only Son. On the other hand, Paul's perspective on life emphasizes the new life in Christ, resulting from Christ's death and resurrection in the context of the end times. In Paul's view, the new life in Christ is encapsulated in his famous declaration, "Therefore, if anyone is in Christ, he is a new creation. The old has passed away; behold, the new has come" (2 Cor 5:17).

The interpretation of this verse on new creation is often seen as a personal conversion experience. According to this view, the old desires and motivations of unregenerate individuals are somehow replaced by new ones as one becomes a Christian. However, Christians living in the present world are just as, if not more, troubled by the problems of the fallen world, including in desires and motivations, as nonbelievers. Therefore, the implications of understanding the text along the lines of personal conversion experience contradict the reality of Christian life because sinful desires equally beset it, and we have not yet arrived at perfection.

To gain the correct perspective of this particular text in 2 Cor 5:17, or any other biblical text, we must first consider the context in which the verse appears. In verse 17, the first word, "therefore," indicates that verse 17 is a conclusion based on what was said earlier, especially in verses 14–16 that emphasize the impact of Christ's atoning death for all. The implication is that those who live a new life no longer live for themselves but for Christ, who died for them. Verse 17 contains two declarations: (1) if anyone is in Christ, he is a new creation; and (2) the old has passed away; behold, the new has come. These two statements tell the same reality, relying on different images and idioms, and they are presented in parallel repetition for emphasis. "In Christ" does not refer to mystical fellowship but indicates that the believer belongs to Christ. The phrase "new creation in Christ" signifies a significant salvific-historical fact. The second declaration means that the old order or sphere has passed away, and the new order has come. Therefore, the proper context of the verse implies an eschatological and redemptive-historical perspective.

This eschatological and redemptive-historical perspective is not only Paul's viewpoint in particular but also that of the NT in general. To comprehend this theological mindset, we need to consider Paul's background as a Jew who shared the hope of the coming of the Messiah in the future age. Something transformative occurred in Paul's outlook on the world and life. And this change didn't happen gradually but instantaneously during the Damascus road experience. The appearance of Jesus in power and glory as the Messiah revolutionized Paul's understanding of redemptive history. While he continued to anticipate the coming day of the Lord, encountering Jesus the Messiah as the Savior, a key redemptive event with an eschatological nature, led to the conviction that the age to come had arrived through the life, death, and resurrection of Jesus Christ (Eph 1:9, 10; 3:11). This is the fundamental and all-encompassing character of Paul's preaching about Christ. Additionally, Paul's eschatology is entirely determined by God's realized and still-to-be-realized redemptive work in Christ.

Interpreting the passage about the new creation in Christ in 2 Corinthians along this line, we learn that a radically new kind of existence under a new order has been opened up to people as a result of Christ's messianic work on his cross (2 Cor 5:15, 19): new life in Christ. The idea of newness preserves its eschatological character in the NT. The new life means a radical transformation, a passing from a condition of death and slavery into one of life and freedom, which is not to be explained by human effort and moral strength but only by the creative command of God, as was in the creation of the world. This is accomplished by the recreating work of the Holy Spirit received into the hearts and minds of believers.[11] The expression "in Christ" is one of Paul's most unique idioms. Some understand it as a mystical fellowship of individuals with Christ; others interpret it as being in the church. However, as discussed earlier, this expression can be best understood as the objective facts stating what God has accomplished in Christ (Eph 1:4, 7). It includes the totality of salvation, encompassing redemption, justification, sanctification, and glorification.

A parallel but contrasting "in Christ" idiom is "in Adam." "For as in Adam all die, so also in Christ shall all be made alive" (1 Cor 15:22). Paul conceived of two groups of people: those who are in Adam belong to the old eon with its bondage to sin and death, and those who are in Christ belong to the new eon with its life and freedom. In a sense, believers who are in Christ are still connected to the sinful world because they live and die in it. However, from a redemptive viewpoint, they have entered a new life in Christ—the life of a new era or new sphere of redemption. Being in Christ means experiencing the newness of this new era.

The next important question is about the concrete mode of a believer's existence in Christ. Finding the answer to the question requires us to consider two points. First, the person in Christ is "in the Spirit." The opposite of being in the Spirit is being "in the flesh," just as the opposite of being in Christ is being in Adam. To be "in the flesh" has several meanings depending on the context. Still, in this case, it refers only to a physiological and social sense, as seen in Gal 2:20. Being a Christian means having received life through the Holy Spirit and continuing to live in the communion of the Spirit. The believer baptized into Christ is also baptized by the Spirit into his resurrection, death, newness of life, and death to sin. This signifies an eschatological existence—life in the new age. Second, with the proper understanding of the indissoluble bond and the meaning between being in Christ and the Spirit, we need to ask now in what manner, or how, this new life by the Spirit is realized in man and how it makes him into that new man in all the facets that thus emerge. A short and simple answer is that faith is the mode of existence of the new life by the Spirit.

Understanding these two key points will help us grasp the underlying motive and driving force in Paul's life, as shown in his statement from Gal 2:20: "I have been crucified with Christ. It is no longer I who live, but

---

11. See the "*Spiritus Recreator*" chapter in Ferguson, *Holy Spirit*, 115–38.

Christ who lives in me. And the life I now live in the flesh I live by faith in the Son of God, who loved me and gave himself for me." Paul's underlying motivation for whatever he does in his life is the compelling love of Christ (2 Cor 5:14), and it can't be any other way in order for all of us to live a new life, which is opened up for all believers. When believers truly understand the magnitude of Christ's costly sacrificial love, we can commit our lives similarly to a new life worthy of such amazing love.

In summarizing what has been said thus far, note first that "eternal life" and "life" are used interchangeably. To gain eternal life, one must be born again by believing in Jesus as the Savior through the Holy Spirit. Since eternal life involves knowing God and his Son on a deep and intimate level, being born again is the initial step toward establishing a personal and intimate relationship with God and Jesus Christ, which constitutes inheriting eternal life. In John's Gospel, John emphasizes the necessity of being born again to inherit eternal life and explains eternal life as knowledge of God and His Son. In contrast, Paul's redemptive focus is on the believer's participation in the death and resurrection of Jesus Christ. This shared reality is also described as our having died and being crucified to sin and the world. This would take believers into the new-life context of Christ, in which the Spirit rules the orientation of our thoughts and obedience. This entails living a new life as a new creation in Christ through the Holy Spirit. Therefore, eternal life, new life in Christ, and new creation in Christ essentially refer to the same reality but with different emphases and terminology.

To live a new life in Christ through the Holy Spirit requires the renewal of the entire mental process, including the inner direction of thought and mind. This is closely related to the NT word for repentance, which means changing one's mind so that one's life's views, values, goals, and ways are changed and one's whole life is lived differently. Paul exhorts believers to "not be conformed to this world, but be transformed by the renewal of your mind, that by testing you may discern what is the will of God, what is good and acceptable and perfect" (Rom 12:2). The key phrase in this verse, as well as in Eph 4:23–24, is "the renewal of the mind." Paul often speaks of the mind (*nous*) and usually refers to the human cognitive faculty. But in this verse it refers to the inner direction of thought and will and the awareness of the moral consequence of one's decision. So, the inward work of Christ through the Spirit is to be understood not in terms of the complete transformation of the character but in the pouring of divine power, accomplishing a reorientation of the will toward God. The *Baker Expository Dictionary* defines it as the proper disposition of the Christian mind in discerning the will of God: "What is good and acceptable and perfect" (Rom 12:2).[12] Paul claims "But we have the mind of Christ" (1 Cor 2:16) and calls for the renewal of the mind (Rom 12:2, Eph 4:23) and warns against being "quickly shaken in mind" (2 Thess 2:2).

Spurgeon's Sermon: "Eternal Life!"

In concluding this essay on eternal life in the Bible, we want to focus on Charles Spurgeon's sermon titled "Eternal Life!" delivered on February 6, 1878.[13] The two biblical texts used are John 17:3, "And this is eternal life, that they know you, the only true God, and Jesus Christ whom you have sent," and 1 John 5:20, "And we know that the Son of God has come, and has given us an understanding, that we may know Him who is true; and we are in Him who is true, in His Son Jesus Christ. This is the true God and eternal life" (NKJV). The first text is familiar because we have examined it closely in discussing John's view of eternal life.

Spurgeon's sermon is long but contains some very useful and vital insights, so we want to bring a summary to shed further light on eternal life. In an earlier examination of the first text (John 17:3), we explain two constituents of eternal life: the knowledge of only true God and Jesus Christ whom he sent. To put it concisely, eternal life is knowing, or the knowledge of, the true God through Jesus Christ. In his sermon on eternal life, Spurgeon expounds on this and further explains why this has to be so.

After some introductory remarks on eternal life, Spurgeon first raises a question: What is the constituent and integral part of eternal life? He first answers that eternal life consists in the knowledge of the only true God (John 17:3) and of Jesus Christ (John 17:3, 1 John 5:20). The power of his sermon lies in elucidating the truth that there is no other way but to have knowledge of both to gain eternal life.

He then starts to consider the want (not having) of this knowledge. Not having this knowledge, followed by the fall, results in all forms of idolatry. Then he makes two faith statements: (1) man must have a God

---

12. Longman and Strauss, "*Kainos, Neos*," *BED* 546. See also, Bromiley, "*Kainos* (New in Nature), *Kainotes* (Newness), *Anakainoo* (To Make New), *Anakainnosis* (Renewal)," *TDNTA* 388–89.

13. Spurgeon, "Eternal Life!"

for he cannot be happy without one; and (2) there is a great superior being, our Creator and Judge. These two statements touch on fundamental philosophical and theological questions debated for centuries. However, we should note that these two statements reflect a monotheistic belief system of major religions, including Christianity, Islam, and Judaism.

Spurgeon then raises the second question about the meaning of this knowledge. His answers consist of four parts: (1) It is not eternal life to merely know that there is a God. One may know that there is a Queen of England, but this does not mean that one knows her. (2) It is to know him as God—namely, to know him as God to us, which means that we revere him, bow before him, and submit ourselves to his law and commands. (3) And it is to know him on personal terms and intimately. Knowing God in these ways described above will allow us to regard him as our very close, intimate, and cherished friend.

Spurgeon additionally lists several benefits of knowing God for believers in their earthly lives. First, once you come to know God in the way described above, something makes life worth living—a secret bliss. With the intimate knowledge of God, you also have a grand object in life. Additionally, with God, all conditions of life become opportunities for the true and intended life; without him, there is nothing to live for! Furthermore, the person who knows God can explain many things that puzzle others because he has God to rely on when he cannot explain. Spurgeon explained several more benefits, but these are sufficient for our purpose.

Let us recall that the constituent and integral part of eternal life consists in the knowledge of both "the only true God" (John 17:3) and of his Son, Jesus Christ, "the true God" (1 John 5:20, which says, "And we know that the Son of God has come and has given us understanding, so that we may know him who is true; and we are in him who is true, in his Son Jesus Christ. He is the true God and eternal life"). One should pay close attention to the fact that Jesus Christ is "true God and eternal life." Considering these two passages together, we know that knowing God apart from Christ would not be eternal life. Why so? Because apart from Jesus Christ, the God we come to know is an almighty God and infinitely just, whose laws we have violated. God the Father is infinitely loving and unfailingly wise; nevertheless, the penalties of sin must be punished and cannot be reversed. So, knowing God the Father alone without Jesus Christ would be a "knowledge of terror"[14] that would make one move away and avoid

---

14. Spurgeon, "Eternal Life!," 4.

God. When we see God in Jesus Christ meeting us through the lens of our Lord's atoning work on the cross, we realize that the true God demanded a just penalty, yet he himself provided it. John describes this in his epistle: "In this is love, not that we have loved God but that he loved us and sent his Son to be the propitiation for our sins" (1 John 4:10). From this, we know that we have entered into eternal life in the knowledge of God in Christ and God through Christ.

Bibliography

Acorn, Randy. "What Does the Bible Say About Heaven." Eternal Perspective Ministries, Feb. 4, 2010. https://www.epm.org/resources/2010/Feb/4/what-does-bible-say-about-heaven/.

Atkinson, David. *The Message of Genesis 1–11*. Downers Grove, IL: InterVarsity, 1990.

Aulén, Gustaf. *Christus Victor: An Historical Study of the Three Main Types of the Idea of Atonement*. Translated by A. G. Hebert. Eugene, OR: Wipf & Stock, 2003.

Bavinck, Heman. *God and Creation*. Vol. 2 of *Reformed Dogmatics*, edited by John Bolt. Translated by John Vriend. Grand Rapids Baker Academic, 2006.

———. *Holy Spirit, Church, and New Creation*. Vol. 4 of *Reformed Dogmatics*, edited by John Bolt. Translated by John Vriend. Grand Rapids: Baker Academic, 2006.

———. *Sin and Salvation in Christ*. Vol. 3 of *Reformed Dogmatics*, edited by John Bolt. Translated by John Vriend. Grand Rapids: Baker Academic, 2006.

———. *The Wonderful Works of God*. Glenside, PA: Westminster Seminary, 2019.

Baxter, Richard. *The Saint's Everlasting Rest*. Updated and abridged by Tim Cooper. Wheaton, IL: Crossway, 2022.

Beale, G. K. *A New Testament Biblical Theology: The Unfolding of the Old Testament in the New*. Grand Rapids: Baker Academic, 2011.

Beasley-Murray, George. R. "The Kingdom of God in the Teaching of Jesus." *Journal of the Evangelical Theological Society* 35.1 (Mar. 1992), 19–30. https://etsjets.org/wp-content/uploads/2010/07/files_JETS-PDFs_35_35-1_JETS_35-1_019-030_Beasley-Murray.pdf.

Beeke, Joel R. "Appropriating Salvation: The Spirit, Faith and Assurance, and Repentance." In *A Theological Guide to Calvin's Institutes: Essays and Analysis*, edited by David W. Hall and Peter A. Lillback, 270–300. Phillipsburg, NJ: P&R, 2008.

Beeke, Joel R., and Christopher W. Bogosh. *Dying and Death: Getting Rightly Prepared for the Inevitable*. Grand Rapids: Reformation Heritage, 2018.

Billings, J. Todd. *Union with Christ: Reframing Theology and Ministry for the Church*. Grand Rapids: Baker Academic, 2011.

Bright, John. *The Kingdom of God: The Biblical Concept and Its Meaning for the Church*. Nashville: Abingdon, 1981.

Bromiley, Geoffrey W. "Sin." In *ISBE* 4:518–25.

———. *Theological Dictionary of the New Testament: Abridged in One Volume*. Edited by Gerhard Kittel and Gerhard Friedrich. Translated by Geoffrey W. Bromiley. Grand Rapids: Eerdmans, 1985.

Bromiley, Geoffrey W., et al., eds. *The International Standard Bible Encyclopedia*. 4 vols. Rev. ed. Grand Rapids: Eerdmans, 1988.

Brown, Robert McCafee. *Is Faith Obsolete?* Philadelphia: Westminster John Knox, 1979.

Burge, Gary M. "Life." In *The New Interpreter's Dictionary of the Bible*, vol. 3, edited by Katherine Doob Sakenfeld, 655–61. Nashville: Abingdon, 2008.

Calvin, John. *Institutes of the Christian Religion*. Translated by Henry Beverage. Peabody, MA: Hendrickson, 2008.

Campbell, Constantine R. *Paul and Union with Christ: An Exegetical and Theological Study*. Grand Rapids: Zondervan, 2012.

Caragounis, C. C. "Kingdom of God / Kingdom of Heaven." In *DJG* 417–30.

Chesterton, G. K. *Orthodoxy*. Sutton-Alpine, AK: Relevant, 2006.

Clark, R. Scott. "Election and Predestination: The Sovereign Expressions of God." In *Theological Guide to Calvin's Institutes: Essays and Analysis*, edited by David W. Hall and Peter A. Lillback, 90–122. Phillipsburg, NJ: P&R, 2008.

Critchley, Simon. "To Philosophize Is to Learn How to Die." *New York Times*, Apr. 11, 2020. https://www.nytimes.com/2020/04/11/opinion/covid-philosophy-anxiety-death.html.

Demarest, Bruce. *The Cross and Salvation: The Doctrine of Salvation*. Wheaton, IL: Crossway, 1997.

DeYoung, Kevin. *Daily Doctrine*. Wheaton, IL: Crossway, 2024.

———. "Theological Primer: *Pactum Salutis*." Gospel Coalition, Feb. 15, 2019. https://www.thegospelcoalition.org/blogs/kevin-deyoung/theological-primer-pactum-salutis/.

Dunson, Ben C. "The Kingdom of God in the Old Testament: From Abraham to Israel." Ligonier Ministries, June 13, 2015. https://learn.ligonier.org/articles/kingdom-god-old-testament-abraham-israel.

———. "The Kingdom of God in the Old Testament: Kingship and Creation." Ligonier Ministries, Apr. 18, 2015. https://learn.ligonier.org/articles/kingdom-god-old-testament-kingship-and-creation.

———. "The Kingdom of God in the Old Testament: The Prophetic Hope." Ligonier Ministries, June 13, 2015. https://learn.ligonier.org/articles/kingdom-god-old-testament-prophetic-hope.

Edwards, Jonathan. *Heaven: A World of Love*. Pensacola, FL: Chapel Library, 1998. https://www.chapellibrary.org/book/hawo/heaven-a-world-of-love-edwardsjonathan.

———. "Sinners in the Hands of an Angry God," In *The Works of Jonathan Edwards*, vol. 2, edited by Edward Hickman, 7–12. Carlisle, PA: Banner of Truth Trust, 1976.

———. "The True Christian's Life Is a Journey Towards Heaven." In *The Works of Jonathan Edwards*, vol. 2, edited by Edward Hickman, 243–46. Carlisle, PA: Banner of Truth Trust, 1976.

Elwell, W. A. "Election and Predestination." In *DPL* 225–29.

Ferguson, Sinclair B. *The Christian Life: A Doctrinal Introduction*. Carlisle, PA: Banner of Truth Trust, 1981.

———. *The Holy Spirit: Contours of Christian Theology*. Edited by Gerald Bray. Downers Grove, IL: Intervarsity, 1996.

---. *In Christ Alone: Living the Gospel Center Life*. Sanford, FL: Ligonier Ministries, 2011.

---. "What Is the Beatific Vision?" Interview at Ask Ligonier live event. Uploaded July 1, 2022. Ligonier Ministries video, 2:26. https://learn.ligonier.org/qas/what-is-the-beatific-vision.

Fesko, J. V. *The Trinity and the Covenant of Redemption*. Fearn, UK: Christian Focus, 2016.

Foucault, Michel. *The Order of Things: An Archaeology of the Human Sciences*. New York: Vintage, 1994.

Frame, John. *Doctrine of the Knowledge of God*. Phillipsburg, NJ: P&R, 1987.

Garriott, Aaron L. "True Repentance unto Life." *Tabletalk* (Feb. 2024) 64–65.

Green, Joel B., et al., eds. *Dictionary of Jesus and the Gospels*. Downers Grove, IL: InterVarsity, 1992.

Hall, David W., and Peter A. Lillback, eds. *A Theological Guide to Calvin's Institutes: Essays and Analysis*. Phillipsburg, NJ: P&R, 2008.

Hawthorne, Gerald F., et al., eds. *Dictionary of Paul and His Letters*. Downers Grove, IL: InterVarsity, 1993.

Henry, Carl F. H. "Reflections on the Kingdom of God." *Journal of the Evangelical Theological Society* 35.1 (Mar. 1992) 39–49.

Hodge, Charles. *An Exposition of the Second Epistle to the Corinthians*. New York: Robert Carter & Brothers, 1863.

Hyde, Daniel R. "What Does Predestination Mean for the Non-Elect?" Ligonier Ministries, Aug. 29, 2014. https://learn.ligonier.org/articles/predestination-what-does-mean-non-elect.

Jenks, R. Gregory. *Paul and His Mortality: Imitating Christ in the Face of Death*. Bulletin for Biblical Research Supplement 12. University Park: Pennsylvania State University Press, 2015.

Johnson, D. H. "Life." In *DJG* 469–71.

Keller, Timothy. *On Death*. New York: Penguin, 2020.

Kierkegaard, Søren. *Fear and Trembling: Dialectical Lyric*. Translated by Walter Lowrie. Rev. ed. Princeton University Press, 2018.

Kreitzer, L. J. "Eschatology." In *DPL* 252–69.

Ladd, George Eldon. *The Gospel of the Kingdom: Scriptural Studies in the Kingdom of God*. Grand Rapids: Eerdmans, 1959.

---. "Kingdom of God." In *ISBE* 3:23–29.

---. "The Kingdom of God: Reign or Realm?" *Journal of Biblical Literature* 81.3 (Sept. 1962) 230–38.

---. *A Theology of the New Testament*. Grand Rapids: Eerdmans, 1974.

Letham, Robert. "Predestination and the Divine Decree." Gospel Coalition, Jan. 14, 2020. https://www.thegospelcoalition.org/essay/predestination-divine-decree/.

Lewis, C. S. *Mere Christianity*. New York: HarperOne, 2001.

Liefield, W. L. "Salvation." In *ISBE* 4:287–95.

Longman, Tremper, III, and Mark L. Strauss, eds. *The Baker Expository Dictionary of Biblical Words*. Grand Rapids: Baker, 2023.

Lunde, J. "Heaven and Hell." In *DJG* 307–12.

Maile, J. F. "Heaven, Heavenlies, Paradise." In *DPL* 381–83.

Malone, Adrian, dir. *Cosmos: A Personal Voyage*. Episode 1, "The Shores of the Cosmic Ocean." Featuring Carl Sagan. Aired Sept. 28, 1980.

Mark, Joshua J. "Martin Luther's 95 Theses." World History Encyclopedia, Dec. 1, 2021. https://www.worldhistory.org/article/1891/martin-luthers-95-theses/.

Marshall, I. H. "Salvation." In *DJG* 719–24.

McGrath, Alister. *Doubting: Growing Through the Uncertainties of Faith*. Downers Grove, IL: InterVarsity, 2006.

———. "When Doubt Becomes Unbelief." *Tabletalk* (Dec. 1991). https://learn.ligonier.org/articles/when-doubt-becomes-unbelief.

McLaughlin, Ra. "The Church Militant and the Growth of the Kingdom of God." *Tabletalk* (Apr. 2023) 14–18.

Meek, Esther Lightcap. *Longing to Know: The Philosophy of Knowledge for Ordinary People*. Grand Rapids: Brazos, 2003.

———. *Loving to Know: Introducing Covenant Epistemology*. Eugene, OR: Cascade, 2011.

Mohler, R. Albert, Jr. "Moralistic Therapeutic Deism: The New American Religion." 2005. https://albertmohler.com/2005/04/11/moralistic-therapeutic-deism-the-new-american-religion-2/.

———. "The Scandal of Biblical Illiteracy: It's Our Problem." Jan. 20, 2016. https://albertmohler.com/2016/01/20/the-scandal-of-biblical-illiteracy-its-our-problem-4/.

Montaigne. Michel de. "To Philosophize Is to Learn to Die." Translated by HyperEssays, July 14, 2024. https://hyperessays.net/essays/to-philosophize-is-to-learn-to-die/.

Morgan, Christopher. "The Kingdom of God." Gospel Coalition, Jan. 14, 2020. https://www.thegospelcoalition.org/essay/the-kingdom-of-god/.

Murray, John. *Redemption Accomplished and Applied*. Grand Rapids: Eerdmans, 1955.

Nichols, Stephen. *Heaven on Earth: Capturing Jonathan Edward's Vision of Living in Between*. Wheaton, IL: Crossway, 2006.

Nichols, Terrence. *Death and Afterlife: A Theological Introduction*. Grand Rapids: Brazos, 2010.

Nietzsche, Friedrich. *A Genealogy of Morals*. In *The Works of Friedrich Nietzsche*, vol. 10, edited by Alexander Tille, translated by William A. Haussmann, 1–228. London: MacMillan, 1924.

Ort, Phillip. "Who Is Charles Haddon Spurgeon?" Spurgeon Center, June 6, 2018. https://www.spurgeon.org/resource-library/blog-entries/who-is-charles-haddon-spurgeon/.

Packer, J. I. *Concise Theology: A Guide to Historic Christian Beliefs*. Carol Stream, IL: Tyndale House, 1993.

———. *Hot Tub Religion*. Wheaton, IL: Tyndale House, 1987.

———. *I Want to Be a Christian*. Wheaton, IL: Tyndale House, 1981.

———. *Knowing God*. Downers Grove, IL: InterVarsity, 1973.

Parsons, Burk. "Infallible Words." *Tabletalk* (Aug. 2022) 2.

Pew Research Center. "Views on the Afterlife." Nov. 23, 2021. https://www.pewresearch.org/religion/2021/11/23/views-on-the-afterlife/.

Piper, John. "Is Double Predestination Biblical?" In *Ask Pastor John*, produced by Desiring God, uploaded Aug. 26, 2022. Podcast, 16:32. https://www.desiringgod.org/interviews/is-double-predestination-biblical.

Plantinga, Alvin. *Warranted Christian Belief*. New York: Oxford University Press, 2000.

Plantinga, Alvin, and Michael Tooley. *Knowledge of God*. Malden, MA: Wiley-Blackwell, 2008.

Plantinga, Cornelius, Jr. *Not the Way It's Supposed to Be: A Breviary of Sin*. Grand Rapids: Eerdmans, 1995.
Polanyi, Michael. *Personal Knowledge: Towards a Post-Critical Philosophy*. Corrected ed. Chicago: University of Chicago Press, 1962.
Puritan Reformed Theological Seminary. *The Canons of Dort*. Uploaded Oct. 12, 2016. https://prts.edu/wp-content/uploads/2016/10/Canons-of-Dort-with-Intro.pdf.
Rethinking Hell. "Clark Pinnock, Hell and the Holiness of God." Dec. 20, 2014. https://rethinkinghell.com/2014/12/20/clark-pinnock-hell-and-the-holiness-of-god/.
Ridderbos, Herman N. *Paul: An Outline of His Theology*. Translated by John Richard De Witt. Grand Rapids: Eerdmans, 1975.
———. *When the Time Had Fully Come: Studies in New Testament Theology*. Grand Rapids: Eerdmans, 1982.
Rollinson, Philip B, ed. *The Westminster Confession of Faith and Catechisms in Modern English*. Livonia, MI: Summertown, 2004.
Russell, Bertrand. "Why I Am Not a Christian." London: Allen & Unwin, 1957.
Schmucker, Leslie. "The Uncomfortable Subject Jesus Addressed More Than Anyone Else." Ligonier Ministries, May 11, 2017. https://www.thegospelcoalition.org/article/the-uncomfortable-subject-jesus-addressed-more-than-anyone-else/.
Scott, J. J., Jr. "Life and Death." In *DPL* 553–55.
Smedes, Lewis B. *Union with Christ: A Biblical View of the New Life in Jesus Christ*. Grand Rapids: Eerdmans, 1970.
Sproul, R. C. "The Beatific Vision." Produced by Ligonier Ministries, uploaded Jan. 30, 2025. Podcast, 04:59. https://learn.ligonier.org/podcasts/ultimately-with-rc-sproul/the-beatific-vision.
———. *Essential Truths of the Christian Faith*. Wheaton, IL: Tyndale House, 1992.
———. "Is Double Predestination Biblical?" Ligonier Ministries, June 23, 2018. https://learn.ligonier.org/articles/double-predestination-biblical.
Spurgeon, Charles Haddon. "The Deep-Seated Character of Sin." Sermon #812, delivered at the Metropolitan Tabernacle, May 17,1868. https://www.spurgeongems.org/sermon/chs812.pdf.
———. "The Dumb Become Singers." Sermon #3332, delivered at the Metropolitan Tabernacle, Dec. 12, 1912. https://www.spurgeongems.org/sermon/chs3332.pdf.
———. "An Epistle Illustrated by a Psalm." Sermon #2538, delivered at the Metropolitan Tabernacle, Oct. 10, 1987. https://www.spurgeongems.org/sermon/chs2538.pdf.
———. "Eternal Life!" Sermon #2396, delivered at Metropolitan Tabernacle, Feb. 6, 1887. https://www.spurgeongems.org/sermon/chs2396.pdf.
———. "Heart-Knowledge of God." Sermon #1206, delivered at the Metropolitan Tabernacle, Dec. 6, 1874. https://www.spurgeongems.org/sermon/chs1206.pdf.
———. "Our Last Journey." Sermon #1373, delivered at the Metropolitan Tabernacle, Sept. 9, 1877. https://www.spurgeongems.org/sermon/chs1373.pdf.
———. "Precious Deaths." Sermon #1036, delivered at the Metropolitan Tabernacle, Feb. 18, 1872. https://www.spurgeongems.org/sermon/chs1036.pdf.
———. "The Repentance unto Life." Sermon #44, delivered at the New Park Street Chapel, Sept. 23, 1855. https://www.spurgeongems.org/sermon/chs44.pdf.
———. "Sermons from Saintly Death-Beds." Sermon #783, delivered at the Metropolitan Tabernacle, Dec. 1, 1867. https://www.spurgeongems.org/sermon/chs783.pdf.
Stott, John R. W. *The Cross of Christ*. Downers Grove, IL: Intervarsity, 1986.

Strong, James. *The New Strong's Exhaustive Concordance of the Bible*. Nashville: Thomas Nelson, 2001.

Tearle, Oliver. "A Summary and Analysis of George Orwell's 'Politics and the English Language.'" Interesting Literature. https://interestingliterature.com/2021/02/orwell-politics-and-english-language-essay-summary-analysis.

Tolstoy, Leo. *Anna Karenina*. Translated by Richard Pevear and Larissa Volokhonsky. New York: Penguin, 2002.

Van Dixhoorn, Chad. *Creeds, Confessions, and Catechisms: A Reader's Edition*. Wheaton, IL: Crossway, 2022.

Venema, Cornelis P. "Why Five Points?" *Tabletalk* (Dec. 2023) 4–9.

Vos, Geerhardus. "The Kingdom of God." In *Redemptive History and Biblical Interpretation: The Shorter Writings of Geerhardus Vos*, edited by Richard G. Griffin, 304–16. Phillipsburg, NJ: P&R, 1980.

———. "The Structure of the Pauline Eschatology." In *The Pauline Eschatology*, 1–41. Phillipsburg, NJ: P&R, 1994.

Warfield, Benjamin B. *The Plan of Salvation*. Kansas City, MO: Kessinger, 2010.

Warren, Rick. *Created to Dream: The 6 Phases God Uses to Grow Your Faith*. Grand Rapids: Zondervan, 2023.

Waters, Guy Prentiss. *Facing the Last Enemy: Death and the Christian*. Sanford, FL: Ligonier Ministries, 2023.

Watkin, Christopher. *Biblical Critical Theory: How the Bible's Unfolding Story Makes Sense of Modern Life and Culture*. Grand Rapids: Zondervan Academic, 2022.

Wax, Trevin. "Why Should I Believe in Original Sin?" Gospel Coalition, Sept. 29, 2009. https://www.thegospelcoalition.org/blogs/trevin-wax/why-should-i-believe-in-original-sin/.

Wedgeworth, Steven. "How Jesus Disarmed the Devil." Gospel Coalition, Apr. 1, 2020. https://www.thegospelcoalition.org/article/how-jesus-disarmed-devil/.

Westermann, Claus. *Genesis 1–11*. Translated by John J. Scullions. Minneapolis: Fortress, 1994.

Wikipedia. "Salvation in Christianity." Wikimedia Foundation. Last modified Apr. 2, 2025. https://en.wikipedia.org/wiki/Salvation_in_Christianity.

Wilbourne, Rankin. *Union with Christ: The Way to Know and Enjoy God*. Colorado Springs, CO: Cook, 2016.

Yancey, Philip. "Faith and Doubt." 2009. https://philipyancey.com/q-and-a-topics/faith-and-doubt/.

———. *A Skeptic's Guide to Faith: What It Takes to Make the Leap*. Grand Rapids: Zondervan, 2009.

www.ingramcontent.com/pod-product-compliance
Lightning Source LLC
Chambersburg PA
CBHW071438150426
43191CB00008B/1169